RECONNAISSANCE IN SONORA

Reconnaissance in Sonora

Charles D. Poston's 1854 Exploration of Mexico and the Gadsden Purchase

C. GILBERT STORMS

THE UNIVERSITY OF ARIZONA PRESS

TUCSON

The University of Arizona Press
www.uapress.arizona.edu

We respectfully acknowledge the University of Arizona is on the land and territories of Indigenous peoples. Today, Arizona is home to twenty-two federally recognized tribes, with Tucson being home to the O'odham and the Yaqui. Committed to diversity and inclusion, the University strives to build sustainable relationships with sovereign Native Nations and Indigenous communities through education offerings, partnerships, and community service.

© 2015 by The Arizona Board of Regents
All rights reserved. Published 2015
First paperback edition published 2025

ISBN-13: 978-0-8165-5496-6 (paper)
ISBN-13: 978-0-8165-3149-3 (cloth)
ISBN-13: 978-0-8165-0153-3 (ebook)

Cover design by Carrie House, HOUSEdesign llc
Cover images: (top) Charles D. Poston, Tucson. No. 50194, Arizona Historical Society. (bottom) Fort Yuma, 1869, by J. Ross Browne.

[Library of Congress Cataloging-in-Publication Data
Storms, C. Gilbert, author.
 Reconnaissance in Sonora : Charles D. Poston's 1854 exploration of Mexico and the Gadsden Purchase / C. Gilbert Storms.
    pages cm
 Includes bibliographical references and index.
 ISBN 978-0-8165-3149-3 (hardcover : alk. paper)
 1. Poston, Charles D. (Charles Debrille), 1825–1902—Travel—Mexico—Sonora (State) 2. Poston, Charles D. (Charles Debrille), 1825–1902—Travel—Arizona. 3. Sonora (Mexico : State)—Description and travel. 4. Arizona—Description and travel. 5. Gadsden Purchase. I. Title.
 F786.S884 2015
 917.2'1604—dc23
                          2014030799

Printed in the United States of America
♾ This paper meets the requirements of ANSI/NISO Z39.48-1992 (Permanence of Paper).

For Liz

Contents

List of Illustrations ix
Acknowledgments xi
Introduction 3
Chapter 1. Starting Out in Kentucky 9
Chapter 2. San Francisco and the Customs House 15
Chapter 3. The Government Boarding House 21
Chapter 4. Expansionist Dreams and Private Conquests 34
Chapter 5. Planning the Expedition to Sonora 44
Chapter 6. Navachiste and Sonora 49
Chapter 7. A Port on the Gulf 58
Chapter 8. The Sand Desert 71
Chapter 9. The Gila Trail and Colorado City 80
Chapter 10. Deals and Disappointments 95
Chapter 11. Stories of the Sonoran Expedition 106
Postscript: Poston's Story 115
Appendix: Charles D. Poston, "Reconnoisance in Sonora" 123
Notes 155
Bibliography 177
Index 187

Illustrations

Figure 1.	Charles D. Poston	5
Figure 2.	Samuel Haycraft	11
Figure 3.	San Francisco Customs House, 1851	17
Figure 4.	J. Ross Browne, the *Zoraida* at Navachiste Bay	50
Figure 5.	Port of Guaymas	56
Figure 6.	Ehrenberg's 1854 map showing San Juan Bautista Bay and La Labor	59
Figure 7.	Manuel María Gándara	64
Figure 8.	Andrew B. Gray	73
Figure 9.	Ehrenberg's 1854 map showing Adair Bay and Poston's route to the Yuma Crossing	78
Figure 10.	Gila Trail above Oatman Flat	83
Figure 11.	J. Ross Browne, Oatman gravesite	85
Figure 12.	J. Ross Browne, Fort Yuma	86
Figure 13.	Louis J. F. Jaeger	87
Figure 14.	Samuel Peter Heintzelman	88
Figure 15.	Section of Ehrenberg's 1854 map showing Poston's route to San Diego	92
Figure 16.	Colorado City diagram	93
Figure 17.	Poston's Colorado City stock certificate	98
Figure 18.	Charles D. Poston in old age	107
Figure 19.	"Reconnoisance in Sonora" first page	124
Figure 20.	"Reconnoisance in Sonora" envelope	125

Acknowledgments

Many thanks are due to a number of talented and dedicated librarians who helped me to gather documents and information for this book—notably Patricia Hewitt at the Fray Angelico Chavez History Library, New Mexico History Museum, Palace of the Governors, Santa Fe, New Mexico, for her help in locating the original of Poston's "Reconnoisance in Sonora"; the librarians at the Arizona Historical Society archives in both Tucson and Tempe; and the librarians at the University of Arizona Special Collections in Tucson for their help in locating papers and other documents relating to Charles Poston, Herman Ehrenberg, and the other principals of Poston's 1854 adventure.

Special thanks are due also to Raymond S. Cooper for reading and commenting on an early draft of the manuscript, and to Kristen Buckles, acquiring editor at the University of Arizona Press, for her encouragement and advice about this project.

Poston's "Reconnoisance in Sonora" is published here with permission of the Fray Angelico Chavez History Library.

Portions of this book have been published in "Charles D. Poston and the Founding of Colorado City," *Journal of Arizona History* (Winter 2014) © 2014, Arizona Historical Society, and are reproduced here with permission.

RECONNAISSANCE IN SONORA

Introduction

Charles Debrille Poston is a familiar figure in Arizona history, known mainly for his early settlement of Arizona, his part ownership of one of the earliest Arizona silver mining companies, and his efforts to make Arizona a U.S. territory. He was Arizona's first superintendent of Indian affairs and first elected territorial delegate to Congress. But these were the achievements of Poston's mature years, ones that eventually earned him the sentimental title "Father of Arizona."[1] Before any of these things happened, as a young man of twenty-eight, Poston was a frontier adventurer and would-be entrepreneur. And his very first visit to Arizona came by way of a daring and controversial expedition he led into Sonora and the Gadsden Purchase in 1854, the purpose of which was to locate commercial properties for American development. His story is a dramatic one — of a young man who abandoned his family to seek adventure and redemption from scandal at home, and who faced difficult, even dangerous obstacles while trying to make his fortune in the frontier Southwest. Poston's adventure has broader historical significance as well, since it reflects important political and economic trends in mid-nineteenth-century America — the frenzied search for mineral wealth in California and northern Mexico, American expansionist politics, and the drive to build a transcontinental railroad.

The period following the 1846–47 war between Mexico and the United States was a time of expansionism in American politics, when American politicians and newspaper editors proclaimed that it was America's "Manifest Destiny" to expand its boundaries by colonization, by purchase, or by force of arms. It was a time when Americans of all regions and political views were calling for a transcontinental railroad to be built across the United States. Public debate continued for years about the most promising route for such a railroad, and prospective investors eagerly competed to purchase the rights to develop different routes.

It was partly to acquire the land for a southern transcontinental route that in 1854 President Franklin Pierce sent James Gadsden to Mexico City to negotiate with Mexican president Antonio Lopez de Santa Anna the purchase of a portion of northern Mexico. The news of Gadsden's negotiations stirred men to seek to acquire land in northern Mexico that would soon be located within the United States and thus could be developed by American capital under American laws.

Much of this acquisitive spirit had, of course, been inspired by the California gold rush of the late 1840s and early 1850s. The gold rush had drawn tens of thousands of people from all over the world to California seeking their fortunes either in the goldfields or through some other form of adventuring, particularly in northern Mexico, where for centuries fabulous gold and silver mines were rumored to have existed, waiting to be exploited by those with the skill and daring to find them. These reports were so compelling that in the 1850s, not only did some try to acquire Mexican land legitimately, but French and American "filibusters" entered northern Mexico and tried to seize portions of the country by force.

Charles Poston had a passion for travel and adventure and, like many young men of his time, was attracted by the prospect of finding his fortune in the American West. However, he also was driven by other motives — the need to support a wife and daughter in Kentucky and to erase the embarrassment of failed real estate investments and unpaid debts. Having left his home for California and obtained a position in the San Francisco customs house, Poston was drawn into the freewheeling speculation over commercial opportunities in northern Mexico. Inspired by discussions among companions at his San Francisco boardinghouse, he resolved to lead an expedition into Sonora to locate the Iturbide Grant, an enormous grant of land awarded by the Mexican government to the family of former Mexican emperor Augustine Iturbide.[2] Locating the grant on lands that would be included in the Gadsden Purchase would not only benefit the Iturbide family by providing them with lands that might either be sold to, or developed by, Americans, but could make Poston and his friends rich by giving them an "inside track" either to develop the lands themselves or to act as agents for their development.

Poston said that he formed a "syndicate" of San Francisco businessmen to support the expedition. However, the syndicate altered Poston's objectives, directing him away from the Iturbide Grant and instead sending him

Figure 1. Charles D. Poston. Photo courtesy of the Arizona Historical Society, Tucson.

into Sonora to find other properties that could be exploited directly by American investors without the involvement of the Iturbides once the land became U.S. territory. Specifically, Poston was to locate a site for a port city on the Gulf of California as well as abandoned silver and gold mines that could be reopened. Poston sailed to Mexico with a party of twenty-five men, making an unplanned landing when his ship ran aground on the west coast of Sinaloa. He then journeyed north into Sonora, cultivating the acquaintance of wealthy landowners and searching for the types of properties that would interest his backers.

In Sonora, Poston negotiated with some of these landowners a concession to develop a port city at San Juan Bautista Bay that could become the terminus for a transcontinental railroad line to be built by the Texas Western Railroad. He then traveled north into the Gadsden Purchase and down the Gila River to the Colorado, where he and his companion on the expedition, German mining engineer Herman Ehrenberg, surveyed the port of Colorado City and sold shares to investors. However, when Poston returned to San Francisco, he was unable to interest his syndicate in either San Juan Bautista Bay or Colorado City. His plans were too risky and vulnerable to the maneuverings of railroad speculators and the complex politics of Mexican-American relations. Subsequently, Poston tried to find support for Colorado City among politicians and investors in the East, but again without success, and the reconnaissance in Sonora ended, leaving as its legacy only the stories of its remarkable events and ambitious schemes.

Poston told of his 1854 adventure in two major published sources. One was "Poston's Narrative," a chapter in J. Ross Browne's 1869 book *Adventures in the Apache Country*. The chapter purports to be the transcription of a journal Poston showed Browne during their 1864 tour of Arizona Territory.[3] Another version of the story appeared in Poston's article "Building a State in Apache Land I: How the Territory Was Acquired," the first of four articles that Poston wrote about the development of Arizona for the *Overland Monthly Magazine* in 1894.[4] Poston also briefly described aspects of the expedition in other writings later in his life.

However, the earliest and most detailed account of the 1854 expedition is Poston's "Reconnoisance in Sonora," a report dated September 15, 1854, that he wrote upon his return to San Francisco, probably for the supporters of his expedition.[5] While the "Reconnoisance" relates Poston's adventures exploring Sonora and the Gadsden Purchase for commercial opportunities, it also attempts to persuade his readers that they should acquire rights to land in those territories on which a transcontinental railroad could be built and develop a new port city as its terminus. In the process, it reveals the relationships of power in mid-nineteenth-century border politics and the imperialist reach of nineteenth-century American enterprise, with its supporting myths of Manifest Destiny, Mexican mineral wealth, and the redemptive power of the transcontinental railroad.

The purposes of this book are to describe Poston's 1854 expedition in more detail than has previously been possible and to explore the origins of the expedition in Poston's early life in Kentucky and his attempts to prosper in San Francisco. The book will also discuss the connections between Poston's adventure and the larger historical issues mentioned earlier—American expansionism, the Gadsden Purchase, the quest for mineral wealth in northern Mexico, the drive to build a transcontinental railroad, and the activities of the Mexican filibusters. Finally, the book will compare the various narratives that Poston composed concerning the expedition, exploring the differences among them and how, in particular, the "Reconnoisance" clarifies the chronology and significance of the 1854 expedition. Once the expedition's projects—San Juan Bautista Bay and Colorado City—failed, Poston rarely mentioned them again. So an examination of the "Reconnoisance" is valuable in bringing to light these efforts by Poston and his associates to make their fortunes by exploiting both the Gadsden Purchase and the ambitions of American speculators to build a transcontinental railroad.

Dealing with Poston has been difficult for historians because of his practice of retelling stories of his experiences and because the retellings were often embellished or inaccurate. In fairness it must be said that as Poston aged his memory failed him.[6] And as he more frequently played the role of the former pioneer reminiscing about his frontier experiences, he tended to invent more. Some of his additions in later tales of the expedition were legitimate in that he included incidents and personal observations that would have been inappropriate in the "Reconnoisance." That document was meant to persuade its audience of the possibilities for commercial development in Mexico and Arizona. The later narratives were intended to relate the pioneer experience in unusual or dramatic stories. Thus, Poston created the narratives of the 1854 expedition at different times and in response to different exigencies in his life. The result is a patchwork of Poston tales about the expedition that have sometimes confused historians who did not understand their different purposes and have led to misconceptions about what Poston did in 1854 and why he ventured into Mexico at all.

To aid in validating Poston's narratives about the 1854 expedition, I have surrounded his stories with a variety of corroborating sources—letters and journals of other travelers in Mexico and Arizona, some going back to Spanish colonial times; reports of surveys and military expeditions; and newspaper stories concerning contemporary events and political and economic issues related to Poston's trip. I believe that by examining all of these sources, the book will give a new and richer sense of Poston's Sonoran adventure and its meanings.

CHAPTER ONE

Starting Out in Kentucky

Charles Poston's 1854 Sonoran expedition was not simply the activity of a restless adventure seeker or ambitious fortune hunter but had its origins in the circumstances of his early life. Poston was born near Elizabethtown, Hardin County, Kentucky, on April 20, 1825. His mother was Judith Dibrelle, a descendant of a prominent South Carolina family. Her mother, Elizabeth Lee Dibrelle, was a member of the Lee family of Virginia. Elizabeth was either the sister or aunt of Henry "Lighthorse Harry" Lee, whose son, Robert E. Lee, would thus have been a distant cousin of Charles.[1] The Poston family was a large one. Charles had two older sisters, Lee Ann Debrelle and Elizabeth Ann; an older brother, Sanford James; and a younger brother, John Lee. Another sister, Mary Elvira, and a brother, John Anthony, died in infancy.[2]

When Charles was seven his family moved to Elizabethtown, about forty-five miles south of Louisville, where his father, Temple Poston, edited and published the *Western Sentinel* newspaper. As a boy, Charles worked for his father as a news carrier and printer's devil. His only formal education was to be tutored, from 1832 to 1837, by an itinerant teacher named Robert Hewitt. In January 1837, when Charles was twelve, his father apprenticed him for a six-year term to Samuel Haycraft, chief clerk of the Hardin County Court at Louisville and the county's circuit courts. The Haycrafts were a respected though not wealthy family with a two-story home in Elizabethtown. Not only did Charles work in Haycraft's office as deputy clerk of the Hardin County Court from 1837 to 1843, but on July 17, 1837, he went to live with the Haycraft family.[3]

A month later, in August 1837, Judith Debrille Poston died. Poston later said that he was orphaned at the age of twelve, but this was not true. Poston's father was still living in 1837 and was a constable and justice of the peace in years following. He may have lived until 1864.[4] But for reasons unknown, Temple Poston seems to have thought that his son would be better off in the care of the Haycrafts. Charles doubtless benefited from this arrangement. He gained a home and foster family in addition to a profession. But however comfortable Charles may have been with the Haycrafts, the fact that he later claimed to have been orphaned in 1837 suggests that in some way he felt abandoned by his parents. The experience may have contributed to the insubstantial connection he had with his own wife and daughter and the wandering, adventure-seeking life that he later pursued, one of the first manifestations of which was the expedition to Sonora and the Gadsden Purchase.

Poston seems to have been well treated by the Haycrafts, and on September 14, 1848, he literally became a member of the family when he married Samuel Haycraft's second-youngest daughter, Margaret. Their first child, a daughter, was born in Elizabethtown on November 3, 1849, and the name her parents chose for her reflected Charles's pride in both his old and new family connections: Sarah (Margaret's mother's name) Lee Poston.[5]

With his legal training Poston might have been expected to pursue a career in the law. He built upon this training after his six-year apprenticeship with Haycraft by working for another year (1844–45) as a deputy clerk in the law office of James P. Clark of Nashville, clerk of the supreme court of Tennessee.[6] In the courts at Louisville and Nashville, Poston would have met some of the leading attorneys, judges, and political figures of Kentucky and Tennessee. And Poston seems to have been adept at cultivating these kinds of relationships. Though young and from rural Kentucky, he was outgoing and sociable. John Myers Myers says that at this time Poston appeared to be "an exceptionally bright young man with a gift for drawing the favorable notice of influential men," one who "would have gone far along the track available to talented lawyers and achieved standing as an upper class political figure."[7]

However, after his Nashville clerkship Poston steered away from the law and pursued business ventures, some of which involved trips to eastern and southern cities. Poston's journal of 1847–50 records four such trips, two that he took before his marriage and two after. In his journal Poston calls these journeys "business" trips and refers several times to business that he conducted during each one, but he never describes his business activities specifically. Poston biographer Roy Goodale says that in his journal Poston

Figure 2. Samuel Haycraft. Photo from Samuel Haycraft, *History of Elizabethtown.*

seems far more interested in travel and the prominent people he met than in any business obligations he may have had.[8]

Two of Poston's trips, the first and third, made a circuit of "Eastern cities": Cincinnati, Wheeling, Baltimore, Philadelphia, New York, Albany, Syracuse, Buffalo, Niagara Falls, Sandusky (Ohio), and Cleveland. On his second and fourth trips he traveled south, to Natchez and New Orleans. On his first Natchez visit Poston attended to the "sale of stock" but does not say what sort of stock. On his last trip Poston says that he "parted company" with his "trading companion, Frank Slaughter." Who Slaughter was or what business he and Poston were in is not known, but Poston seems to have been working for or with him, perhaps as early as 1847.[9]

On this final trip Poston returned home by way of St. Louis and St. Joseph, Missouri. Poston describes St. Joseph as "the principal disembarking place for California and western emmigrants [sic]—Many of them were encamped here now and thousands more coming, it is estimated that one hundred thousand will cross the plains this spring."[10] Clearly, Poston was excited by the emigrants' presence, and his envy of the westbound travelers is evident in his journal.

In keeping with his new business ambitions, Poston engaged in real estate speculation in Kentucky, but Samuel Haycraft said that these activities "proved unfortunate."[11] Poston's older brother, Sanford James Poston, had been appointed sheriff of Hardin County in 1843 by Kentucky governor Robert P. Letcher, and it appears that the brothers began to speculate in land in the mid-1840s. Goodale suggests that the Postons may have been acquiring land by the payment of delinquent taxes, and reports at least four purchases in 1846–47. Whatever the nature of these transactions, they resulted in debts that the brothers could not pay. Charles's debt remained unpaid as late as 1869.[12]

The public embarrassment of these circumstances must have been painful for Charles, whose social standing in Elizabethtown was already ambiguous. The motherless boy with the aristocratic Southern heritage and the father who had abandoned him had been taken up by the Haycrafts and given advantages hardly available to most young men in rural Kentucky. But in his mid-twenties Charles had stumbled. He had rejected the opportunity for a legal and political career provided by Haycraft. Instead, eager for wealth, he had ventured in over his head, failed to fulfill the expectations created by his family connections, and now was unable to support his wife and daughter.

Given these facts, it is not surprising that sometime in 1850 Poston decided to go to California to seek his fortune. Like many young men of his time, Poston was going west to escape a dubious reputation at home and get a fresh start in a place where his past would not confront him at every turn. In doing so, he was forgoing any attempt to repair his fortunes at home and was taking a still bigger risk to try to accomplish this in the land of the gold rush. Such a trip meant that he had to leave Margaret and Sarah in Elizabethtown and in the care of his in-laws. But since it was common at the time for young men to go west to improve their fortunes, Goodale speculates that neither Margaret nor her father would have opposed Charles's decision.[13] Samuel Haycraft expresses no criticism of Poston for the departure and says matter-of-factly that Poston went west because of the unpaid debts he had accumulated.[14]

Ironically, leaving his new family behind probably damaged Poston's reputation more than his debts. Poston's grandson Colonel Benjamin Pope says that the judgment of some in Poston's family was severe: "The entire subject of Charles D. Poston was taboo in our family due to puritanical disapproval by our father of his having deserted his wife and daughter ... leaving them with his wife's family in Kentucky while he went adventuring, with ultimate failure his only reward."[15] This opinion was shared by others in Poston's hometown. In an article in the *Louisville Sunday Courier* in the late 1980s, Dick Taylor writes that over 150 years later Elizabethtown residents who remembered Poston at all called him by the mocking nickname "Dib," evoking his aristocratic heritage, and remembered him as the man who deserted his family and ran off to California: "As far as Elizabethtown residents were concerned 'Dib' Poston deserted Margaret Haycraft ... [and] never mounted [sic] to much in Elizabeth town [sic] anyhow. People here forgive all sins of the locally successful, but never those of local failures. ... You don't desert a Haycraft here and get away with it."[16]

These are harsh judgments, but once he left for San Francisco in 1850, Poston became virtually an absentee husband and father, rarely returning to Kentucky or visiting his family. Another grandson, Gustavus Pope, says, "I do not remember seen [sic] my grandfather after I was a very small boy, for though he corresponded with my mother [Sarah Lee Poston Pope], he did not, I think, visit us. She always spoke of him with affection and admiration but regretted, too, that he chose to live so far apart from us."[17] The reason for Poston's absence is not known. Was it his father's legacy—some mistaken notion that, in the effort to succeed, a husband and father should leave his family in the care of others while he sought to improve his standing? Was it a fear that he would never measure up to the Haycrafts' standards or that he could not face the disapproval that he knew existed in Elizabethtown and even in his own family?

There were exceptions to the self-imposed exile. During two brief intervals Poston lived again with his wife and daughter. One was in 1858 when they resided at "Dr. Frales health establishment on Laight St. near St. Johns Park" in New York City after Poston had contracted an eye infection in Arizona. The second was in 1862 when Poston took his family to New York and "maintained at Doctor Taylors in 38th St."[18] Gustavus Pope says that Charles also wrote periodically to Sarah Lee, paid for her to go to boarding school in New York City, and took her with him to Europe in 1867. For her wedding he gave her a beautiful silver chest made by Tiffany from silver mined in Arizona.[19] But aside from these contacts, Poston's absence from his family continued for the rest of his life.

It appears likely that Samuel Haycraft, as he had always done, helped Poston before the young man left for California by arranging recommendations that would be useful to Charles in the West. In his journal Poston says that when he left Elizabethtown on November 21, 1850, he stopped first in Louisville and obtained letters of introduction from two former acquaintances from his Hardin County Court days: Judge Larue and Judge (later U.S. senator) Joseph Rogers Underwood.[20] In a January 24, 1868, letter to Secretary of State William Seward, Poston said that Senator John Jordan Crittenden of Kentucky also helped him to secure employment in San Francisco.[21] Poston could have obtained these recommendations on his own. However, it is equally likely that Haycraft approached these men on Charles's behalf and asked them to help his son-in-law get a start in California.[22] However the letters were obtained, with them in hand Poston was ready to start for California.

CHAPTER TWO

San Francisco and the Customs House

Poston arrived in San Francisco on January 23, 1851.[1] He probably spent the next month investigating job opportunities in the city, using the letters supplied by his Kentucky contacts. As Poston explored San Francisco he would have seen the city starting to develop beyond its beginnings as a tent city with planked streets.[2] Meanwhile, ships by the hundreds sailed into San Francisco Bay, and the waterline kept moving outward, away from the original settlement, as "water lots" were filled in and built upon.

Poston would also have seen throngs of men who poured through the streets, going to and coming from the goldfields:

> Many of those crowding the streets and saloons had been broken in the diggings, and wracked by disease, hard work, and skimpy diets, had straggled back to San Francisco to await steerage home to the States. . . . Many had the look of those . . . unable to go back and without means to move on. Others had somehow sensed that there was more gold in lumber, dry goods, foodstuffs, hardware, fine wines and clothing than in the average long tom and had set up brick warehouses well-stocked with goods, along Battery and Front Streets. Every manner of goods and services were available for a price, and as the place blossomed before the eyes of the first comers, real estate spiraled, speculation became commonplace, and violence was a matter of daily course. Mission and

Howard Streets became promenades on pleasant days for throngs of fashionable men and women of pleasure, idlers, loafers, gamblers and drunks on foot or in vehicles of every description. The custom house, city hall, post office, and the more gorgeous saloons with cigar shops, fancy stores and livery stables were on Kearny Street—a street also of loafers, litigants, lawyers, officials, politicians, and, of course, the idle and the unemployed.[3]

Poston himself joined this crowd, one of the thousands who hoped to find their fortune in the growing city.

Finally, on February 17, 1851, Poston took a position in the new San Francisco customs house at the corner of Montgomery and California streets. Probably because of his legal and business background, he leapfrogged the usual entry-level positions of customs inspector and clerk, and started as a chief clerk at a salary of three hundred dollars a month, under the collectorship of Thomas Butler King, the former Whig congressman from Georgia.[4] He worked in the office of Hart Fellows, surveyor of customs.[5] That Poston did not seek or accept this position immediately upon arriving in San Francisco contradicts the suggestion by some that the job was a political appointment he had obtained before leaving Kentucky.[6]

In the customs house Poston had a front-row seat to observe the burgeoning commerce of the West Coast's busiest port, as well as contact with the wealthiest merchants and most influential politicians of the nation's newest state. The customs house, says Goodale, was a center of commercial and political activity in California. Here ships newly arrived at San Francisco registered their cargoes, had them inspected, paid millions in import duties, and got clearances to sail. Poston had landed in just the right place to be at the center of commerce and cash flow in and out of the new state, as well as a fulcrum of political influence and planning. Goodale says that Poston's "observation of the methods and modus operandi of successful bureaucrats, speculators, investors, politicians and adventurers . . . and the prospect of vast new unexplored territories being opened to exploitation were a heady combination he could neither ignore nor soon forget."[7]

However, life in the customs house was not all excitement and opportunity. The collector had a staff of some two hundred subordinate officers and other employees, all hoping—and maneuvering—for advancement. Poston's duties were ordinary, consisting of making up reports and bills for customs fees and taking care of the surveyor's correspondence.[8] Customs house clerks made relatively little money, and employment was mainly a matter of political or regional connections. Caspar T. Hopkins, a clerk in

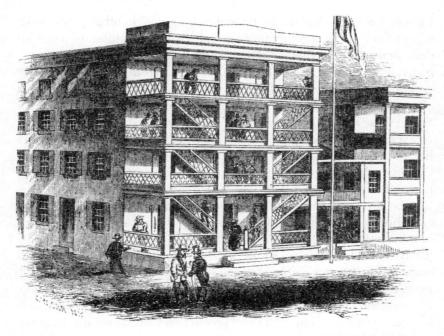

Figure 3. San Francisco Customs House, 1851. Illustration from Soulé, Gihon, and Nisbet, *The Annals of San Francisco.*

1852 during Poston's time, said that the place was known as the "Virginia Poor House" because most of the staff were either Southerners or Northerners with Southern sympathies. Hopkins complained that "looseness and favoritism" prevailed in most departments, the clerks' work was "poorly done," and accounts were kept in a "careless and bungling manner." Also, because of the prevalence of Southerners, quarrels over personal honor were common and duels often fought to resolve them: "The pistol, rifle and horsewhip were the ever ready tools for the suppression of calumny and the self-protection of rogues who were not courting investigation."[9]

Despite this volatile social environment, Poston found work in the customs house stultifying and soon became bored with the daily routine. On November 21, 1851, the anniversary of his having left Kentucky, he reflected in his journal on his life since arriving in San Francisco, concluding that "since the 17th of February [when he began work at the customs house] my life has been very even and monotonous, having been engaged in the same service which I then commenced without suffering any of the vicissitudes so consequent to this Country—being pleasantly engaged without seeing much of the World or travelling any." In other words, while other men were prospecting for gold and having adventures, he sat at his desk along with hundreds of other customs house employees, shuffling papers and dreaming of how he might get ahead. He also was homesick: "It is difficult to realize how fast the time has passed away except on account of my absence from home and my family & friends, which makes it seem an age since I left; but a little time."[10]

Even before this anniversary a major change had taken place in Poston's life, but one that that hardly seemed to touch him. When Poston left for California, Margaret had been pregnant with their second child. On February 10, 1851, a week before Poston started work at the customs house, Elizabeth Ann Poston ("Bettie"), was born. However, only eleven days later, on February 21, Margaret suffered an attack of paralysis, which extended eventually to the entire left side of her body. John Goff thinks that the paralysis was the result of a stroke; Myers, that it was a form of Parkinson's disease. Whatever the cause, Margaret survived and lived for another thirty years, but as an invalid requiring the care of her family. The infant Bettie, too, was overtaken in the tide of misfortune. She died of unknown causes five months later, on July 30, 1851.[11] Poston never saw his second daughter.

Far away in California, Poston would not have received word of Bettie's birth or death or Margaret's illness until well after they had occurred, but he must have known of all three events before he set out on the Sonora expedition. Why he did not return to Kentucky but chose to pursue his fortunes in the West is not known. Perhaps he thought it best to try to "make good" where he was in order to support his family. Perhaps his pride and embarrassment over his Kentucky business failures were still too great for him to go back. Perhaps he feared that because of his "desertion" of his family, the new disasters would be blamed on him. In any case, neither homesickness nor the tragedies at home induced him to return to Kentucky.

Instead, Poston continued working at the customs house and, undaunted by his Kentucky mistakes, once again bought and sold real estate.[12] Apart from striking it rich in the goldfields, probably the most popular way of seeking one's fortune in California was speculating in San Francisco real estate. Caspar Hopkins, who struck out for the goldfields when he first arrived in California, later said, "Had I known then what I do now, and what business men knew then, I would have immediately put . . . money into a lot, and held onto that lot."[13] This was because property values in the city rose dramatically after 1849. From twelve dollars for fifty-vara lots, prices rose to "hundreds, thousands and tens of thousands of dollars; so that large holders of such properties became on a sudden millionaires."[14] It was not just the value of the land that contributed to this sudden wealth. It was the extravagant rents people were willing to pay for land and buildings that made San Francisco real estate speculation so attractive: "In a couple of years, the building speculator in real estate had all his outlay returned to him in the shape of rents. Henceforward his property was a very mine of wealth. As rents rose, so did the prices of property. The richest men in San Francisco have made the best portion of their wealth by the possession of real estate."[15]

It is uncertain how much money, if any, Poston made in San Francisco real estate. Wiser, perhaps, after his Kentucky problems, he seems at least to have kept his head above water, because he declared in his journal that he was able to send modest sums of money home to his family.[16] Whether the money went to support Margaret and Sarah or to settle Poston's debts is not known. But if he was investing in real estate, it is not likely that Poston sent much home. Caspar Hopkins reflected the fever for making money at that time that infected all young men with a little cash to invest: "I sent no money East, for its use was too valuable in San Francisco, and I fancied that by using all I made in trade I should be doing far better . . . than by stopping interest at only 6 per cent per annum a few months sooner."[17]

But success in real estate could not erase Poston's sense of frustration at the customs house. All around him men seemed to be making fortunes in the goldfields or in real estate, by brokering ships' cargoes, or in other speculative ventures. Meanwhile, Poston sat at his desk in the customs house, seemingly unable to get in on the action. He desperately needed to succeed, if only to pay off his debts and show the doubters and scoffers in Elizabethtown that he was a person of ability.

However, Poston was not for the drudgery of the goldfields, and he did not have the capital to make highly profitable real estate investments in San Francisco. His greatest talent seemed to lie in cultivating business and social contacts and later in brokering enterprises that might bring profit to investors. With the right connections, he might have done well in politics. But Poston's political connections were Whig, and after the national election of 1852, Democrats controlled both the White House and Congress. So Poston found it impossible to rise at the customs house. Instead, he joined the ranks of others victimized by the power shift in Washington. Poston's boss, Hart Fellows, was replaced as surveyor by William Van Voorhies, and a reshuffling of lesser posts took place. On June 10, 1853, Van Voorhies replaced Poston as chief clerk with Thomas E. Buchanan. To add insult to injury, another Democrat, "Colonel" J. J. Bryant, was put ahead of Poston in salary and importance on the customs house roster.[18]

Poston wrote a letter protesting the demotion to Treasury Secretary James Guthrie on June 10, 1853, claiming that he was now doing the same work he had done before, but for less money. Poston also complained that Bryant was a "professional gambler" and not qualified to be chief clerk, and he asked to be restored to his former salary. Because of the influence of a Kentucky friend, Major Thomas B. Eastland, who wrote to Guthrie on Poston's behalf, Poston's salary was increased from twenty-six hundred to three thousand dollars a year, but he was not returned to his position as chief clerk.[19] In any case, it appeared that Poston's career at the customs house, such as it was, was blocked for reasons beyond his control and that if he wanted to improve his situation, he would now have to look elsewhere.

CHAPTER THREE

The Government Boarding House

A way out of Poston's stagnation at the customs house appeared to him, oddly, in the form of a political discussion group at the boardinghouse where he lived. Like most young men in San Francisco in the early 1850s, Poston lived in rented rooms. In his second year in San Francisco, 1852, he moved to a place at the northwest corner of Stockton and Washington streets that he called the "Government Boarding House" because it was home to mostly lower-level government officials and civil servants like himself. They included, Poston said, a former member of Congress, several California senators and their families, the U.S. marshal for California, and several lesser officials.[1]

At the boardinghouse Poston became part of an informal group of men who discussed politics after dinner.[2] In summer 1853, at about the time Poston suffered his demotion at the customs house, their discussions turned to commercial possibilities in northern Mexico, where land and mining opportunities promised extraordinary wealth. It was these discussions that eventually led to the Sonoran expedition. But the discussions—and the expedition—were stimulated by many circumstances. Foremost among these, Poston said, was the negotiation known to be taking place in Mexico City over what would become the Gadsden Purchase, which many hoped would produce the greatest opportunities for wealth in the West since the gold rush. As Poston later said, "A new California was hoped for on the southern boundary."[3]

On August 4, 1853, James Gadsden arrived in Vera Cruz, Mexico, sent by President Franklin Pierce to negotiate a new boundary between Mexico and the United States. According to the 1848 Treaty of Guadalupe Hidalgo, negotiated at the end of the war with Mexico, the boundary between the two countries ran from the Gulf of Mexico along the Rio Grande River to the southern boundary of New Mexico just north of the town of El Paso del Norte (present-day Juarez, Mexico). It then went west three degrees of longitude from the river, north to the nearest branch of the Gila River, and down the Gila to its junction with the Colorado River at present-day Yuma, Arizona. From there, it continued west to the Pacific, following the established boundary between Upper and Lower California.[4]

However, this boundary, along with some other provisions of the treaty, was unacceptable to many Americans. Wealthy eastern businessmen dreamed of constructing a transcontinental railroad connecting eastern business centers with a port on the Pacific Ocean. The acquisition of California and New Mexico in the Mexican War had fed their ambitions, and in the late 1840s and early 1850s, several possible routes for such a railroad were being discussed. Southern Democrats in Washington wanted a southern route for the railroad, and Article VI of the Treaty of Guadalupe Hidalgo said that a railroad could be built through present-day Arizona along the Gila River, within one marine league of either bank, pending agreement between the two governments. The railroad had to "serve equally for the advantage and use of both countries."[5] But supporters of the southern route did not consider the narrow strip of land along the Gila described in the treaty adequate for development of a railroad. The State of Texas had encouraged construction of a railroad across its territory by providing land grants to companies that would build the railroad to its western border. But for those favoring the southern route, it appeared that there was no way of extending this road to the Pacific except through Mexico.

The significance of the "southern route" in American politics in the 1840s and 1850s is difficult to overstate. In fact, it was central to the controversy concerning the U.S.-Mexican boundary in southern New Mexico that had simmered ever since the signing of the 1848 treaty. Because of the southern route's critical importance in understanding Poston's expedition, it is worth discussing here in some detail.

According to Article V of the Treaty of Guadalupe Hidalgo, the new boundary between the United States and Mexico was to be determined by a joint boundary commission.[6] In 1850 that group was supervised by commissioners John Russell Bartlett of the United States and General Pedro Garcia Condé of Mexico. The treaty negotiators had set the boundary based upon the "Map of Mexico" published in 1847 by John Disturnell, a New York book and map publisher. However, unknown to the negotiators,

Disturnell's map was incorrect. It was the product of a series of plagiarisms—a reproduction of an 1828 map, taken from an 1826 imprint of an 1822 map of North America published by H. S. Tanner in Philadelphia. Tanner's map placed El Paso del Norte (hereafter, El Paso) thirty-four miles north of the town's actual site, and over a hundred miles farther east than it really was. And subsequent versions of the map all repeated the error.[7]

Bartlett believed that the southern boundary of New Mexico should run just eight miles north of the true location of El Paso, at latitude 31°52′, but Garcia Condé thought that the town's location on the Disturnell map should prevail. So they compromised. To satisfy Condé, the initial point of the boundary was fixed at forty-two miles north of El Paso, at latitude 32°22′, as shown on the Disturnell map. To satisfy Bartlett, the line ran west three degrees of longitude from the actual location of the Rio Grande, then north until it reached a branch of the Gila, then down the Gila as described in the treaty.[8] The decision gave six thousand square miles of territory to Mexico, in which about three thousand people lived, most in an area along the Rio Grande known as the Mesilla Valley.[9] Bartlett believed that he had given up land of no value while gaining the site of the celebrated Santa Rita del Cobre copper mines and perhaps some gold and silver mines.[10]

However, the boundary decision was not Bartlett's and Condé's alone to make. The two governments had agreed that decisions of the joint commission had to be approved not only by the commissioners but by the official surveyors for each side. The surveyor for the American commission was Andrew B. Gray, who had been delayed in arriving at El Paso by illness. When he arrived and was able to view the relevant documents, he opposed the compromise, believing that the initial point of the boundary should be where Bartlett had originally said, eight miles north of the actual location of El Paso, at 31°52′. He expressed his disapproval in reports to Bartlett and Secretary of the Interior Alexander H. Stuart and refused to sign the compromise.[11]

Stuart, who had already accepted the compromise, agreed that the land below 32°22′ was worthless and dismissed Gray as surveyor for the commission.[12] However, Stuart's acceptance of the compromise aroused the ire of Southern politicians in Washington, for whom a southern route for the transcontinental railroad was critically important. Thus, it was no surprise that in July 1851 the Senate Foreign Relations Committee, led by Senator James Mason Murray of Virginia, asked Stuart for a full report on the activities of the Bartlett commission and, on July 26, 1851, began a full-scale investigation of the commission. Eventually, the committee rejected the Bartlett-Condé line as being in violation of the 1848 treaty.[13]

All of the prominent politicians who subsequently opposed the Bartlett-Condé line in the Senate and House of Representatives were Southerners, and Texans especially opposed the compromise boundary on grounds that Bartlett had given away the best land for building a southern route for the transcontinental railroad. Their opposition was sharpened by the expectation that Texas would benefit if the eastern terminus of such a line were located at San Antonio, Galveston, or Houston. Other Southern politicians supported the Texans, since if such a line were extended eastward to the Atlantic, other Southern cities would benefit.[14] Andrew Gray himself was a Southerner, from Virginia, who had adopted Texas as his home state. Proposals for developing a portion of the transcontinental railroad through Texas and on to San Diego had been discussed and approved in the Texas legislature since 1848 and thus would have been familiar to all Texas politicians, and to Gray.[15]

Nor were the Texans' expectations empty ones. On February 16, 1852, the Texas Western Railroad Company was chartered by the Texas legislature and planned, with a grant from the state, to build a railroad from the eastern boundary of Texas to El Paso, a circumstance of which Texas legislators in Washington surely were aware.[16] Now aroused and in full-throated opposition to Bartlett-Condé, compromise opponents attached an amendment to the 1852 appropriation bill that cut off funding for the Bartlett commission until the boundary was fixed not further north than the line Gray had suggested, at 31°52'.[17]

Once the Democrats had won the 1852 election and Franklin Pierce had moved into the White House, the president decided that the only sensible way to deal with the boundary mess in New Mexico was to invoke Article XXI of the Treaty of Guadalupe Hidalgo, which said that if any disagreement arose between the two nations regarding the treaty, they would resolve it through negotiation.[18] Hence, Pierce appointed Gadsden to travel to Mexico City, negotiate a new boundary with Mexico, and settle other issues relating to the treaty. Gadsden, too, was a Southerner (from South Carolina and Florida), president of the Louisville, Charleston, and Cincinnati Railroad from 1840 to 1850, and a supporter of the southern route since at least 1845.[19]

There were, of course, other reasons for the Gadsden negotiations, almost all of which stemmed from problems with the Treaty of Guadalupe Hidalgo. They included the inability of the United States to prevent Apache raids into northern Mexico as promised in Article XI of the treaty, the settlement of mutual claims of Mexican and U.S. citizens against each other's governments following the war, and the awarding of a concession to an American company to build a road across the Isthmus of Tehuantepec in the southernmost part of Mexico.[20] However, Secretary of State William L. Marcy instructed Gadsden that acquiring land for a transcontinental railroad route was the most important U.S. aim and that Gadsden should, in one treaty, negotiate a new boundary between the United States and Mexico, obtain release for the United States from Article XI of the 1848 treaty, and settle all claims between the two countries, absorbing the resolution of all issues into the boundary negotiation. For such a settlement, the United States was prepared to pay a substantial sum of money.[21]

The head of the Mexican government, who ultimately had to approve any such agreement, was President Antonio Lopez de Santa Anna, who had a long and checkered history as a Mexican military and political leader. Santa Anna was a Mexican army officer who had served as president of Mexico three times before—in 1833–36, 1841–44, and in 1846–47, during the war with the United States. On all three occasions he was overthrown in revolutions and exiled from Mexico. Each time he returned and found his way back into power. Most recently, he had been recalled to Mexico and elected president in 1853, after which he governed the country as a dictator with only a council to assist him.[22] Many Mexicans already despised their government for having ceded Texas, New Mexico, and Upper California to the United States in the Treaty of Guadalupe Hidalgo, and this made Santa Anna a cautious negotiator.[23] But Santa Anna's reluctance to give up any more Mexican territory was overcome by his need for cash to run his impoverished government and maintain the military force necessary to defend it from yet another revolution that might sweep it away.[24]

Pierce had given Gadsden six possible boundary lines to negotiate, each allowing more or less territory for the United States.[25] Negotiations were concluded and a treaty agreed upon in December 1853, but the debate over ratification in the U.S. Senate continued into 1854 while Poston planned and made his trip through Sonora. While no one could tell where the new boundary would be until the treaty was ratified by both governments, it was widely assumed that some part of northern Mexico, perhaps all of Sonora, Chihuahua, or Baja California, would soon become U.S. territory. All through fall 1853 and the first half of 1854, rumors about the progress of the treaty flew. The subject was much discussed in American newspapers, and Poston and his boardinghouse companions would have been well acquainted with the various popular opinions concerning the purchase.

For example, President Pierce favored a boundary that would include northern portions of the states of Sonora, Chihuahua, and Coahuila, and all of Baja California. California senators wanted a substantial acquisition of Mexican territory and a port on the Gulf of California. Some Northern senators insisted that the boundary be extended south to the twenty-seventh parallel, which would take in most of the states of Sonora and Chihuahua and about half of Coahuila, including the port of Guaymas on the Gulf of California and the silver mines of Sonora. Some Southern senators wanted only a boundary that secured a workable southern transcontinental railroad route. But others wanted to take enough of Mexico to create a new "slave state" in order to offset California's admission to the union as a "free state."[26]

Most California newspapers favored American expansion, and Poston and his friends would have seen in their San Francisco papers a steady flow of articles and editorials favoring either purchase or outright annexation of parts of Mexico. For example, the *Daily Alta California* for September 2, 1851, declared that territory from northern Mexico would be brought into the United States "by conquest or by purchase," while the September 20 edition criticized the U.S. government for failing to annex Baja California in the Treaty of Guadalupe Hidalgo but assured readers that the government would do so soon. On December 19, 1852, the paper confidently asserted that a large portion of Mexico would be annexed to the United States and the frontier moved as far south as Sinaloa. On June 21, 1853, the paper declared that Mexico was ripe for annexation and that many Mexican businessmen and landowners favored it. Three months later, on September 19, it declared that annexation of all Mexico by the United States was inevitable, especially if Mexicans wanted to escape dictatorial rule by Santa Anna.[27] Not to be outdone, the *Sacramento Daily Union*, on November 16, 1853, declared that it supported U.S. territorial acquisition in Mexico—but by purchase or negotiation, not by force of arms.

Such an expansion of U.S. territory meant that speculation in northern Mexican properties might bring enormous profit. One can imagine the scrambling on both sides of the border during the Gadsden negotiations: American speculators trying to get a foothold in northern Mexico in anticipation of territory being purchased by the United States and a transcontinental railroad being built through the region, and Mexican landowners trying to negotiate favorable deals with American developers in order to maximize the value of their land, or at least protect its value in an uncertain legal environment. From the American speculators' point of view, profit must have seemed astonishingly easy. All one would have to do is purchase Mexican land before any U.S. takeover. The purchase might involve tracts for mining or farming, a prospective port on the Gulf of California, or a railroad route. And as Goodale explains, this was the right time to make such arrangements with northern Mexican landowners, before the new

U.S.-Mexican boundary was determined: "Until the region was securely confirmed by Senate ratification of Gadsden's treaty, agreements and concessions might easily be arranged with one or more of the contending local factions or private parties which would provide substantial financial advantages to future investors."[28]

This was the aim of the Poston expedition: to acquire wealth by speculating in Mexican properties before the Gadsden Purchase was completed, especially land on the Gulf of California, where a port city might be built, or abandoned gold or silver mines that might be exploited.[29] This was just the sort of deal that Poston thought he might bring off given his legal and business background. And it was the sort of opportunity that very shortly came his way.

Poston and his friends at the Government Boarding House fed their speculations by researching accounts of early Spanish explorers in northern Mexico. "Old Spanish history was ransacked," Poston says, "for information from the voyages of Cortez in the Gulf of California to the latest dates," and the group would have found no lack of stories about the mineral wealth of Sonora.[30]

For almost three hundred years, since the time of Coronado and the legends of El Dorado and the Seven Cities of Cibola, stories had circulated about the fabulous mineral wealth of northern Mexico, treasure both buried in the ground and held by native peoples.[31] These stories included not only ancient legends about rich silver and gold deposits in what are now Sonora and Arizona but also more recent accounts of mineral discoveries and abandoned mines that promised untold riches to be had for relatively little investment or effort. It is ironic, but fitting, that the boardinghouse group would have rehearsed these narratives, since such stories fundamentally authorized exploitation of the land by implying that the treasure to be found existed to be gathered by the ingenuity of Europeans or, later, Anglo-Americans.[32]

One of the most potent and persistent of these legends concerned the fabulous *bolas y planchas de plata* (balls and slabs of silver) found in October 1736 in the mountains of northern Sonora by Antonio Siraumea, a Yaqui Indian mine worker and prospector. Siraumea's discovery was fifteen miles southwest of the old Spanish mission of Guevavi in southern Arizona and about ten miles below the present-day international border. The *bolas y planchas* were chunks of almost pure silver, lying partially exposed on the ground or nine to eighteen inches below the surface. One enormous slab reportedly weighed nearly one and a quarter tons. The discovery, of course, caused a rush by local miners to the site. The *planchas* were, in some instances, so large and so pure that Juan Bautista de Anza, chief justice of Sonora, captain-for-life of the Fronteras presidio, and the highest-ranking government official in the region, suspected that they were not a natural vein of silver, but a buried treasure or products of a clandestine smelting operation. If this were true, they would have been the property of the Spanish crown and off-limits to miners. So Anza banned all mining at the site and confiscated the silver already found there. Later, on orders from the viceroy in Mexico City, he returned to the site with a team of six mining experts, all of whom declared that the silver was, indeed, a natural deposit. Anza then reopened the site and returned the impounded silver to the finders.

In describing the location of the discovery, Anza referred to "Arizona," the residence of his deputy chief justice in the area, Bernardo de Urrea, a Basque rancher, storekeeper, and miner. Urrea's ranch was about fifteen miles southwest of the discovery site, near a small mining village called Agua Caliente. Anza had ordered the impounded silver stored at Urrea's ranch and made the ranch his headquarters while taking depositions about the discoveries. "Arizona," in the Basque language, means "the good oak tree," an appropriate name in a region of canyons and ridges covered by oaks. Later, the discovery location was mistakenly referred to by writers as "Arizonac," "Arizuma," or "Arizumea" and was described as the site of rich silver "mines," even though the original *bolas y planchas* were found just below the surface of the ground, and virtually no additional silver was found after the first discoveries. Despite these facts, the site became celebrated among Spanish colonists and travelers through the region. And for more than a century afterward, tales of the *bolas y planchas de plata* lured seekers of wealth such as Poston and others to northern Mexico.[33]

The German Jesuit missionary Juan Nentvig wrote about the *bolas de plata* ("*Las Bolas*") as early as 1762 in his *Rudo Ensayo*, in which he also described several other gold and silver deposits in Sonora. In a claim typical of those made by travelers through Sonora, Nentvig declared that there was no part of the region that did not offer silver and gold, "almost on the surface, to those who have the patience to dig and separate the ore from the dirt. . . . There is an inexhaustible source of these and other metals."[34] Anza's son, Juan Bautista de Anza, referred to the famous "site of Arizonac" in the diary of his 1774 expedition from Sonora to California and reported "good gold and silver mines" near Arivaca, "which were worked until the year 'sixty-seven [1767], when they were abandoned because of greater persecution by the Apaches. From that time henceforward grains and good-sized nuggets of pure gold have been found in the neighborhood, for I have seen them."[35] The British chargé d'affaires in Mexico City, Henry George

Ward, referred to the *bolas de plata* in his popular book *Mexico in 1827*.[36] Andrew B. Gray, whose expedition surveying a southern route for the Texas Western Railroad was in Sonora at the same time as Poston's, reported being told of the *planchas de plata*, "a river of placer where enormous pieces of virgin silver were found very near the surface many years ago."[37]

Poston would not have read Nentvig's, Anza's, or Gray's works before his Sonoran expedition, since none was published in the United States until after his return.[38] However, in their research Poston and his friends would have had access to several other books describing the mineral wealth of northern Mexico. Some hints as to what these were appear, oddly enough, in an 1856 report of the Sonora Exploring and Mining Company of Cincinnati (SEMC), whose founders included Poston, Major Samuel Peter Heintzelman, William Wrightson, and Edgar Conkling. The company's report was designed to attract new investors, and to this end, it cited three authors—Alexander Von Humboldt, Ward, and Robert A. Wilson—whose works celebrated the mines of northern Mexico. Though not named in the report, Humboldt's *Political Essay on the Kingdom of New Spain* (1814) detailed the vast quantities of gold and silver taken from Mexican mines from the late seventeenth to the early nineteenth century. And references to Humboldt in the report suggest that someone involved in preparing the document knew of his work. Ward's *Mexico in 1827* (1828) and Wilson's *Mexico and Its Religion* (1855) are quoted extensively in the report.[39] While it is not known if Poston read Humboldt's or Ward's works before his Sonora expedition (Wilson's book would have been published too late), he and Heintzelman are the most likely to have suggested them to the other principal investors, who were Cincinnati businessmen, not explorers or mining enthusiasts.

In his *Political Essay on the Kingdom of New Spain*, Humboldt claims that "from 1777 to 1803, the quantity of silver annually extracted from the Mexican minerals, has almost constantly been above two millions of marcs of silver."[40] In a manner typical of Europeans exploring the Americas, Humboldt argues that industrious Europeans would easily outdo Mexicans in developing the country's natural wealth. In examining the travel writings of nineteenth-century British visitors to South America, Mary Louise Pratt finds that "Spanish American society in general . . . is relentlessly indicted for backwardness, indolence, and above all, the 'failure' to exploit the resources surrounding it."[41] Thus, New Spain, Humboldt assures readers, "under a better administration, and inhabited by an industrious people, will alone yield in gold and silver, the hundred and sixty three millions of francs, at present furnished by the whole of America."[42]

Ward, in 1828, promises similarly that the mines of northern Mexico offer to European investors and scientists "a field . . . superior in richness to any the New World has yet presented." Sonora, in particular, is a land that "can hardly fail, in the course of a few years, to acquire great and permanent importance." Acquiring mining concessions and extracting the mineral wealth in this region, Ward declares, should be relatively easy: "In all these districts [in Sonora] the depth of the mines is inconsiderable, their former riches acknowledged, and the causes by which their working was interrupted, known. The advances necessary in order to bring them into activity are small. . . . No unreasonable expectations are entertained by the Mexican proprietors, and no onerous conditions proposed: while their respectability and influence in the country are the best possible guarantee to the adventurers that their operations will be conducted with good faith, and can meet with no interruption. The success of the enterprise appears to me unquestionable."[43]

Another resource that Poston may have consulted before his expedition is retired British naval lieutenant R. W. H. Hardy's *Travels in the Interior of Mexico in 1825, 1826, 1827 & 1828*. Hardy visited Mexico in the 1820s to inspect pearl fisheries along the Gulf of California for the General Pearl and Coral Fishery Association of London and to prospect for new pearl fishing sites.[44] Andrew Gray read Hardy's book before undertaking his expedition through Sonora, and Poston may have done so, too.[45] Hardy describes the gulf's pearl fisheries but also promotes the numerous silver and gold mines of Mexico, which he did not visit but knew only by rumor and legend. Among the many silver mines he describes, is the "Arizona," which is "supposed to abound in balls of silver," including one weighing "ten thousand pounds!!!" Gold, he promises confidently, "can be obtained by every class of people with little comparative industry."[46]

Poston and his friends did not have to rely on legends or books by early travelers to hear of the reputed mineral wealth of Sonora. Contemporary California newspapers often carried stories of Mexico's riches. The historian Joseph A. Stout says that California newspapers reported Sonora as being even richer in resources than California. Supposedly, five million dollars' worth of gold had been exported from Guaymas in 1848, and although this decreased by half in 1851, many Californians believed that one could still find easy wealth in the mines of Mexico.[47] On October 27, 1852, the *Daily Alta California* praised both the rich silver mines and agricultural potential of Sonora. It cited the province's silver mines again in its April 3 and December 10, 1853, issues. And on January 3, 1854, only weeks before Poston left for Sonora, a writer identifying himself as "N" wrote to the paper that Sonora's silver mines were, "almost without exception, of an enormous value. I have seen pieces of native silver weighing several arrobas." However, he warned that "the working of these mines requires a fortune: the rich Mexicans will not expose theirs, (and besides they have no cash) and foreign capital is not to be had."[48]

Old legends and new rumors notwithstanding, the story that Poston said precipitated the Sonoran expedition was one that appeared in the November 24, 1853, *Daily Alta California*, telling about the famous Iturbide Grant in Mexico. The Iturbides, a wealthy and prominent Mexican family, had been offered a grant of land by the Mexican government worth one million dollars as an indemnity for the execution in 1823 of General Augustin de Iturbide, a revolutionary leader, who in 1820 had fought against Spanish rule. In 1822, after the Spanish had been overthrown and before the new republic could firmly establish itself, Iturbide declared himself emperor of Mexico. When the Mexican people became restless under Iturbide's severe rule, rebel leader Vicente Guerrero, in alliance with Santa Anna, set up a republic against him. Iturbide was forced to abdicate and was deported to Italy on a pension. When he returned to Mexico the following year, he was arrested, tried for treason, and executed.

In recognition of his services to Mexico, and to forestall any opposition that might form around the Iturbide family, the Mexican republic granted the family an indemnity of one million dollars, which, because the government lacked the cash to pay, it translated into a grant of land. The grant was first offered in Texas, but the Iturbides failed to locate the grant before Americans moved into Texas, rebelled against Mexico, and Texas became independent. The Mexican government then offered a grant to be located in New Mexico or Upper California. But again the family delayed, and the United States acquired those territories through the 1846–47 war and the Treaty of Guadalupe Hidalgo. Finally, the Mexican government offered the Iturbide family "thirty leagues square of land, to be located by them or their agents on government land, in a body or in separate parcels in the States of Sonora, Sinaloa, or Lower California."

The *Alta California* article reported statements made by "the heirs" of Augustin Iturbide supporting Poston's contention that a "representative" of the family visited San Francisco at that time.[49] The article did not say who spoke for the family, but it may have been Salvador Iturbide, the younger son of the former emperor, who came to San Francisco in 1852 to claim land that would make up the Mexican grant. Since the grant was not formally located while Upper California was part of Mexico, Iturbide's claim could not be validated by the California Board of Land Commissioners, and his visit was in vain. The Iturbides did not pursue their claim in California after 1852, so why a member of the family would have been in California again the following year is unclear. But the visit was well publicized and inspired potential speculators like Poston and his companions.

The Iturbide article emphasized the value of the grant, which, it pointed out, could be located on land likely to become part of the United States and thus developed through the industry of an Anglo-Saxon people:

> The immense value of this land can scarcely be estimated, located, as it may be, in a multitude of places which will be the centres of great trade and commerce within ten years. Nine hundred square leagues, more than five millions of acres, which may be located on land where soon the star-spangled banner will wave, where the land shall bloom like a garden, whither ships shall bear freight from every land, where the railroad car will bear off the mineral produce, and the manufactures of a busy Anglo-Saxon population. . . . The grant is made in good faith, and of its legal validity there can be no doubt, so soon as it may be properly located. If it be written in the book of fate that the United States shall obtain any further portion of Mexico, we would hope that the claim of the Iturbides may be located upon that portion.

Poston and his boardinghouse colleagues were thoroughly absorbed by the legends of Sonoran wealth and the opportunity for riches that the Iturbide Grant represented. In language that captures both the romance of legendary Mexican riches and the opportunity for wealth and political power that justified their taking, Poston explains how he and his friends readily concluded that

> the Gulf of California was the Mediterranean of the Pacific and its waters full of pearls. That the Peninsula of Lower California was copper-bound, interspersed with gold and minerals, illustrated with old Spanish Missions, and fanned by the gentlest breezes from the South Pacific. That the State of Sonora was one of the richest of Mexico in silver, copper, gold, coal, and other minerals, with highly productive agricultural valleys in the temperate zone. That the country north of Sonora, called in the Spanish history "Arizunea," (rocky country) was full of minerals, with fertile valleys washed by numerous rivers, and covered by forests primeval. . . . That the Southern Pacific Railroad would soon be built through the new country, and that a new State would be made as a connecting link between Texas and California, with the usual quota of governors, senators, and public officials.[50]

The group also quickly grasped the speculative strategy outlined in the *Alta California*: "It was urged that the Iturbide Grant could be located so as to secure the best sites for towns and cities in the new State, and the rest distributed to settlers as an inducement for rapid colonization." Poston admits that, in his discouragement over his situation at the customs house, he was attracted by the opportunity the unfulfilled grant represented: "It must be admitted that an alluring prospect was opened for a young man idling away his life over a custom house desk at three hundred a month; and in the enthusiasm of youth I undertook to make an exploration of the new territory and to locate the Iturbide Grant."[51] It remained for him now to determine how to take his exploration out of the realm of fantasy and turn it into a genuine expedition.

CHAPTER FOUR

Expansionist Dreams and Private Conquests

The boardinghouse discussions of Poston and his friends concerning northern Mexico would have taken place amid a stew of opposing political ideas and attitudes bubbling on both sides of the border. Mexican sensibilities toward Americans were still raw after the 1846–47 war, a grinding, bloody, two-year conflict in which the American army fought its way through Mexico until it took possession of the capital at Mexico City. Subsequently, in the Treaty of Guadalupe Hidalgo, Santa Anna ceded half of Mexico to the United States, a surrender over which many Mexicans still were bitter in 1854. Mexican politicians, journalists, and intellectuals were all critical of what they viewed as American contempt for Mexico and the danger of America trying to conquer all of Mexico and annex it.

From Mexico's beginnings as a republic in 1821, Mexican attitudes toward the United States had been, in the words of the American historian Gene M. Brack, a "dichotomy, compounded of admiration and fear." At first, Mexicans envied U.S. independence and growing prosperity, which contrasted starkly with Mexican poverty and political instability. Consequently, when Mexicans created a constitution after winning independence, they substantially followed the American model.

However, when the United States supported the 1836 Texas revolt, Mexicans feared that the United States was bent on taking over part or all of their country, either by gradual colonization or by force, and increasingly they distrusted American political aims toward Mexico. Instead of lengthy, admiring articles on American political institutions and economic success, Mexican newspapers after 1836 were filled with anti-American sentiments. America became the "colossus of the north," a term suggesting "a powerful, overly materialistic and aggressive nation which harbored slavery, eradicated Indians, and exploited weaker neighbors, callously disregarding the sensitivities and peculiar problems of Mexico. . . . In general, foreigners, especially Americans, were not cordially received in Mexico, and Mexicans did not travel much in the United States."[1]

Mexicans especially feared American racism, which they believed included Mexicans, and they viewed American slavery as "the most obvious and cruel manifestation of an intense Yankee ethnocentrism" that would devastate Mexico should the United States decide to annex their country. Over the years, Mexicans had become aware that many Americans, especially those who most loudly advocated expansion, saw Mexicans as inferior to them. This had frightening implications, for it was clear that Americans did not respect the rights or culture of those they considered inferior. They were in the process of exterminating their native peoples and kept African Americans in slavery. Mexicans feared that they would suffer the same consequences if Americans were to take over part or all of Mexico.[2]

These fears were not without justification. Since the 1840s American newspaper editors and politicians had written and spoken at length about what John L. O'Sullivan, editor of the *Democratic Review*, called the United States' "Manifest Destiny," the idea that it was historically destined that the country should expand its borders north to the fifty-fourth parallel, west to the Pacific Ocean, and south to . . . no one was quite sure where. O'Sullivan had said that it was the United States' "Manifest Destiny to overspread the continent allotted by Providence for the free development of our yearly multiplying millions."[3] He was speaking of the American settlement of California. But some editors and politicians talked of annexing all of Mexico, or at least Baja California and Sonora. Many, like the editor of the *Daily Alta California* on September 20, 1851, felt that the United States should have taken Baja and Sonora after the 1846–47 war. The full scope of Manifest Destiny was voiced with typical enthusiasm by the *New York Morning News* on October 13, 1845:

> Our way lies not over trampled nations, but through desert wastes, to be brought by our industry and energy within the domain of art and civilization. We are contiguous to a vast portion of the globe, untrodden save by the savage and the beast, and we are conscious of our own power to render it tributary to man. . . . It has been laid and acted upon, that

the solitudes of America are the property of the immigrant children of Europe and their offspring. Not only has this been said and reiterated, but it is actually . . . the basis of public law in America. Public sentiment repudiates possession without use, and this sentiment is gradually acquiring the force of public law. It has sent our adventurous pioneers to the plains of Texas, will carry them to the Rio del Norte, and even that boundary . . . will not stay them on their march to the Pacific, the limit which nature has provided. In like manner, it will come to pass that the confederated democracies of the Anglo American race will give this great continent as an inheritance to man.[4]

Patricia Nelson Limerick points out the racism inherent in the concept of Manifest Destiny and how the desire for more territory, especially a port on the Pacific coast, combined with this racism to support the assumption that Mexico would readily surrender territory to the United States.[5] Americans felt especially superior to Mexicans when it came to the latter's apparent lack of industry. Mexicans seemed not to realize that "time was money," and their evident lack of ambition in developing their own resources seemed to justify Americans moving in and doing it for them. To American visitors, Mexican mines, in particular, were underworked, and it appeared that American ownership and American workers would get from the mines many times what Mexicans had been able to obtain.[6]

Mexicans were well aware of these sentiments. Therefore, after the war, when a group of prominent Mexicans gathered to assess the causes, consequences, and implications of the war, they had little doubt about what American intentions toward Mexico had been since long before the conflict. The United States had wanted to "extend their dominion in such manner as to become the absolute owners of almost all this continent." They would do this by "bringing under their laws and authority all America to the Isthmus of Panama." The war had been a consequence of this "spirit of aggrandizement," combined with American confidence in its ability to overcome Mexico by sheer military force. Now, the brutal consequences of the war—the extensive damage to Mexican towns, roads, and ports; the thousands of military and civilian casualties; the loss of land; and the humiliation of having their cities occupied by American troops—all had taken a devastating emotional, as well as economic, toll on the Mexican people. And Mexicans had little doubt of future U.S. intentions: "We will see ourselves overwhelmed anew, sooner or later, in another or in more than one disastrous war, until the flag of the stars floats over the last span of territory which it [the United States] so much covets."[7]

Some Americans—and persons of other nationalities—were more than willing to fulfill Mexican expectations. Between 1852 and 1854, before and during Poston's Sonora expedition, several armed expeditions, called "filibusters," entered northern Mexico from the United States and attempted to seize Mexican territory by force.[8] Some of these groups were led by Americans, some by French or other nationalities. Sometimes the filibusters sought to overthrow the Mexican government, sometimes to seize territory that could later be annexed to the United States, and sometimes just to take part of Mexico and exploit it for personal gain.

Joseph A. Stout Jr., who has written extensively about the Mexican filibusters, points out that political and social conditions in both the United States and Mexico encouraged filibustering. In the United States, expansionist politics, the war with Mexico, and undisguised racism convinced many that invasion and annexation of parts of Mexico were appropriate, if not inevitable, and that only "Anglo Saxons from north of the border could bring stability and modernization to Mexico."[9]

Simple greed also contributed to the filibustering impulse. Some filibusters had made fortunes in the West, then lost them; others had come west to seek fortune but had found the going too difficult. These men crowded the cities of California, and many of them saw filibustering in Mexico as an easy path to riches.[10] Northern Mexico seemed an especially inviting target. The many revolutions following Mexican independence in 1821 had made the national government unstable and too weak to defend its northern states from filibusters, bandits, and raiding Apaches. Much of northern Mexico was thinly populated and undeveloped; many of the people were poor and lived marginal lives.[11] It seemed to ambitious outsiders as though the land was available for the taking. Invasion promised "a taste of flavorful adventure, a sense of lifting oppression from the shoulders of an inferior people, and a hope of quick wealth." However, although they sometimes professed a desire to advance the values of American democracy and economic enterprise or to help "oppressed" Mexicans, the filibusters were not driven mainly by political ideals but by a desire for personal power and wealth.[12]

In the early 1850s four filibustering expeditions into northern Mexico received ample publicity in California and probably influenced the course of Poston's expedition. Three of these were organized by Frenchmen and attempted to take advantage of Mexican leaders' desire to populate their northern states with foreign immigrants.

The first of the French filibusters attempting to take advantage of Mexican openness to foreign settlement was that of Count Charles de Pindray in 1851. Pindray was born to a wealthy French family but as a young man quickly spent his inheritance and fled to America to avoid the consequences of debt and illegal financial activities. He was not alone. From 1848 through 1852, thousands of French immigrants came to California and Mexico to improve their conditions or escape political turmoil at home. Predictably, not all succeeded, and, as with the Anglo-American forty-niners, there was a large group of unemployed, dissatisfied Frenchmen in California looking for wealth and adventure.[13]

Pindray himself was a failed gold seeker, who had learned of Mexican colonizing opportunities and thought that they might enable him to re-create his fortune. Santa Anna's government had authorized colonization to populate the northern frontier.[14] The government welcomed French settlers but would not admit Americans. Having learned that the Mexican vice-consul in San Francisco, William Schleiden, was looking for colonists to settle in northern Mexico, Pindray volunteered to recruit and lead a French expedition. The Mexican government gave Pindray's party permission to settle in Sonora, and the Sonoran government granted the Frenchmen three leagues of land near Cocóspera, where the expedition settled in March 1852.

Unfortunately for Pindray, even before his expedition arrived, the venture had begun to look suspicious to Sonoran authorities. Persistent reports in California newspapers suggested that many of Pindray's men were not French but American and that Pindray's "colony" was really a filibustering expedition. When Pindray's men left the colony to prospect for gold and silver, Mexican authorities decided that these "colonists" were not what they claimed to be. General Miguel Blanco, the Mexican military commander for Sonora, cut off Pindray's supplies, and the colony collapsed. After a brief confrontation with Mexican militias at Ures, Pindray and his men retreated to the village of Rayón, where Pindray died mysteriously, supposedly shooting himself in the head while suffering from a high fever. Many of Pindray's men returned to California, and some joined the expedition of Count Gaston Raousset de Boulbon, which was then forming in California.[15]

Raousset had had a career similar to Pindray's. He was born into a wealthy French family, squandered his inheritance, failed in French politics, and joined the California gold rush, expecting to get rich quickly. However, as a French nobleman, he did not care to do the hard manual labor required in mining. While looking for easier opportunities to make money, he met Pindray in a San Francisco bar. Both men were interested in obtaining power and wealth, and Pindray may have offered Raousset a place in his expedition. But most likely both wanted to lead, and Pindray's party left California without Raousset, who formed his own expedition.

Like Pindray, Raousset had a contract with the Mexican government that allowed him and his men to colonize in northern Sonora. The agreement was approved by Mexican president Arista, and the expedition had financial backing from the French-American banking firm of Jecker, Torre, and Company. Among other things, the contract allowed Raousset's party to locate and work abandoned mines near the storied "Arizonac" site, taking the mines from the previous owners by force if necessary. Also like Pindray, Raousset found it easy to recruit for his colony among unemployed Frenchmen in San Francisco and was able to gather nearly two hundred men. All were promised a share of land and of any mineral wealth found. As with Pindray's expedition, Americans were excluded, since Mexican law forbade them from colonizing.

On February 17, 1852, Raousset's expedition left San Francisco for Mexico and was welcomed by citizens at Guaymas, who hoped that the colonists would keep both Apaches and land-hungry Americans beyond Mexico's northern border. But state authorities' doubts were aroused when the French debarked in full military style, displaying artillery and other arms in defiance of their agreement with the Sonoran government. Raousset also began calling himself the "Sultan of Sonora," confirming suspicions that he and his men were not legitimate colonizers, but filibusters.

After continued clashes with Sonoran officials over where his expedition could and could not go, Raousset attacked Hermosillo, occupied the city, and raised a flag declaring "Liberty to the State of Sonora." However, Raousset received an arm wound in the fighting and later suffered a severe attack of dysentery. With most of their officers now dead or ill, Raousset's men asked their remaining two officers to lead them out of Mexico. When the French reached Guaymas, they surrendered to General Blanco and asked to be allowed to leave the country. Most returned to California. Raousset remained in Mazatlan, recovering from his illness, but did not give up on his plans. He returned to San Francisco in January 1853 to plan a second filibuster.

After failing to persuade Santa Anna to make him military governor of Sonora, Raousset took a large force to Sonora in two separate parties, one in April and another in July 1854. News of Raousset's expedition ignited a firestorm of condemnation in Mexico City newspapers, which called it "'villainy,' 'treason,' and an attempt to establish an 'iniquitous' government on Mexican soil." Newly chosen Mexican president Santa Anna issued a decree that "no armed foreigners should be allowed to disembark anywhere in Mexico, and that North Americans living along the coast were to be watched carefully." General José María Yáñez was appointed military commander of Sonora to defend the state against Raousset, and his men crushed Raousset's forces in Guaymas on July 13. Most of the Frenchmen left Mexico. Raousset was court-martialed on August 9, convicted of conspiracy to overthrow the Mexican government, and executed by firing squad three days later.[16]

Raousset's 1852 filibuster probably inspired American William Walker to try to acquire some of northern Mexico for himself. Walker, from Nashville, practiced law briefly in New Orleans and edited the *New Orleans Crescent* newspaper. Like Poston, he went west with the gold rush and arrived in San Francisco in 1850, where he obtained a job as assistant editor of the *San Francisco Daily Herald*. In 1851 he moved to Marysville, California, and practiced law there with his partner, Henry P. Watkins.

After Raousset failed in 1852, Walker and Watkins decided to try filibustering in Mexico. Unlike his French predecessors, Walker made no pretense of seeking Mexican permission to colonize. He planned from the start to seize Baja California and Sonora and proclaim the "Republic of Sonora." He raised money by selling bonds for the new "republic" as early as May 1853 and found plenty of failed miners, gamblers, and drifters in California willing to sign up for his expedition. By the end of September 1853, Walker had completed his arrangements, including chartering the brig *Arrow* to transport the expedition from San Francisco. He was delayed when troops commanded by General Ethan Allen Hitchcock, acting under a personal order from President Pierce to stop filibusters from entering Mexico, seized the ship on September 30. But the delay was only temporary. On October 16, Walker and forty-five men left San Francisco on a smaller ship, the *Caroline*, which landed at Cape San Lucas at the southern tip of Baja California. Sailing back and forth between Cape San Lucas and La Paz, Walker arrested the Mexican governor of Baja, Colonel Rafael Espinosa, and his replacement and fought with the local inhabitants, some of whom resisted his attempts to "liberate" them. He also proclaimed the newly independent "Republic of Lower California" and began promulgating laws for the new state.

Realizing that he could not hold La Paz or Cape San Lucas, Walker sailed north to Enseñada, where he was again opposed by local residents led by the bandit-turned-patriot Guadalupe Melendrez. Undaunted, Walker proclaimed the annexation of Sonora to Baja California on January 18, 1854, and changed the name of his new state to the "Republic of Sonora."

Walker's clumsy maneuverings and lack of supplies caused his men to desert in large numbers. By February he had only 130 men left. With those he tried to revive his expedition by invading Sonora. He marched north to the Colorado River, about seventy miles south of Fort Yuma, then turned east for a short distance into Sonora. But when still more of his men left him, Walker was forced to return to Ensenada with a force of only twenty-five. There, he was surrounded by Melendrez's men. Walker fought Melendrez while retreating to the U.S. border, where he and his men made a frantic charge through the Mexicans and managed to get across the line. They were arrested by soldiers led by Major J. McKinstry and taken to San Francisco, where Walker was tried for illegally leading a military expedition into Mexico.[17]

The French and American filibusters in Mexico had several implications for Poston's expedition. First, they showed Poston what men of action might dare and drew him, as they did others, to seek the celebrated riches of northern Mexico. Poston said later that Raousset's 1852 filibuster, in particular, was a stimulus for his own expedition.[18] But the 1850s filibusters that preceded Poston, although celebrated in the press as daring and ambitious, had all failed, and what they attempted was expensive, illegal, and dangerous.

Poston's expedition was not a "filibuster." His men were armed, but their numbers were small, and their intent was not to take or hold Mexican territory. Moreover, as the preceding paragraphs have shown, they would not have succeeded had they tried. Mexican authorities were aware of the filibustering expeditions and successfully defeated all of them. California newspapers reported publicly on Raousset's and Walker's expeditions. In some cases, meetings of filibustering organizations were advertised in the newspapers and were open to the public. Moreover, Mexican officials in the coastal cities of Mexico and California were adept at gathering intelligence about filibusters. One of their methods was to take sworn statements from ship's captains and passengers who landed at ports along the Mexican coast.[19]

It was not lost upon Mexicans that these expeditions, whether French or American, originated on American soil. It also seemed clear that although the U.S. Congress had passed a neutrality law in 1818 forbidding military incursions from the United States into foreign countries with whom it was at peace, the government did little or nothing to stop the filibusters.[20] Some Mexican authorities thought that the U.S. government was secretly financing and supporting the filibusters.[21] There is no evidence for this, but American enforcement of the neutrality statute was inconsistent at best. It became more aggressive in 1853 when Presidents Fillmore and Pierce ordered their Pacific military commanders, Generals Hitchcock and John E. Wool, respectively, to stop filibustering expeditions leaving California for Mexico.[22] In any case, the brutal Walker filibuster and Raousset's fatal second venture both happened almost simultaneously with Poston's expedition, and both would have brought suspicion and scrutiny of Poston's activities by Mexican authorities, forcing him to be very careful about his entrance into Mexico and about what he said and did while there.

Walker's 1853 Baja invasion, for example, created a crisis in international relations, greatly complicating Gadsden's negotiations and endangering the lives of Americans in Sonora. Juan Robinson, U.S. consul at Guaymas, warned Gadsden that Walker's expedition was a threat and asked if Walker's men could be kept off the Mexican mainland. Gadsden responded by ordering American warships in the waters off Mexico to stop any suspicious ships containing large groups of men or supplies that might be intended for Walker. Despite these measures, on November 17, 1853, Robinson told Gadsden that Guaymas was "an armed camp" because the Mexican military commander there had recruited "all able bodied men to repel the filibusters."[23]

Not long after, the American schooner *General Patterson* was denied permission to discharge its American passengers at Guaymas unless the ship paid a special duty. The ship was suspected of having landed American filibusters along the Gulf of California.[24] Once news of Walker's invasion reached Guaymas, Mexican citizens there threw stones at Americans and shouted "Death to Americans," while two thousand Mexican army regulars massed near the port, awaiting orders to cross the gulf to Baja California and drive the filibusters out.[25]

Individuals thought to be sympathetic toward the filibusters were singled out for retribution. In January 1854 two Polish American citizens with naturalization papers and passports were expelled from Guaymas by the prefect of the city. The two, who had been living in Guaymas for six months, were forced to leave behind their business, worth about five thousand dollars. One of the two, named Walter (similar to Walker), was thought by Mexican authorities to be part of Walker's forces and to know his plans.[26]

Even U.S. consul Robinson was not exempt from punishment. Because the *Caroline*, the ship that had transported Walker's men to Baja, was owned by Robinson's son, Mexican opinion went heavily against the Robinsons. Mexican authorities demanded that Juan Robinson pay a large sum of money as a contribution toward the war against Walker. Many foreigners thought that had the British warship *Virago* not arrived at Guaymas just then, Mexicans would have killed Robinson because he was suspected of favoring the filibusters. Eventually, Robinson was forced to leave Guaymas, and the U.S. government had to appoint a new consul.[27]

As the Walker filibuster dragged on, conditions for all foreigners in Guaymas became grim. In January, Mexican authorities ordered all foreigners in Guaymas to register with the government and form a company to fight Walker. It was thought that the Mexicans intended to put the foreigners in the front rank when fighting began so that they would serve as a shield for Mexican troops. The foreigners did register but refused to take up arms against the filibusters.[28]

While the French and American filibusters in Mexico may have exhibited daring, their leaders were self-absorbed, impractical, and overreaching. They also created serious difficulties for foreigners who happened to enter Mexico while the filibustering expeditions were under way. And they ensured that any who sought wealth in that country would have to pursue a very different course than the one of deception and force used by the filibusters.

CHAPTER FIVE

Planning the Expedition to Sonora

The first step in planning the Sonoran expedition, Poston said, was to form a "syndicate" of influential men in San Francisco who would support it and be potential investors in developing the Iturbide properties once they were located.[1] Actually, it is not clear whether Poston formed the syndicate or the syndicate found him. Poston researcher Benjamin Sacks says that Poston "was selected" by the syndicate to make the journey into Sonora.[2] In either case, members of the syndicate must have been impressed with the young man who would implement their plans. Twenty-eight years old, eager for adventure, having both a legal and commercial background in the international business environment of the customs house, and apparently able to charm his way into or out of most any situation, Poston must have seemed made to order for an exploration of northern Mexico and the pending new American territory.

As for the syndicate, it is not known who or how many they were. Poston never identified them. They may have been men Poston knew from his work in the customs house, men with sufficient wealth to develop any resources that the expedition found or with the personal contacts to attract such support. John C. McLemore, to whom the "Reconnoisance" is addressed, was probably one of the syndicate, perhaps its head. Other members may have included the signers of a presidential petition, discussed later in this chapter, recommending that Poston be appointed the new U.S. consul at Guaymas.

Whoever the syndicate were, evidence suggests that once they entered the picture, they steered Poston away from his original aim of locating the Iturbide Grant and toward goals they considered more profitable. This was a sensible course. The Iturbide Grant had to be located in Mexico for the family to claim it, but American entrepreneurs would have preferred investment on soil that would be American once the Gadsden negotiations were complete. The Iturbide family and their grant are not mentioned once in the "Reconnoisance in Sonora," suggesting that the focus of the expedition had shifted from the grant to the Gadsden Purchase and that the expedition's objectives had been changed to exploring investment opportunities on lands that would become part of the United States once the Gadsden Treaty was ratified.

Historians and biographers have not said much about Poston's syndicate because Poston himself said so little. It is difficult to make generalizations about them, but with the help of the "Reconnoisance" and Poston's later accounts of his expedition, it is easier to see what the syndicate's role was, especially in setting objectives for the expedition: a railroad terminus for the transcontinental railroad on the Gulf of California, far enough north to be included in the Gadsden Purchase, and access to the silver mines of Sonora.[3] These objectives were quite specific, not generalized or wishful thinking like the Iturbide project. The Gadsden Purchase would provide a legal context for acquiring the properties the syndicate wanted. Avoiding the excesses of the filibusters, Poston and his associates would plan carefully, keep a low profile, and operate within the law—both American and Mexican. They would seek out wealthy landowners in Sonora and negotiate legally binding land concessions. That is where Poston, with his legal knowledge, social skills, and customs house experience, came in. Although young and lacking in frontier knowledge, as a negotiator he had the skills that the syndicate needed. And the trail experience the expedition lacked might come from elsewhere, as it did once Poston recruited the members of his party.

Poston began making specific preparations for the expedition late in 1853. He obtained financial support from two French bankers.[4] How Poston chose these bankers is not known. They may have been recommended by the syndicate, or they may have been contacts Poston made while working in the customs house. Poston says that he was influenced in his planning by Raousset's 1852 filibuster, which had been financed by the French-American bankers Jecker, Torre, and Company. Perhaps this circumstance led Poston to seek out French bankers.

Poston also appears to have begun raising cash for the expedition on his own, buying and selling real estate in a bullish San Francisco market. Real estate prices in the city peaked in the last months of 1853, but Goodale says that by February 1854 the market collapsed in a wave of speculation: "Unimproved town lots became unsalable at any price, rents plummeted, and for the first six months of 1854, a commercial depression blighted the city."[5] Clearly, Poston had learned something about real estate dealings from his Kentucky experience. He escaped financial disaster by keeping his investments limited and getting out of the market when prices began to fall. In the process, he managed to raise about one thousand dollars for the expedition.[6]

On January 6, 1854, Poston resigned his position at the customs house.[7] The expedition had probably been in the planning stages for a couple of months by this time, and Poston's resignation was one of the final steps before the expedition left San Francisco. About this time, Poston probably began recruiting men for the expedition. Like the filibusters that had preceded him into Mexico, he did this from the many unemployed fortune hunters and adventure seekers populating San Francisco. Poston says that he assembled a party of twenty-five, a "rather tough cargo of humanity . . . not so bad as reckless; not ungovernable, but independent."[8]

Poston never identified any of these men but one—Herman Ehrenberg, who was arguably the most important member of the expedition. Ehrenberg was a German mining engineer, surveyor, and mapmaker. He was also a true adventurer, who had served in the war for Texas independence (on the Texans' side), survived the Goliad massacre, fought in the battle of San Jacinto, traveled the Oregon Trail, performed surveys for King Kamehameha III in Hawaii, served under John C. Fremont in the California Bear Flag Revolt, and prospected in Mexico. He was only four years older than Poston, and like Poston, he was working a humdrum job in late 1853 as a lithographer for Zabreski Alexander & Company in San Francisco. But his engineering skills and his experience as a soldier and explorer made him critical to the expedition's success.[9]

To calculate Ehrenberg's importance to the expedition, one need only consider the many things that Poston, the customs house clerk, did not know about frontier exploration. Although nominally the expedition's leader, Poston had no experience in frontier travel. He had bought and sold farm property in Kentucky and city lots in San Francisco and understood legal contracts, deeds, and ships' manifests. But he had never sailed the west coast of Mexico, climbed a mountain range, or led a group of starving men on a do-or-die march across a waterless desert, all of which he had to do on the expedition. He had never prospected, never seen a silver or gold mine, never navigated a seaport, and never surveyed a harbor or town site. He had never had to negotiate with officials of a foreign government on their native soil and in their own language. In fact, except for the journey from Kentucky to San Francisco, he had never been outside the United States.

As for Ehrenberg, there would have been few better qualified to advise Poston on how to plan and provision the expedition, what sorts of men to recruit, how to read a map and plot a route, and what to expect when they actually struck the trail. As a mining engineer and surveyor, Ehrenberg knew how to assess a mine's potential and survey a plot of land—and did both on the expedition. For all these reasons, Ehrenberg became Poston's right hand on the journey. And Poston came to trust him, so much so that they remained friends after the expedition and partnered in the development of the Sonora Exploring and Mining Company.

It is not known how Poston and Ehrenberg met. It may have been through Frederick J. Goerlitz, a ship's broker, whose office was not far from the customs house and whose business advertisement appeared frequently in the *Daily Alta California*. Goerlitz was the coordinator for passengers and freight on the *Zoraida*, the ship on which Poston's expedition sailed from San Francisco. He advertised for both in the *San Francisco Daily Herald* of January 29, 1854.[10] Although a native of Germany (and thus a countryman of Ehrenberg), he was a naturalized American citizen, whose business at the customs house may have brought him into contact with Poston. He also was proprietor of an English-language newspaper, *The Times*, which he intended to publish in Guaymas.

On February 17, the *Daily Alta California* announced that "the *Zoraida* will leave today for Guaymas. She takes a number of passengers, among whom are H. Ehrenberg and F. Goerlitz, pioneers in California. Ehrenberg goes to Mexico as a 'surveyor.'"[11] Goerlitz surely was aware of Poston's expedition, but Poston's name is not mentioned in the notice, nor is any information given about the expedition. Perhaps mindful of General Hitchcock's seizure of the *Arrow* and the U.S. government's recent opposition to filibustering, Poston may have deliberately tried to reduce his party's visibility in order to avoid scrutiny by potential competitors and the army.

The syndicate also may have tried to help Poston and the expedition at this time with something more than money and organization. In a January 1854 petition to President Pierce, several individuals recommended that Poston be appointed U.S. consul at Guaymas to replace Juan Robinson. The document says that because all business transacted with Americans in Guaymas is with the port of San Francisco, it is important that "the U.S. Consul there should be one intimately acquainted with San Francisco, its merchants, and its mode of doing business, as well as a practical and experienced man. Mr. Poston possesses all these qualifications. He has been a merchant and man of business, has been connected with the administration of the duties of the Custom House here, has been a resident here for three years, is intimately acquainted with business and business men, and is a man of integrity and principle and irreproachable character." The petitioners add that Poston sought the position "not as a means of enabling him to proceed to Guaymas but in consequence of his determination to proceed to that port and establish himself in business." The petition was signed by W. Van Voorhies, surveyor of customs; John C. McLemore; John McDougal; Sam Bridges; O. P. Sutton; Thomas T. Henley; Alpheus Felch; E. C. Marshall; Phillip A. Roach; T. W. Fenton; C. L. Weller; and G. W. Guthrie, deputy surveyor of customs.[12]

Some of these men, particularly McLemore, may have been members of Poston's syndicate. Several were lower-level customs officials (appraisers) and thus might have been fellow residents at the Government Boarding House, persuaded to help Poston by Van Voorhies, McLemore, or others. The petition was probably intended to give Poston an official position at Guaymas as a basis for his operations, making it easier for him to enter Mexico legally and move about the country. Van Voorhies's place as first of the signers suggests that when Poston left the customs house, Van Voorhies knew that he was leaving to lead the Sonora expedition and wanted to support him.

Whatever its reason for being, the petition was not successful. Poston did not get the appointment. But the expedition's plans were laid, and it was now ready to embark for Mexico.

CHAPTER SIX

Navachiste and Sonora

Six weeks after his departure from the customs house, on February 19, 1854, Poston and his party sailed from San Francisco for Guaymas on the *Zoraida*. He was setting out on the journey that would, finally, make his fortune in the West. It was what he would do instead of prospecting for gold, investing in San Francisco real estate, or climbing the ladder of patronage appointments at the customs house. But something unexpected happened during the passage to Guaymas that nearly destroyed the expedition before it was well started. Poston explains that on March 9 the *Zoraida*, having run short of provisions and water, attempted to make the harbor of Navachiste, on the gulf coast of Sinaloa, but was stranded off shore. The passengers took refuge on the nearby island of Macapule.[1]

That the *Zoraida* would have run short of supplies is surprising, since its voyage from San Francisco to Navachiste took a normal amount of time. An analysis of shipping notices in the *Daily Alta California* between 1850 and 1854 shows that most voyages between San Francisco and Guaymas took seventeen to twenty-one days. In February–March 1854, the *Zoraida* took an unsurprising fifteen days to reach Navachiste. But nearly three months passed before it reached Guaymas, enough time that stories circulated that the ship had sunk. On May 29, 1854, the *Daily Alta California* announced that the *Zoraida* had landed safely at Guaymas and that the rumor circulating that the ship had been "lost" was false.

Whatever the ship's condition after it ran aground, Poston and Ehrenberg probably saved the expedition by leaving the *Zoraida* at Navachiste rather than continuing to Guaymas. Poston's supplies and money for the

49

Figure 4. J. Ross Browne, the *Zoraida* stranded at Navachiste Bay. From Browne, *Adventures in the Apache Country.*

expedition were limited. He could not have afforded a delay of weeks or months waiting for the *Zoraida* to resume its voyage while his resources dwindled and his men returned to California or drifted off to find other employment in Mexico.

Even before Poston left San Francisco, California newspapers had told of the anti-American sentiment at Guaymas because of the Walker filibuster. And Poston seems to have been aware of Santa Anna's 1853 order that no armed foreigners should be allowed to land in Mexico.[2] In either case, Poston may have been glad of a chance to avoid the hostile reception that an armed party of Americans surely would have received in Guaymas. Entering Mexico two hundred miles to the south, dealing with Mexican officials in Sinaloa rather than in Sonora, and approaching Guaymas overland, as travelers already in the country legally, may have seemed an easier course.

Navachiste, Poston said, was the principal port for towns in northern Sinaloa.[3] Goodale says that it was known as a local debarking point for passengers sailing between California and Guaymas and a place where contraband was smuggled in and out of Mexico.[4] Poston found the harbor accessible but good enough only for "contraband trade, small coasting business or oyster gathering."[5] In several places in the "Reconnoisance," Poston mentions the smuggling that took place in Mexican gulf ports. In fact, smuggling was rampant along the Sinaloan and Sonoran gulf coast in the mid-nineteenth century, some of it engaged in by the most prosperous merchants of the region, such as Manuel Iñigo in Sonora and the Vega family in Sinaloa, who used their commercial and political influence to avoid duties on goods brought into Mexico.[6]

At Navachiste, Poston had landed in a more rural setting than the crowded port of Guaymas. The landing place was a ranch belonging to a Spaniard who had come from Manila in colonial times, and Poston seems to have been well received by the local citizens, some of whom helped the expedition. Needing animals for his party, Poston turned to a "Mexican gentleman of Culiacan," who had been a fellow passenger on the *Zoraida*. With his aid, they obtained mules from a nearby ranch, rounding up about two hundred and picking out "twenty five of the best looking" to carry them and their supplies.[7] Once the expedition moved north through Sinaloa, Poston and his men stayed at the estate of a General la Vega and were treated "with hospitality and kindness."[8]

The Vegas were one of the wealthiest and most powerful families of Sinaloa from the 1830s through the early 1850s. Headquartered in Culiacán, Sinaloa's capital, they worked diligently to further their own economic interests and those of friends, supporters, and their city. In 1835 the family masterminded a political coup that put Manuel de la Vega in the governor's office. Shortly afterward, the port of Altata, thirty-seven miles west of the city, opened to coastal trade, promoting the flow of commerce through Culiacán to the interior of the state. The Vegas and their friends imported large quantities of contraband through the port. Manuel was succeeded in the governorship by his older brother Rafael in 1844 and his younger brother Francisco in 1847. Federalists in politics, favoring stronger, independent state government and weaker central government, the Vegas were removed from office in 1853 when Santa Anna assumed the dictatorship of Mexico. But they were still a very wealthy and powerful family in Sinaloa when Poston visited the Vega hacienda early in 1854.[9] It was his first contact with the notable families of northern Mexico.

Poston and his party continued north to Villa del Fuerte on the Fuerte River, where they met the first Mexican authorities on their trip and obtained permission to pass through the country, "having presented our passports and caused the usual hubbub."[10] Though this encounter sounds easier than what Americans were facing in Guaymas, Poston admitted that he did not escape difficulty with officials when armed Americans showed up in the interior of Mexico without having first passed one of the usual ports of entry.

Poston found the land near Fuerte full of agricultural potential, with "soil rich enough to produce cotton or sugar equal to Alabama or Louisianne." This comparison of Sonoran land to American is something that Poston does repeatedly in the "Reconnoisance." In the process, he addresses a common concern in planning a railroad route—the region's ability to support the line with arable land for raising crops and livestock, as well as water, timber, and materials for building settlements. In this case, Poston characterizes the land as worth possessing for its value as part of the American economy. He does this by imagining the land as already in some sense "American." This proprietary interest is even more obvious in his description of the land near Navachiste as rich bottomland that produces "a considerable quantity of corn beans cheese stock & poultry for exportation to California."[11]

A week after leaving Navachiste, Poston's expedition arrived at the old colonial city of Alamos, Sonora, which "had been a very rich and prosperous mining town in the days of the monarchy, but had decayed and crumbled into ruins like everything else under the mismanagement of the Republic." Poston is charmed by the remnants of Spanish colonial culture in Alamos, particularly the cathedral, which displayed the "Royal Arms of Spain." The place, he says, had "the appearance of a primitive Mexican city, with all the customs and costumes of a people who have little or no intercourse with the outside world."[12] But here as elsewhere in the "Reconnoisance," Poston loses few opportunities to point out Mexican government incompetence. In fact, his characterization of Alamos contains elements reminiscent of the filibusters' arguments—that they were taking over parts of Mexico in order to "liberate" Mexicans from an oppressive and inept government and improve their lives.

In Alamos the party had a more serious encounter with Mexican officials than the casual business in Villa del Fuerte. One evening, Mexican soldiers suddenly appeared at the house where they were staying and demanded that Poston and his men appear before the *alcalde*, or mayor, and explain what they were doing in Mexico. Fortunately, Poston said, the alcalde was "a gentleman of wealth, intelligence, and liberality—old José Almada, the owner of the rich silver mines of Alamos."[13] Like the Vegas of Sinaloa, the Almadas were one of the richest and most influential families in their state. José Almada was head of the family, one of four brothers who had immigrated to New Spain in 1815. Their holdings included hundreds of thousands of acres of land, nearly all of the land in and around the city of Alamos, and the richest silver mines in the region. The Almadas were allied by marriage with the Vegas, and Poston may have won the alcalde's cooperation by mentioning his recent acquaintance with the Vega family.[14]

Like Pratt's British travelers in South America, Poston typically praises the Mexican elites for their hospitality, aristocratic heritage, and generous treatment of Americans. But the Mexican population in general he looks down upon for its indolence and failure to exploit the country's resources. Because of economic decline during the war for Mexican independence (1812–21), mining in Sonora had failed. Mines filled up with water, shafts collapsed, and workers who had drifted away to work on farms and ranches could not be lured back to the brutal and dangerous work of the mines. Quicksilver and other materials necessary for processing silver were in short supply, and there were no minting facilities in the state for processing silver bullion into coin.[15] The Almadas' mines seem to have been among the few that remained open. But having only limited understanding of economic conditions in northern Mexico, and judging Sonoran mines only by the legends of their richness, Poston took the reduced operation of the Almada mines as a sign of Mexican indolence. Almada, he observes in the "Reconnoisance," owns fifty or sixty mines, few of which are being worked but which, nevertheless, yield about two ounces, or thirty-two dollars, to 250 pounds of ore. His miners "abandon working a mine which yields less than one Marco or about eight dollars to the cargo of ore."[16] American industry, Poston implies, would not permit such inefficiency.

Nevertheless, Poston expresses admiration for Almada—not surprisingly, since the alcalde treated the Americans courteously and allowed them to pass after a pro forma show of their passports and a letter of introduction written by Rubio, a fellow passenger on the *Zoraida*. The letter explained that Poston's men were not filibusters but immigrants, who had been stranded with him on Macapule. It asked, on the immigrants' behalf, for the "hospitality and protection of the . . . Mexican government."[17] Hardy says that such letters were "indispensably necessary" for foreigners traveling through Mexico.[18] And, indeed, Poston found that Rubio's letter almost magically afforded both hospitality and free passage to his party: "We were treated with great courtesy and furnished with letters of security to protect us from future interruption."[19] Subsequently, Poston found that he could ease the progress of his party through northern Mexico by using the endorsements of powerful families like the Vegas and Almadas, whose names commanded respect and cooperation from local authorities and invited the hospitality of other prominent Sonorans.

Leaving Alamos, Poston's party found the Yaqui River, a large stream originating in Chihuahua and emptying into the Gulf of California about sixty miles below Guaymas. The Yaqui was Poston's first really promising find. Its mouth looked like it might make a good harbor for small boats, and the river could be navigated by steamboats for about one hundred miles. In addition, the river bottom was "the most extensive and valuable body of land in Sonora," fifty miles wide and extending one hundred fifty miles up the river. It had soil, Poston says, "equal to any on the Mississippi or Missouri" and yielded wild cotton, sugar cane, and a variety of fruits.[20]

The river's appeal faded somewhat when Poston learned that the land in the river valley was held by the Yaqui Indians, who had defended it successfully against Spanish and Mexican attempts to settle it and permitted no intrusion by non-Indians. The Yaquis had first rebelled against Spanish government control and the encroachment of Spanish settlements in 1740. And while the Yaquis were defeated later that year, they rebelled again in 1825, and remained almost continuously in rebellion against Mexican authorities through 1833.[21]

On his trip through the region, Poston saw that the Yaquis controlled the broad, navigable river. But reluctant to reject any promising commercial site, he assures his "Reconnoisance" readers that while the Yaquis have resisted Spanish and Mexican rule, they constitute no obstacle to American commerce. They command the river by levying "a tax on all vessels entering or navigating the river and . . . duties upon all imports and exports," but these charges are "very simple and easily settled." In fact, Poston found that the Yaquis practiced republican politics, in pueblos "well regulated and governed by an alcalde elected annually by the 'popular suffrages.'"[22] In "Poston's Narrative," they are practically exemplars of civilization with familiar American virtues—cultivating crops, raising livestock, weaving their own clothing, and practicing the Christian religion: "Churches in every village attest the zeal and industry of these pioneers of Christianity."[23]

Poston's view of the Yaquis is partly a superficial understanding of their resistance to Spanish and Mexican control and partly naïve misinterpretation of the special nature of their acceptance of Catholicism and Spanish-Mexican law and governmental practices. Like most other Indians in northern Mexico, the Yaquis absorbed much of Spanish culture and politics and resorted to armed rebellion only as a last resort to preserve control of their lands and their political and cultural autonomy.[24]

Jesuit missionaries had colonized the Yaquis in the mid-seventeenth century, establishing agricultural communities around eight Indian towns along the Yaqui River and setting boundaries between these communities so that no land was open to individual settlement. They instituted Yaqui election of their own town "governors" and a captain general to command the combined military force of the eight towns. The Jesuits also strengthened the Yaquis' conviction that the Indians held exclusive rights to their land, water, and resources and the right to elect their own officials, who had the authority to govern them independent of outside control.[25]

The Yaquis accepted much, if not all, of Jesuit religious teaching, and their religious fervor suggested to Poston that they were devout Christians. Their election of leaders "by the popular suffrages" seemed to Poston remarkably American in character. But Yaqui acceptance of Christianity did not replace adherence to their traditional religious beliefs.[26] And their adoption of elections, the historian Edward Spicer says, was likely because "there was considerable compatibility between what the Indians had or were aiming at in the form of leadership and what the missionaries . . . [and] the Spanish government wanted."[27] The Yaquis maintained a coherent tribal identity. Their sense of connection with their land was strong, and their resistance prevented substantial access by non-Indian settlers to the Yaqui Valley.[28] While willing to work in the mines and ranches of Sonora, the Yaquis were determined to resist every attempt to make them subordinate to the Mexican state.[29] Moreover, they had learned their Jesuit lessons well. They were literate, understood Spanish culture and political organization, and had learned how to use Spanish political mechanisms (such as petitions to the viceroy and church authorities and, later, appeals to the Mexican government) to defend their towns and their autonomy.[30] Poston doubtless met Yaquis, since he traveled through their territory along the Yaqui River. But the tribe was not likely to have behaved antagonistically toward him because, unlike the Spaniards and Mexicans, he posed no threat to their land or autonomy. Thus, he reports them as "friendly" to Americans.

From the Yaqui valley, Poston's party proceeded to Guaymas, their original destination. Poston says that he and his men registered as U.S. citizens at the American consulate. Perhaps because of the "letters of security" provided by José Almada, he seems to have had no difficulty with Mexican officials, who he says were "polite but not cordial."[31]

Almost certainly, Poston would have inquired at the U.S. consulate about the status of the Gadsden negotiations, since approval of the treaty and the new border it set between the United States and Mexico were critical to his expedition. He could not acquire land or mining concessions that would fall within the new U.S. boundary if he did not know where that boundary was. Poston would have known that the treaty draft Gadsden

Figure 5. Port of Guaymas. Photo courtesy of the Arizona Historical Society, Tucson.

brought to Washington on January 19 proposed a boundary just south of today's U.S.-Mexican border and did not include a port on the Gulf of California.[32] The full text of the draft had been published by the *New York Herald* on January 20, a month before Poston left for Mexico. But because the treaty had not been ratified by the U.S. Senate, and because of the vigorous and extended debate in the United States about where the new boundary should be, Poston could not assume that the line proposed in the draft would be the final one.

Exactly when Poston arrived in Guaymas and visited the American consulate is not known. But he found no news about the treaty there. Perhaps because no new American consul had been appointed to replace Juan Robinson, no official communications were being sent to the consulate. Whatever the reason for the lack of information, as Poston's expedition went forward, he remained uncertain about where the new boundary would be and which portion of the territory he was exploring would, eventually, become part of the United States.

As for Guaymas itself, Poston says that he found it a "miserable Mexican seaport town." And because the deepwater area in the harbor was relatively small and far from land, he gives the port only a modest rating. Poston also found the country for a hundred miles around Guaymas a wilderness unsuited for settlement: "a blasted barren desert entirely destitute of wood water and grass, producing only cacti and a stunted growth of mesquite." The water of Guaymas, too, he says, had a brackish taste and often made travelers sick.[33] Both as a port and a potential place of settlement, Guaymas was a disappointment.

In contrast, Poston found his next destination, Hermosillo, in the valley of Horcasitas, "one of the most beautiful cities in the northern states of Mexico" and a model of civilization in its commerce, architecture, and agriculture. It was a promising commercial site, being "the principal depot and distributing point for the northern portion of the state, and part of Chihuahua." Shipping, Poston says, was conducted through Guaymas, but "the wealth and fashion of the state is . . . concentrated at Hermosillo." The city had "many large and costly houses constructed of stone brick and adobes well finished and furnished in the interior with the best and most costly European furniture." It also featured gardens and an ample water supply and was located in a fertile valley, in which "the soil is very rich . . . highly cultivated and very productive." The principal crop, Poston says, was wheat, but he also found an astonishing array of fruit crops, and the local vineyards produced about twenty-five hundred barrels of brandy a year. Unfortunately, Poston observes, the potential wealth of the region had been limited by governmental incompetence and the indolence of the Mexicans. Cotton and sugar were once grown in the valley, but their cultivation had been abandoned "for lack of any protection from the government or enterprize in its citizens."[34] Nevertheless, nearby, Poston found the port site he had been looking for—and the wealthy Sonorans who could help him to acquire it and thus achieve his, and the syndicate's, goals.

CHAPTER SEVEN

A Port on the Gulf

Hermosillo was about sixty miles from the Gulf of California and San Juan Bautista Bay, the first bay Poston found that he thought might be developed into the port he sought. San Juan Bautista Bay was the long, narrow body of water that lay between the mainland and the island of Tiburon. It had been named by Father Eusebio Francisco Kino and Captain Blas de Guzman in 1685.[1] At a length of fifty miles and a width of two to ten miles, the bay was large enough to accommodate a large number of oceangoing ships. Poston told the syndicate that it was "the largest and best harbor in the Gulf of California and much superior to Guaymas as San Francisco is to Monterey." Tiburon on the west formed a breakwater against storms and provided a location for piers, while the mainland was suitable for building a sizable city. Poston's plan of acquisition apparently included military defense of the port, since he notes that the island would make a good site for a "naval station and impregnable fortress." The port's "usefulness and adaptability for commercial purposes is doubtful on account of its isolated position but it has several good harbors and an abundant supply of running water which would be very convenient for supplying vessels going to sea."[2] A port here would have been the only port of entry on the gulf north of Guaymas.

Poston knew about the existence of the bay before he went to Mexico, since he says that he was familiar with reports on it by three naval officers: Mexican commander Tomas Spence, Lieutenant Hardy, and American lieutenant Stanley. Stanley had mapped the bay during the war with Mexico and had reported on the region to the secretary of the navy in case the United States were to acquire the country. Poston had spoken with Stanley

58

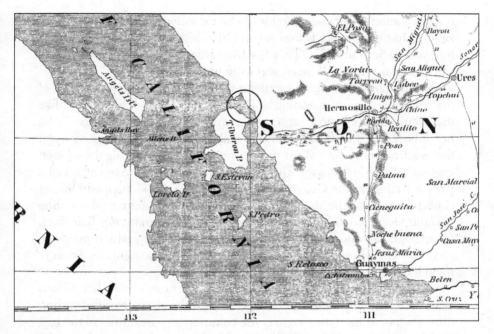

Figure 6. Section of Herman Ehrenberg's 1854 "Map of the Gadsden Purchase," showing San Juan Bautista Bay and La Labor. Courtesy of the Arizona Historical Society, Tucson.

about the bay before leaving California, and Stanley had drawn a map of the region for him and given him "much valuable information of the Island [Tiburon] and vicinity."[3]

Unfortunately, here, as in the Yaqui valley, opposition appeared in the form of the local Seri Indians, nomadic fishers, hunters, and gatherers who occupied Tiburon and the coast of the Gulf of California from Guaymas north to Rio de la Concepción.[4] The Seris were feared and hated both by the colonial Spanish and, later, by the Mexicans of the early republic. Along with the Apaches of northern Sonora, the Seris were the only native people in the region the Spaniards and Mexicans were unable to subdue and assimilate into their culture. Even the Yaquis, who resisted Spanish and Mexican domination, accepted Catholicism, joined the Sonoran economy as farmers and laborers, and employed Spanish political institutions to preserve their independence. But for the most part the Seris, like the Apaches, wanted no part of Spanish or Mexican society.[5] They hunted, gathered, and fished, living off the desert and the sea. To the Spanish, the Seris were savages—animal-like and anarchic—who exhibited no qualities of "civilization." In the words of Father Adam Gil, a Franciscan missionary killed by dissident Seris in 1773, "They live like cattle, without God, without law, without faith, without Princes, and without houses."[6]

Poston's language when describing the Seris reflects Mexicans' fear of the tribe and their exasperation at being unable to subdue them. Unlike the Yaquis, the Seris, to Poston, are "a savage and sanguinary tribe," who not only defend their land fiercely but make "the most savage inroads upon the ranches on the Petic River murdering the men and taking the women captive."[7] In 1854, perhaps while Poston was in Sonora, Seris attacked a party traveling on the Guaymas-Hermosillo road and kidnapped Dolores (Lola) Casanova, the daughter of a prominent Guaymas family. She became a legend in Sonora, remaining with the Seris, marrying their chief, Coyote-Iguana, and bearing him three sons. Her story, which provoked revulsion among upper-class, white Sonorans, may account for Poston's melodramatic description of Seri raiding practices.[8]

Of course, to the Seris, as to the Yaquis, American visitors like Poston were no threat to their independence. And in the absence of Indian hostility, Poston, in his optimism over the commercial possibilities of the bay, could easily overlook the long history of Seri resistance toward those who had invaded their lands and tried to change their way of life. Like land speculators elsewhere in the frontier West, Poston exhibited an astonishing facility for looking past Indian claims to their own land and seeing only the possibilities for commercial development. Thus, while Poston observes that Mexicans near Hermosillo "live in continual dread of these inhuman and remorseless savages," the Seris, like the Yaquis to the south, pose no threat to American development. He portrays them as friendly to Americans and British and seems to view them, in their poverty, as more pitiable than dangerous.[9]

Far more important to Poston was that the region of the bay invited development. The bay itself, Poston says, abounds in fish and oysters, and the mainland offers stone and other materials necessary for building a large settlement. Further inland, the Petic River provides water for irrigation, and the soil is "rich sandy loam." Thus, the Petic valley was potentially rich agricultural land that already supported civilization. The area contained the largest estates of Sonora and a majority of the towns and villages, including Hermosillo, the principal city of the state, and Ures, its capital.[10]

Poston found land at the northern end of the bay that was an "eligible site for a large city." The site contained an area of about seven leagues (twenty-one miles). Its boundaries ran from Sergeant's Point, opposite the northern end of Tiburon, north three leagues, east five leagues, south to the water, and then northwest to Sergeant's Point again. The land was owned by Joaquin de Astiazarán, "an intelligent and liberal minded gentleman of Hermosillo," who had practiced law in Mexico City eight or ten years earlier but was now "living upon his paternal estate near Hermosillo in the enjoyment of an immense income and every refinement and luxury that can be introduced into that remote province."[11]

Astiazarán's wealth and class recommended him as a partner in the syndicate's plans. That Poston intended to contact large landholders in Sonora is supported by the fact that he showed the landowners whom he met "testimonials from Mexican citizens of Calif^a" in order to win their trust.[12] Poston says that he met Astiazarán in Guaymas and later spent two weeks at his hacienda, La Labor. Astiazarán was one of the leading landowners in Sonora, and Poston was not the first foreigner to visit La Labor.[13] Hardy visited in 1826 and reported a "charming" estate with well-cultivated gardens and a library including books on agriculture. Astiazarán, he said, "has about him more the appearance of an English country squire than any person I have seen since I have quitted my native land."[14] Henry George Ward visited the following year and described "the neatest place that I met with in Sonora," including a redbrick house that "strongly resembled the very large comfortable farms in some parts of England," extensive gardens laid out in the English style, and productive farm fields irrigated by a canal dug from the river. Ward said that he and his party were served dinner on silver plates with "a profusion of excellent things" and that "everything was of a piece in this comfortable establishment for the beds that they provided us were most luxurious."[15]

Poston says that the San Juan Bautista land had been given to Astiazarán "under a grant made by His Excellency Manuel María Gándara Governor of the State of Sonora in November 1851 with conditions of colonization &c."[16] The grant may have been given to Astiazarán directly as a gift, or it may have been land purchased by Astiazarán from the State of Sonora under Gándara's administration. Most likely, it was the result of a *denuncia*, or declaration that the lands were unoccupied, filed by Astiazarán, who then would have purchased the land from the Sonoran government. The *denuncia* was a device increasingly used by non-Indian settlers in Mexico in the eighteenth and early nineteenth centuries to acquire either unassigned royal lands or unused land in the public domain. The proceeds from such sales helped to fill empty state treasuries.[17] The Astiazarán land, just north of Tiburon, was in Seri territory. But the Seris had no legal title to it, so according to Mexican law, it could be "denounced" as vacant and purchased by a private citizen for no more than five hundred pesos. The conveyance with "conditions of colonization, &c." may have meant that the land had to be occupied and put to productive use, a requirement for some state-issued grants.[18]

Poston proposed to Astiazarán, Gándara, and a few other wealthy Sonorans that a port city be built on Astiazarán's land on the northern end of San Juan Bautista Bay and that negotiations be opened with the Texas Western Railroad, who were known to be building a transcontinental line through Texas to the Pacific. The negotiations would aim at making the proposed port the western terminus of the line.[19] That Poston proposed the Texas Western connection suggests that the syndicate knew about the Texas Western's objectives from the start of the expedition and hoped to draw the company into a port city project.[20]

Who were these Sonorans whom Poston had sought out to partner with the syndicate? They called themselves "notables," meaning "prominent families of a community who predominated in its economic activities, directed its public affairs, and maintained its tone of refined taste in style and manners." They were wealthy landowners and merchants descended from Spanish immigrants, who came to Sonora and Sinaloa in the late eighteenth century. They made their fortunes in ranching, mining, and trade, and dominated commerce and politics in the towns of the two states.[21] Poston had already met members of two of the notable families of northern Mexico, the Vegas of Culiacán and the Almadas of Alamos.

Becoming a notable, or continuing as one, was a game of alliances, created either by marriage or commercial partnerships. These alliances enabled the notables to survive politically or economically unstable times or declines in their fortunes. The alliances were typically complementary: merchant families would marry into those with land; those with land would marry into others with capital, town property, a military command, or a political office. Through these marriages, notable families combined into a network, which resembled something like a modern corporation in that it was an association of power and money formed to accomplish business objectives.[22]

Going into politics was popular among second-generation notables, since by holding office they controlled their fates and protected themselves from government interference in their affairs. The most popular offices for notables were local ones, such as alcalde, or state offices, such as governor or commander general (military commander) of state military forces. Some notables held offices in *ayuntamientos* (town councils), state legislatures, or the congress in Mexico City.[23] Notables holding political office could place other family members or allies in positions of influence in government or the courts. Local government offices offered opportunities for political control in the administration of municipal land, supervision of water rights, and notarization of business and legal transactions. At the state and district levels, political officeholders could determine the amount and kinds of taxes people paid, the conduct of customs operations, the awarding of tax concessions and monopolies, and the securing of loans to the state treasury, which were often made at high rates of interest. Notable merchants could import contraband through a port such as Guaymas with the connivance of friendly customs officials and exclude competitors by vigorously enforcing the customs laws against them. With relatives and allies placed in judgeships in the state courts, merchant notables could enforce payment from their debtors and avoid payment to their creditors, thus using the courts to help their friends and punish their enemies.[24]

The most successful of the family networks in northwest Mexico was that of the Gándara, Iñigo, and Aguilar families, who were related by marriage and commerce and dominated Sonoran politics from the 1830s through the 1850s. Their economic activities were frequently carried out in partnership with relatives and through the influence of family members in local and state offices. The network's leading member, Manuel María Gándara, was born in Sonora in 1800. His father, Juan Gándara, had emigrated from Spain in the late eighteenth century, settled near Ures, and married Anna Gortari. In 1830 Manuel married Dolores Aguilar, daughter of Victor Aguilar, the head of a prominent Sonoran commercial family. The marriage increased Manuel's wealth, and he eventually became a major landowner with hundreds of acres along the Sonora River and large herds of livestock. Because Gándara was a leader among Sonoran landowners, Mexican president Anastasio Bustamante appointed him governor of Sonora in 1837, after which Gándara was appointed or elected governor repeatedly until 1855.[25]

Related to the Gándaras and Aguilars by marriage were the Iñigo family, probably the most powerful merchant family in Sonora, who controlled most of the commerce in the port of Guaymas. The family's head was Fernando Iñigo Ruiz, a wealthy landowner, whose son-in-law Manuel Rodriguez moved to Hermosillo and became one of its most successful merchants by the time of Mexican independence. Fernando's son Manuel was a subdelegate in the Horcasitas *ayuntamiento* and conducted business in that city before 1830, when he moved to Guaymas and formed a merchant firm with branches in Horcasitas and Hermosillo. This firm included Fernando Iñigo's son-in-law (and Manuel's cousin) Fernando Cubillas, and a son and daughter, respectively, of the Aguilar and Gándara families. From the 1830s to the 1850s, members of the Iñigo family held revenue posts and

Figure 7. Manuel María Gándara. Photo from http://upload.wikimedia.org/wikipedia/commons/ 2/21/Manuel_maria_gandara_retrato.jpg.

financed the Sonoran treasury as well as the military forces led by Gándara when he had to fight to maintain control of the governorship.[26]

Joaquin Astiazarán was part of this family network. He married the daughter of Fernando Iñigo and received La Labor as part of his wife's marriage settlement. His son Fernando married the daughter of Manuel María Gándara, so that the Astiazaráns were tied to both the Iñigo and Gándara families by marriage. In addition to acquiring the San Juan Bautista grant, in 1838 Joaquin purchased the enormous Sopori grant, nearly 140,000 acres, on the west bank of the Santa Cruz River in present-day Arizona. The land was purchased from the State of Sonora while Gándara was governor. Thus, the sale may have been the result of a *denuncia*. The San Juan Bautista Bay and Sopori acquisitions, taken together, made Astiazarán one of Sonora's largest landowners.[27]

The settlement Poston reached with Astiazarán was not easily accomplished. It took two or three weeks of negotiation, Poston says, in addition to presenting his written testimonials, to convince Astiazarán to enter into an agreement. Eventually, Poston had a contract drawn up giving him power of attorney to present the land-and-railroad deal to American investors (presumably the syndicate). According to this agreement, Mexican and American investors would each get half the proceeds from the negotiation with the Texas Western Railroad.[28]

Just as Poston had his San Francisco syndicate standing behind his negotiations, Astiazarán had his family network to support him. Poston says that five Mexicans were "interested" in the San Juan Bautista Bay land concession, three in addition to Astiazarán and Gándara. All five were wealthy men with an aggregate value in land worth over one million U.S. dollars and the necessary "social and political influence to control the destiny of the state."[29] Except for Astiazarán and Gándara, Poston never revealed who these men were. But that the group existed indicates that the political and economic implications of the agreement in Mexico were complex. Astiazarán may have been sole owner of the San Juan Bautista Bay property, but because of the size and importance of the deal, he was obligated to involve his family network. And for the deal to succeed, it required the financial and political support of the Gándara-Iñigo-Aguilar clique, especially if Sonora were to become detached from Mexico and become part of the United States, either by purchase or by secession and annexation. Thus, it would be surprising if members of the Gándara, Iñigo, and Aguilar families were not in the group with whom Poston negotiated.[30]

As we have seen, these discussions took place in an environment of considerable political instability, including the Gadsden Treaty negotiations, with their attendant uncertainty over what part of Mexico would become U.S. territory, and the Sonoran filibusters. If these were not complication enough, a national revolution had begun in the state of Guerrero just eight days before Poston landed at Navachiste and continued all during his time in Mexico. On March 1, 1854, liberal Mexican revolutionaries in Guerrero proclaimed the Plan of Ayutla, calling for the overthrow of the detested Santa Anna and establishment of a liberal, decentralized government.

This revolution was the outgrowth of a conflict that had raged in Mexico since the 1830s between "centralists," who favored a strong central government, and "federalists," who favored stronger, more independent state governments that would act to solve their own problems. The liberals of the 1854 revolution took up the federalist agenda of the 1830s. They were antimilitaristic and against the traditional privileges of the army and the Catholic Church, which they regarded as feudal, not republican. Their opponents, the conservatives, kept to the centralist line, favoring a dominant central government and "strong executive rule" as in colonial times. They favored the army, the Catholic Church, and the creole upper classes, to which Gándara and many other notables belonged.[31]

Gándara was a conservative by birth who believed that strong central government control would favor the Sonoran notables' commercial interests and thus improve the state's fortunes. However, in practice he was a political pragmatist, who was committed neither to federalism nor centralism, but simply wanted to hold onto political power and increase his personal wealth and that of his family network.[32]

By 1854 Gándara had been for many years the controlling political power in Sonora. However, once the Plan of Ayutla was proclaimed, Gándara's political path became rougher. In March 1854, shortly after the revolutionaries' plan was announced, Gándara was removed from the governorship by Santa Anna and replaced by General Yáñez, who was named both governor and military commander of Sonora. Yáñez was monitoring Raousset's forces at Guaymas at the time. Under the looming cloud of revolution, Santa Anna needed allies in the north who were loyal and respected. In Yáñez, he saw not only a popular and skillful military leader, who could defend the state against filibusters and Apaches, but also a more trustworthy ally than Gándara, whose political sympathies could change with the weather, and whose reputation among other notables in the northern states had suffered because of his practice of using Yaqui and Mayo Indians as military forces whenever he needed to defend his governorship against rivals.[33]

Because of these circumstances, when Poston met with the Sonoran notables and talked with them about building a port city on the Gulf of California, Gándara was out of the governor's office—for a short while. In 1855, after Santa Anna had been driven from Mexico, Gándara embraced the Plan of Ayutla and was chosen governor of Sonora—this time by liberals, who had proclaimed the revolution in Sonora.[34] In mid-1854 he was still a potent force in Sonoran politics, and fifty years later, Poston remembered him as an impressive figure, "a sedate and dignified man, much respected by the natives, and especially polite and hospitable to foreigners."[35]

The Sonoran notables Poston dealt with were friendlier than the officials he had met at Guaymas and also took a rather different attitude toward Mexican-American relations. Poston, like other travelers in Sonora, found disparate attitudes toward Americans there—hostility and suspicion among some Mexicans, mostly in Guaymas, but greater tolerance and even friendliness elsewhere, usually among the notable families.[36] Some frontier landowners and political leaders welcomed American interest in northern Mexico. American settlement and investment, they thought, would help to populate their state, improve their chronically poor economy, and protect their farms and ranches from Apache raids. The notables Poston met with, he says, were willing not only to sell their land to American buyers but to do whatever they could to promote annexation of Sonora by the United States. The historian Stuart Voss explains that with economic progress stalled in Sonora after the war with the United States, and Santa Anna and centralism about to be swept aside by the Revolution of Ayutla, Sonoran notables looked to some entity outside Mexico for help in preserving their way of life. Well aware of American ambitions toward northern Mexico and the rumors of a new boundary to be set by the Gadsden negotiations, some concluded that "annexation by the United States was inevitable and the only viable choice open to them."[37]

Poston and the syndicate may have relied on these annexationist leanings as they planned the Sonoran expedition. They probably had read newspaper articles like the one in the June 21, 1853, *Alta California* asserting that Mexican landowners and businessmen favored annexation. Poston similarly assures "Reconnoisance" readers that "the Mexicans interested in this scheme [at San Juan Bautista Bay] as well as a large majority of the influential citizens of Sonora are . . . in favor of annexation to the United States." Accordingly, Poston says, American partners to the agreement must have "sufficient interest and ability to produce the results anticipated, *viz.*, the location of the western terminus of the continental railroad at this point, the establishment of a port of entry and the building of a city at this place and the consequent and necessary transfer of the sovereignty of the country to the United States."[38]

Poston's observation about the Mexicans interested in his scheme suggests that the Sonoran notables were working as diligently as Poston and his syndicate to take advantage of the Gadsden negotiations in ways that would benefit them. Goodale says that the notables had their own motives for involving themselves in Poston's plan, which included the need to prepare themselves for annexation and protect themselves from the liberal revolution: "They were opportunists enough to want the best for themselves; realistic in recognizing the decided possibility that Sonora might fall to *yanki* purchase or force, and diplomatic in concealing from the Americans the uncertainties of their own political fortunes."[39]

One of the group's motives might have concerned the value to them of a new port on the gulf coast. The Gándara-Iñigo-Aguilar network already controlled commerce through the port of Guaymas. If they could use the Americans to establish and gain control of another port north of Guaymas, both their power and their fortunes would be increased.

Poston did not make his annexation suggestion naïvely. He acknowledges both the financial risk and dubious political morality of the San Juan Bautista Bay arrangement, warning readers that "this is an undertaking which might well make the boldest operators and most ambitious speculators pause and reflect before embarking on the enterprize." His justification? That the project's goal—completing a major link in the American transcontinental railroad—seems worth the risk: "The great and profitable ends to be accomplished seem much more worthy of the expenditure of time and money than most of the more ordinary pursuits of life."[40]

Those Government Boarding House discussions had taught Poston the American passion for building a transcontinental railroad, and in a rambling series of paragraphs he draws out for his "Reconnoisance" readers the argument that the Gadsden Purchase had been negotiated in order to enable a southern route for the transcontinental railroad, "as necessary to the United States as [to] the defenceless Mexicans." For the Mexicans, the railroad would provide a "commercial barrier against the Indians." From an American point of view, more northerly routes for the railroad were simply impracticable because of adverse terrain and climate.[41]

A natural course for a railroad to follow to the sea, Poston thought, was the well-used "Emigrant trail" through Mexico to California. This trail went through Guadalupe Canyon west of El Paso to San Juan Bautista Bay. The wagon road on this route was one of the best in the country and had been traveled regularly since Spanish colonial days. It was the old military road in the region and had been used more recently for commercial purposes. Bartlett's boundary commission traveled it in 1851. It passed through the most inhabited parts of Sonora and the most fertile agricultural lands in the state.[42]

Echoing the glowing, early 1850s newspaper predictions concerning Sonora, Poston declares, in his best promotional rhetoric, that the mountains near San Juan Bautista Bay have "probably the richest mineral deposits of any mineral region in Mexico and are considered inexhaustible in mines of gold, silver, copper, quicksilver, and precious stones." Thus, the old narrative of northern Mexico's riches, which Poston had internalized, now contributed to the newer one of a southwestern commercial route to the gulf. And like other writers before him, Poston revived the claim that Sonora was the "new California." Gándara and other Mexicans, he says, are confident that Sonora would surpass California in mine production if the mines were worked with the same freedom and technology as in the United States and that the Sonoran mines would yield a more stable output than those of California.[43]

Poston points out that a railroad route to the gulf would be shorter than any other proposed route and therefore more profitable.[44] A fundamental and recurring argument for American expansion to the Pacific at mid-century was that it would provide easier access to Asian markets.[45] Even the Mexicans who had analyzed the causes of the 1846–47 war understood that Americans intended "opening an overland passage to the Pacific Ocean, and making good harbors to facilitate its navigation. By this plan, establishing . . . an easy communication of a few days between both oceans, no nation could compete with them."[46] Thus, it is not surprising to find Poston arguing in the "Reconnoisance" that the proposed port at San Juan Bautista Bay would be nearer than San Francisco to the line of navigation to Asia, the Pacific Islands, Australia, and the western coasts of Mexico and South America. It would more efficiently serve trade with China and the East Indies, and bring together the treasure of the Western Hemisphere, including gold from California and silver from the west coasts of Mexico and South America. In short, Poston promises, such a port would "revolutionise the commerce of the world."[47]

While Poston was negotiating with Astiazarán and his friends—approximately between March 13 and April 25, 1854—the U.S. Senate was debating the Gadsden Treaty, and Poston and the Sonorans might have imagined that San Juan Bautista Bay would, eventually, fall within U.S. territory.[48] However, by the time Poston wrote the "Reconnoisance" (September 15), the treaty had long since been ratified, and Poston knew that San Juan Bautista Bay was well south of the new border. So he takes a different tack in his report, arguing that Mexican envy of a transcontinental railroad north of their border and their dissatisfaction at receiving no benefit from it could be used "to induce them to take any steps that may be necessary to secure to the United States the right of way for the road, the opening of ports, or in fact the *sovereignty of the country* [emphasis Poston's] by cession or annexation." Thus, for the second time in six pages, Poston recommends Sonoran secession or annexation by the United States and predicts that such measures would yield lucrative concessions for the Texas Western Railroad: "In case of the people of Sonora declaring their independence of the Mexican government, any grant of lands, mines, or commercial prevaleges [sic] that might be desired by the projectors of the road to aid in its construction could be easily obtained."[49]

These concessions, Poston says, could be won by offering free use of the railroad and its facilities to "prominent citizens of Sonora, several of whom are already interested in this scheme." A company as large as the Texas Western Railroad, he assures readers, can afford to fund such an offer from the profit it would make on the line. Poston then plays a distinctly American political card—a reference to the growing division in the cultures of American North and South: "The Texas Road will never terminate in California if a more southern route can be secured, the institutions of the two states are uncongenial." The "institution" Poston mainly had in mind, of course, was slavery, and his implied argument is that amid the growing tension between "slave" and "free" states, a railroad company chartered and funded by a slaveholding state, such as Texas, would prefer to build a railroad through Sonora rather than through a state prohibiting slavery, such as California: "It would seem to one a breach of faith to that great state [Texas] which by her generous and princely liberality has breathed this magnificent enterprize into existence to make a western terminus in a state having different institutions and antagonistic principles."[50]

Poston then breaks off his discussion, perhaps realizing the controversial nature of the ideas he has been proposing ("It is unnecessary to discuss the subject further at present") and leaves the matter to McLemore: "I place the matter in your hands for the purpose of making two parties besides yourself interested in the grant of land at San Juan Bautista."[51]

To make the project happen, Poston says, would require "more mature deliberation and another interview" with the interested Mexican parties, "as well as some concerted course of action by some corporate body having control of both financial and political power." Poston here names "the projectors of the Texas Railroad" as the "proper persons to approach on this subject," since he is "confident their views will coincide to some extent with those already expressed in the foregoing condensed statement."[52]

Having negotiated the San Juan Bautista Bay agreement, Poston must have felt both rewarded and vindicated. His belief in the Sonoran expedition appeared to have paid off in a potentially lucrative land deal. And while he had not yet profited in financial terms, he had demonstrated that he could successfully negotiate such arrangements with rich and powerful men. He had come a long way—both literally and figuratively—from the business failures of his northern Kentucky days and his stagnation at the customs house. Still, the expedition was hardly over, and a humbling and near-fatal experience awaited him in northwestern Sonora.

CHAPTER EIGHT

The Sand Desert

From Astiazarán's hacienda, Poston returned to Hermosillo and spent the month of May prospecting silver mines in northern Sonora. Exactly where he went is something of a mystery. In the "Reconnoisance," Poston originally wrote that he went to "northwestern" Sonora, but later wrote an "Ea" over the "we" in "northwestern," changing it to "northeastern."[1] In "Poston's Narrative," which Ross Browne says came from a manuscript Poston showed him in 1864, Poston says that he visited silver mines in "north-western" Sonora.[2] Why and when Poston changed his story can only be guessed at. As late as the 1870s, Poston was showing the "Reconnoisance in Sonora" to prospective investors in a trans-Mexican railroad. The simplest explanation for Poston's change is that in reviewing the document at some later time, he saw he had made a mistake and corrected it.

In the "Reconnoisance," Poston says that the mines he saw were "very rich and will someday be worked with good machinery and yield a remunerating and permanent income on capital and labor invested." Moreover, investors could get "interests of one undivided half . . . at nominal prices" in return for providing machinery to work the mines. Like Gándara, Poston was confident that "the silver mines of Sonora will prove a more regular and permanent source of wealth than the placeres of Calif[a],"and he promised a separate report on the mines.[3] Poston never gave the names or locations of the mines he supposedly found, and he appears never to have written the follow-up report or provided ore samples to validate his claims.

Poston returned to Hermosillo on June 1, 1854, complaining of having had to pay out of his own pocket for his expedition's travel and raising the

71

question of what sort of financial support, if any, he was receiving from San Francisco. More important, the uncertainty of the new boundary between Mexico and the United States continued to haunt him. Poston says that he had had "no reliable news of the conclusion of a treaty defining the limits of the Gadsden Purchase," and since no new U.S. consul had arrived in Mexico to clarify the boundaries, "the prospects of consummating any arrangements in a satisfactory and legal manner were considerably embarrassed."[4] In other words, because San Juan Bautista Bay was not known for certain to be in U.S. territory, Poston could not consider "final" the deal he had made to build a port there. A revised version of the treaty was passed by the U.S. Senate on April 25, about the time that Poston concluded his negotiations with the Sonoran notables. But final ratification by President Pierce did not come until June 29. Mutual ratifications of the treaty by the two nations were formally exchanged at the Mexican legation in Washington on June 30.[5] So it was not until then that Poston could know for certain where the new U.S.-Mexican border was, and in the Sonoran Desert he could hardly get current intelligence on developments in Washington and Mexico City.

Moreover, at this time a cloud appeared on Poston's horizon in the person of Andrew B. Gray, now employed by the Texas Western Railroad to survey for a railroad line along the thirty-second parallel to the Pacific Ocean. Gray, of course, had known about the southern transcontinental route since the 1840s. After his opposition to the Bartlett-Condé line in 1851, he had been relieved of his position as chief surveyor on the Bartlett commission and sent to assist Lieutenant Amiel Whipple in surveying the U.S.-Mexican border along the Gila River. However, in 1853 Gadsden conferred with Gray about the desirability of a southern transcontinental route through the disputed Mesilla Valley in New Mexico and twice asked Secretary of State Marcy to appoint Gray to explore the area and gather data that Gadsden could use in negotiations. Gray wanted this assignment and described to Marcy how he would explore New Mexico in the region of the Rio Grande and the Gila, determine the best route for a railroad, and report to Gadsden. Marcy rejected both men's proposals.[6]

However, in May 1853 Gray wrote a report to the then secretary of the interior Robert McClelland, promoting the Mesilla Valley and the territory west of it along the Gila River as a passage for a transcontinental railway. In his report, Gray concludes that this is "the shortest and most possible route for a railway through our present territory" that would comply with the terms of the Treaty of Guadalupe Hidalgo. This is because such a route would be free of steep grades and heavy snows, and would allow uninterrupted communication along the line year round. As Poston did

Figure 8. Andrew B. Gray. Photo courtesy of the Arizona Historical Society, Tucson.

in promoting Sonora as a site for American development, Gray declares the Mesilla Valley "one of the most beautiful and fertile along the whole course of the Rio Grande. . . . producing the grains and fruits of our most thriving States."[7] Like Poston, too, Gray praises the economic promise of the territory to be acquired, assuring readers that "the fine cotton region of the Gila, the rich copper, silver, and gold mines of New Mexico and Sonora would be at once developed, bringing a vast district of country into cultivation which now presents a fruitless waste." As was customary in Southwest promotion, Gray compares these lands to California, which also had seemed a wasteland before Americans transformed the region into productive agricultural land.[8]

However, the route Gray promotes most strongly in his report is one that extended beyond the boundaries established by the Treaty of Guadalupe

Hidalgo. This route, Gray says, could be completed more quickly and cheaply than any along the Gila and "when finished would develop the resources of the adjoining country." This is a route extending from the Rio Grande, through the Mesilla region southwest to the Gulf of California, where it would access shipping from the Pacific Ocean. By this route, Gray points out, the gulf is only five hundred miles from the Rio Grande and could be reached without having to cross any mountain ranges, swamps, snow, or ice. Mountains could easily be avoided, valleys and streams are "advantageously situated," and a healthy climate prevails year round.[9]

In a sweeping vision, Gray predicts a network of railroad lines connecting New York, the Chesapeake, Charleston, New Orleans, St. Louis, the east coast of Texas, El Paso, and the Gulf of California. The whole will "bring the commercial emporium of the Atlantic within seven days of the great harbors of the Pacific, over a route having a genial climate, free the entire year from the drifting snows of the north, and the malignant diseases of the tropics." Such a route, Gray promises, would give the United States access to the "immediate trade of China, India, and the Pacific islands, and the western coast of Mexico. . . . The trade of the east, to a great extent, together with the India and China travel from Europe . . . would thus become part of our western trade."[10]

Gray soon had an opportunity to test his theory. In December 1853 he arrived in San Antonio, Texas, hired by the Texas Western Railroad to survey a southern route for their railroad from San Antonio to the Pacific Ocean.[11] In late February or early March he began exploring a route from El Paso through the Guadalupe Pass and northwest to Tubac, Arizona. From there, Gray knew that there were two possible routes the railroad could take: north through the Santa Cruz valley to the Gila River and along the Gila to its junction with the Colorado, or southwest through northern Sonora to the Gulf of California. He was already familiar with the Gila route, having surveyed it with Whipple in 1851. So at the Bosano Ranch, fifty miles southwest of Tubac, he divided his expedition, sending one party north along the Santa Cruz River to the Gila and taking another party himself southwest across the Altar Valley of Sonora to the gulf. The two parties were to meet at Fort Yuma, the U.S. Army post at the junction of the Gila and Colorado rivers.[12]

Like Poston's syndicate, Gray was calculating that some or all of Sonora would become part of the United States and that therefore either route might be possible for a railroad. The fact that he chose to lead the gulf-bound party indicates how seriously he took prospects for that route and development of a port city on the gulf, precisely the project that Poston was proposing for San Juan Bautista Bay. As previously noted, the "Reconnoisance" shows that Poston had heard about the Texas Western's plan to build a railroad along this route and used that information to interest Sonoran notables in creating the San Juan Bautista Bay port. But he seemed surprised to learn that the railroad was conducting its own survey in Sonora and quickly moved to get more information.

Gray reportedly had gone to the town of Altar near the gulf to search for a port site, and Poston now fretted that Gray would locate one north of San Juan Bautista Bay and thus undermine his plans for that location: "Fearing that my design would be superceded by the discovery of a port above Tiburon on the gulf as there were vague rumors of a port called 'Adair's Bay' I immediately organized a company for the purpose of exploring the Gulf of California by land in search of such a port and a proper site for a town hoping the same would fall within the limit of the treaty then pending." Poston organized an expedition of fifteen men to explore the region and must have been at least partly relieved when he arrived at Altar and learned that Gray had left.[13] Apparently, the Texan had decided that Altar and any port near it would fall south of latitude 31°, rumored to be the southern boundary of the United States set by the Gadsden Treaty. The rumor was both good and bad news—good in that it had driven Gray away from the vicinity of Altar, but bad in that if it were true, it would mean that the San Juan Bautista Bay site would be outside the Gadsden Purchase and thus useless as the port site the syndicate was seeking.[14]

Poston investigated another possible port site he had heard of called Ensenada de Lobas, at latitude 30°15'23", longitude 112°30', but found it "little better than an open roadstead protected slightly on the northwest by a sandspit." He then followed Gray north to the village of Sonoita near the present international border, where he learned that Gray had explored from there to Adair Bay and then gone north to Fort Yuma. Determined to see what Gray had seen, Poston traveled sixty miles west to Adair Bay, "crossing a coast range of mountains called the Pinacates (black beetles) and then through about fifteen or twenty miles of sand hills to the beach."[15]

Poston's trek might have been considered folly, even dangerous, for in the early Spanish exploration literature, which Poston said he had read, the Pinacates, and particularly the "sand hills," were well documented as a hazardous place to travel. The Pinacates are a range of extinct volcanoes in extreme northwestern Sonora. They are composed of a jumble of rugged black lava flows that radiate from their highest point, Mount Pinacate. East of the range, Mexico Route 8 runs south to Puerto Peñasco and the Gulf of California. To the west, a vast sea of sand dunes extends to the gulf and the mouth of the Colorado River. The naturalist and explorer Carl Lumholtz, who crossed the dunes in 1909, says that they were 185 to 200 feet high and looked like "a sea when exposed to a strong gale." The combination of lava and dunes stopped early explorers who tried to open a route from Sonora to the Colorado River and on to Alta California. Only during the years of the California gold rush did large numbers of people try to cross the Pinacates, often with deadly results.[16]

The Pinacates and the dunes were well known to the Hia C-eḑ O'odham, or "Sand Dune People," who lived among them and knew the best routes through the lava flows and the places where water could be found.[17] Herbert Bolton says that Father Kino made four trips into the Pinacates, which he called the "Santa Claras." On March 21, 1701, Kino recorded his journey across "very great sand dunes, in which our pack animals traveled with difficulty. The water supply which we found was three little springs of somewhat brackish water."[18] Father Juan Maria Salvatierra, who accompanied Kino, was more descriptive. The lava field, he says, "looked more like ashes than earth, all peppered with boulders and . . . entirely black, all of which formed figures, because the lava which flows down solidifies, stops, and assumes shapes. . . . Indeed I do not know that there can be any place which better represents the condition of the world in the general conflagration."[19]

Daytime temperatures here in summer, when Poston crossed, could reach 130 degrees Fahrenheit and soil temperatures 160 degrees. Frost formed on the rocks at night, even when daytime temperatures reached 100 degrees, and summer monsoons could bring as much as five inches of rain in just two or three hours, a condition that, ironically, made travel across the region in summer preferable to that in winter. Because of the heat and haziness in the air, mirages were common, especially near the gulf. Most distressing to travelers, however, were the "*nortes*," winds from the north, common near the head of the gulf, which usually brought sharp drops in temperature (twenty degrees or more), a rapid increase in humidity, and a substantial decline in visibility because of blowing sand. The wind was raw because of the sudden cold and blowing sand and could last from half a day to ten days. Even the durable Father Kino complained of "continuous, violent, and most pestiferous wind" during his journey across the dunes.[20]

In the account of his own expedition, Gray acknowledges the harshness of the sand hills, "the most desolate and forlorn-looking spot for eighty miles around the head of the Gulf, the sand hills looking like a terrible desert." As for Adair Bay, Peter R. Brady, who accompanied Gray, says that it "did certainly not amount to anything," and Poston found it no harbor at all. To make matters even less promising, the ship channel for vessels going to or coming from the Colorado River ran on the west, or "California side," of the gulf, so that these ships did not come anywhere near Adair Bay.[21]

Poston says that he "followed Gray's trail" to Adair Bay, but he did not.[22] The writer William K. Hartmann believes that Gray followed the "standard route to Adair Bay," down the east side of the Pinacate range, across its southern flank to water at Cuervo Tanks, and then on to the bay, a route pioneered by Father Kino in 1698 and 1701.[23] In doing so, Gray says that he traveled about sixty-two miles.[24] But Poston says that his party traveled eighty miles to the bay. Ehrenberg's 1854 "Map of the Gadsden Purchase" shows two routes from Sonoita to Adair Bay—one circling round the southern end of the Pinacates, then turning southwest to Adair Bay and ending at the notation "Col. Gray & Party." This, presumably, was Gray's route. The other route led around the northern end of the Pinacates and picked up Gray's route to the bay. It bears the notation "Ehrenberg Poston & Party." That this route covered about eighty miles suggests that it was the one Poston took.[25]

Brady reveals that Gray's expedition was guided by an O'odham chief named Hormiga.[26] Poston and Ehrenberg also probably were led by an O'odham guide, who would have known the northern route to the gulf.

Adair Bay, as Poston found it, was "nothing but desolation, neither water, grass, wood, or any kind of vegetation for our animals, nothing but a desert of sand as far as the eye could reach up and down the coast, extending at least two hundred and fifty miles by a width of twenty five to thirty."[27] Poston, of course, did not explore 250 miles up and down the gulf coast, but his exaggeration can be taken as a metaphor for his intimidation by the barrenness of the coastal desert. There would be no port here, nor any further exploration. From the gulf, Poston had hoped to travel north along the Colorado River to Fort Yuma but found himself in impassable terrain. As the early missionary fathers had discovered, mules and men kept sinking into the soft sand of the dunes, the only water available was brackish and salty, and Poston's men were exhausted and demoralized. Ehrenberg's 1854 map shows the Poston-Ehrenberg route leading haplessly off into the "Great Sand Desert" to the northwest—and stopping. Poston recounts how he climbed a sand hill to determine his position:

> We took an observation of our locality and found ourselves some forty or fifty miles distant from the mouth of the Colorado without the hope of reaching it with our broken down animals, and even that accomplished, it would have been impossible to proceed along its banks as the whole country for ten to fourteen miles around is cut up with sloughs and back

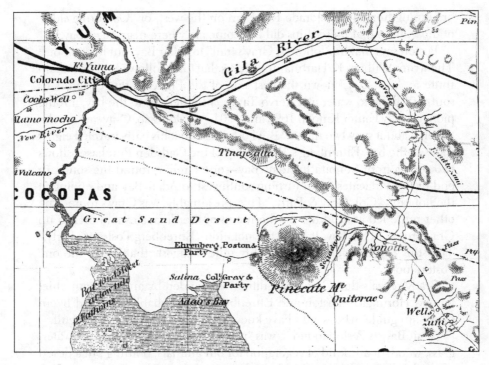

Figure 9. Section of Ehrenberg's 1854 "Map of the Gadsden Purchase," showing Adair Bay and Poston's route to the Yuma crossing. Courtesy of the Arizona Historical Society, Tucson.

water rendering the country impassable and the water unfit for use. The whole country for sixty miles up the river is subject to overflow and consequently can never form the site for a town or commercial city.[28]

The geologist and geographer Ronald Ives says that Poston could not have seen the mouth of the Colorado from Adair Bay.[29] Poston probably learned of the impassability of this area when he arrived at Fort Yuma. However, others had made the same discovery before him or at about the same time. In March 1702 Fathers Kino and Thirso González had difficulty negotiating the "enormous bogs" near the mouth of the Colorado.[30] Hardy, who had located and named Adair Bay in 1826, sailed up the lower Colorado and found both banks "a jungle-like tangle of mesquites, willow, poplar, and acacia, with many dead branches rooted in the soil, and a profusion of reeds."[31] When Lieutenant Nathaniel Michler explored the lower Colorado late in 1854, he found that a heavy tidal bore rushing up and down the river from the gulf made passage by small boats extremely dangerous and that spring flooding caused heavy sloughs (ponds or lakes), collapsing river banks, and marshy ground difficult to cross.[32]

Having struggled to the beach at Adair Bay, short of supplies, and with men and animals suffering, Poston and his men found it "impossible to continue the exploration" and returned, with difficulty, to Sonoita.[33] Poston was hardly the first to have been defeated by the Pinacates. Fathers Kino and González, in their 1701 expedition, had tried, unsuccessfully, to reach the head of the gulf by way of the Pinacates.[34] And Gray's party had to make a similar, desperate retreat through the sand hills.[35]

Overall, Poston's men found the trip so dispiriting that the party disbanded. Poston says that all of the Mexicans in the party went home, leaving only five of the original party to travel north from Sonoita, through the new Gadsden Purchase, to Fort Yuma.[36]

CHAPTER NINE

The Gila Trail and Colorado City

Poston and Ehrenberg left Sonoita near the end of June, entering the territory of the Tohono O'odham, or "Desert People." The region, Goodale says, was "a cheerless and inhospitable land of mesquite, palo verde and cacti, broken by dry, sandy arroyos and shimmering mirages." Water was to be found only in "tanks" (rock or sand pools) in the mountains to the west. To the east, the region was bounded by Baboquivari Peak, beyond which were the Apaches, and to the south was Sonora. Far to the northeast were the mission of San Xavier del Bac and the Mexican settlement of Tucson. Tohono O'odham villages were located throughout the region.[1]

Probably warned by Tohono O'odham guides, Poston and Ehrenberg veered away from the desolate territory to the west, the route to California known for centuries as the "Camino del Diablo" (Devil's Road). They took, instead, a route that ran northeast, through the Sauceda Mountains, then north to the Gila River, which they struck about 130 miles above its junction with the Colorado, near the site of present-day Gila Bend, Arizona.[2] On July 3 they reached the Sauceda villages (Poston uses the names "Son Saida," "Sans Saida," and "Sous Saida"), which Ives says were just two miles north of the summit of a pass between the Sauceda and Sand Tank mountains.[3] The Indians there, Poston says, "were as friendly as brothers, the Chief Tomas having our horses taken out to graze and offering every security and hospitality." They spent July 4 at the villages and the next day traveled sixty miles to the Gila River, reaching the river by midnight.[4]

Once at the Gila, they followed the Gila Trail downriver until they reached the confluence of the Gila and Colorado rivers at Fort Yuma, making, in all, about a three-hundred-mile circuit through the western part of the Gadsden Purchase.[5] Poston and his party may have traveled by themselves, although in a June 13, 1891, article in the *Florence Arizona Enterprise*, Poston says that he was traveling "with a train," suggesting that his party may have joined a wagon train going down the trail, perhaps at Gila Bend.[6]

The Gila Trail ran along the Gila River from the "Pima Villages" north of Tucson to the Yuma crossing of the Colorado River and on into California, across the Colorado Desert and the coastal mountains to San Diego and San Francisco.[7] It may have been new to American travelers, but it had been used for centuries before Europeans arrived, by Indians, for trade between New Mexico and the Pacific Ocean.[8] It was later used by early Spanish explorers and missionaries, including Kino and Captain Juan Mateo Manje (1697, 1699), Kino (1700, 1701, 1701), Father Jacobo Sedelmayr (1743, 1744, 1749, 1751), Father Francisco Garcés (1771, 1774, 1761), and Colonel Juan Bautista de Anza (1774, 1775).[9] Many of these parties were guided by Indian traders.[10]

Spanish and Mexican military expeditions led by Lieutenant Colonel Pedro Fages (1781) and Captain José Romero (1823) followed the trail.[11] Mexican traders used it frequently in the 1830s and 1840s; and American trappers, such as Kit Carson, Sylvestre and James Ohio Pattie, Ceran St. Vrain, Ewing Young, and Michel Robideaux, used it between the mid-1820s and 1840s.[12] Some trappers, such as Carson, Jean Baptiste Charbonneau, and Pauline Weaver, guided American military expeditions along the trail during the war with Mexico.[13] The two most important expeditions of this type were General Stephen Watts Kearny's Army of the West, which traveled from Fort Leavenworth to San Diego, and Lieutenant Philip St. George Cooke's "Mormon Battalion," sent by Kearny to build a wagon road from Santa Fe to California that could be used to supply U.S. troops. From that time, the part of the trail that ran along the Gila River to the Colorado and on to the Pacific was known to most travelers as "Cooke's Road."

In 1848 Major Lawrence P. Graham followed Cooke along the Gila, accompanied by Lieutenant Cave Johnson Couts, who kept a journal of the trip.[14] And later, U.S. military survey expeditions used the trail, as in 1849 when Couts escorted Lieutenant Amiel Whipple along the California portion of Cooke's Road to the Yuma crossing, where Whipple surveyed the Mexico-California border, and in 1851 when Whipple and Gray surveyed the U.S.-Mexican border along the Gila for the Bartlett commission.[15]

A significant feature of the trail pointed out by the historian Harlan Hague is that although the route was more than three hundred years old, each group of Europeans and Americans using it seemed to think that they had "discovered" it and were using it for the first time. This is because information about the trail was not passed along the generations or among the nonnative groups that colonized the region. Kino, Sedelmayr, Garcés, and Anza had traveled the area many times, knew the Indians, their trails, watering places, and settlements, and had written extensively about all of these things. But their journals and other accounts were not available to the public for many years, held in private collections or archives until they were discovered by researchers. Like these writings, the trails were abandoned and forgotten as different groups entered and left the region.[16]

The trail received by far its heaviest use in the gold rush years of 1848–50, when tens of thousands of emigrants used it to travel to California. During this time, it was the most popular route to California, used far more often than the trails through Utah to the north or through northern Mexico to the south.[17] Some emigrants were able to employ Mexicans or American trappers as guides, but many more carried with them copies of Lieutenant Colonel William H. Emory's *Notes of a Military Reconnaissance*, a report of his journey with Kearny along the trail in 1846–47, or Cooke's "Journal of the March of the Mormon Battalion, 1846–1847," both of which contained maps of the trail.[18] And while Poston said little about the trail, these narratives, as well as the stories of many of the explorers, soldiers, and gold seekers who traveled it, told what a difficult and dangerous route it was.

Much of the trail between Gila Bend and the Colorado River consisted of deep sand, which made walking difficult for both men and animals.[19] At Gila Bend, Cooke wrote, "This is certainly the most desert, uncouth, impracticable country and river of our knowledge. It took about three hours to advance four miles, winding about through mesquite trees and other bushes, and gullies of very soft clay, and some sand." Grass for animals was hard to find and, when found, was dry and brittle. Worse yet, water and grass for the animals never seemed to be in the same place, the best grass being a mile or more from the river. The route near the river was on soft clay or mud, or on marshy ground, into which horses and mules sank. Often, there were dense thickets of mesquite and other vegetation near the riverbank. The terrain away from the bank was firmer but barren of food for animals and sometimes rocky and too rough for the animals to cross. Where the trail was loose dirt, travelers plodded through dense clouds of choking dust raised by the mules and horses. Each day's progress was a meandering path away from and then back to the river, always looking for the easiest ground to cross and food for the animals. The river itself Cooke

Figure 10. Gila Trail above Oatman Flat. Author's photograph.

found salty, and sometimes the animals would refuse to drink.[20] Many animals died from lack of food and water. In order to save the animals, travelers discarded superfluous articles, so that along the trail Poston and his party would have seen broken wagons, wagon wheels, carriages, log chains, crowbars, cooking stoves, chairs, tents, and gold-washing machines.[21] John Woodhouse Audubon, son of the famed wildlife artist, followed the trail in 1849–50 and summarized the feelings of many when he said that his party arrived at the Colorado after "such travel, as please God, I hope none of us may ever see again."[22]

Along the trail, travelers found messages cut into rocks, carved into boards, or written on paper attached to sticks or trees. Some were for fellow travelers, giving information about comrades who had gone ahead, or concerning the availability of grass and water. One, signed W. S. Bratton, said, "D—n the jackass team that can't eat leather & go to California, D—n such a country.'" Perhaps the most eloquent was a board sign that, referring to hardships past and yet to come, said simply, "Keep a cool head."[23]

On their way down the trail, Poston and his party would have passed several well-known landmarks: Painted Rocks, which displayed a collection of Indian petroglyphs that astonished most travelers, and "Murderer's Camp," where in 1849 a young man traveling the trail stabbed and killed his guardian with a knife. The crime was witnessed by other members of their party, who tried the young man on the spot, executed him by firing squad, and buried him. A board sign at the site told the story to all who passed.[24]

An especially grim landmark that Poston and his party passed was the site of the "Oatman Massacre," a high mesa above the Gila River where Royse Oatman, his wife, and two of their children were killed by Yavapai Indians on February 6, 1851. The Oatmans' daughters Olive and Mary Ann were taken captive by the Indians, while their son Lorenzo was knocked unconscious, thrown off the mesa, and left for dead. Lorenzo later regained consciousness and made his way to a nearby Pima Indian village, where some immigrants nursed him back to health. While he was recovering, two of the immigrants, Kelly and Wilder, two Mexicans, and several Pima men went back to the mesa and buried the bodies of Royse Oatman, his wife, and the slain children. The ground was too hard to dig, so the men simply piled rocks over the bodies to prevent further destruction by animals and left.[25]

The details of this initial burial have always been in question, since later travelers reported seeing skeletal remains scattered on the ground at the site.[26] Poston told J. Ross Browne in 1864 that when he and his party

Figure 11. J. Ross Browne, Oatman gravesite. From Browne, *Adventures in the Apache Country.*

reached the site in July 1854, they gathered up human remains that they found on the ground, buried them in a fresh grave on the flat below the mesa, and put a small fence around the grave. Taking the tailboard from an abandoned wagon, they made a sign memorializing the attack and those slain. Browne drew a sketch of the site as he saw it ten years later when he and Poston visited on their journey through Arizona.[27]

By the time Poston's party reached the Yuma crossing on the Colorado River, they, like many others, had exhausted their food and had to subsist on mesquite beans picked from the surrounding trees. Poston credits this native desert food with saving their lives.[28] However, even with the customary difficulties, Poston and his companions made good time, arriving at the Yuma crossing on July 11. They had traveled the distance from Gila Bend in just six days.[29]

The Yuma site was the most popular crossing point on the Colorado for parties going to California from Texas, New Mexico, and northern Mexico. According to Poston, emigration through the crossing had declined from a high of ninety thousand in 1849 but was still substantial at thirty-five thousand to fifty thousand a year since 1850, "with large numbers of wagons and immense droves of stock." Poston found three ferries and a steamboat currently operating at the crossing, and he found the river above and below

Figure 12. J. Ross Browne, Fort Yuma. From Browne, *Adventures in the Apache Country.*

Fort Yuma navigable to a depth of twenty to twenty-five feet, similar to the Ohio and Missouri rivers. He also reported "large tracts of arable land" on both banks, "capable of producing cotton and sugar." He found the Indians near the fort "under good subjection."[30]

At Yuma, Poston met two individuals particularly important to his future. One was Louis J. F. Jaeger, a Pennsylvanian who had arrived at the Yuma crossing in 1850, helped to establish a ferry across the Colorado as an employee of George A. Johnson, and later bought out Johnson and other investors to operate the ferry in partnership with William Ankrim.[31] He charged one dollar for ferrying a man across the Colorado, two dollars for a horse or mule, and five dollars for a wagon. Soon, he had enough money to purchase wagons and go into the freighting business. He grew rich from these businesses, and his wagons went as far west as San Diego and Los Angeles and as far east as Santa Fe and El Paso.[32] Jaeger also operated a store in which he sold groceries, mining equipment, and other provisions to the army and mining expeditions. He later added farming and ranching to his enterprises, and Ross Browne describes him as owning silver mines in southern Arizona in 1864.[33]

Figure 13. Louis J. F. Jaeger. Photo courtesy of the Arizona Historical Society, Tucson.

The other important person Poston met at Yuma was Major Samuel Peter Heintzelman, commandant of Fort Yuma. The Yuma crossing was a key point for military and surveying parties in the 1840s and 1850s that crossed or ended their expeditions at the Colorado River. Yet the site was a troublesome one for many years because no one could cross the Colorado without the consent of the native Quechan Indians, and sometimes not without using a ferry that the Indians themselves operated. It was to protect the crossing and the emigrants using it that the army sent soldiers there.[34] From California, Heintzelman was ordered in November 1850 to go to the junction of the Colorado and Gila rivers and establish a post there to protect emigrants and suppress hostile Indians. Heintzelman did so and built Fort Yuma on a high bluff on the California side of the Colorado.[35]

His biographer Jerry Thompson says that for most of his life Heintzelman was a "soldier-entrepreneur," serving in the army but always pursuing

Figure 14. Samuel Peter Heintzelman. Photo courtesy of the Arizona Historical Society, Tucson.

mining and business interests.[36] Jaeger and Ankrim had made him a partner in their ferry business for an investment of six hundred dollars.[37] At Fort Yuma, Poston and Heintzelman became good friends. Heintzelman, always interested in prospective mining ventures, was probably attracted by Poston's stories of his experiences in Sonora, and Poston's talk of rich mines in Arizona probably matched tales Heintzelman had heard from other emigrants. Poston doubtless thought that an army officer with Heintzelman's rank and connections could be useful to him. Perhaps he recognized, too, that Heintzelman was the organizer and "detail person" that he, Poston, was not.

Poston's response to his discovery of the transportation nexus at the Yuma crossing was to have Ehrenberg survey a potential port site that he called "Colorado City" on the south bank of the Colorado, opposite Fort Yuma and just below the junction of the Gila and Colorado rivers. He then promoted Colorado City as the port and railroad hub that he had previously sought in Sonora:

> In view of the settlement of the territory acquired by the Gadsden Purchase, the opening of mines in Sonora and New Mexico, the opening of navigation to the vicinity of the Mormon settlements, and the location of the continental railroad to cross at this place [the junction of the Gila and Colorado rivers] this seems to be a point of sufficient local and geographic importance to justify the location of a commercial point. . . . Accordingly a sufficient amount of land was located immediately below the junction of the rivers containing about one thousand acres and a city laid out and called "Colorado City."[38]

This was quite different from Poston's aim of locating a port site at San Juan Bautista Bay. But it was an idea on which Poston seems to have decided even before he arrived at Fort Yuma. Heintzelman's journal for July 11, the day that Poston and Ehrenberg arrived, says that Poston and Ehrenberg "meant to lay out a town here and are backed by capitalists in S. Francisco. They propose an arrangement with Ankrim & Jaeger for a town near the Ferry, or rather to include it. . . . I have sent for Jaeger to talk with him on the subject."[39]

Why would Poston propose to build a port city at the Yuma crossing when he had already negotiated a deal to build one at San Juan Bautista Bay? First, at the Yuma crossing Poston was finally able to get accurate information about the passage of the Gadsden Treaty and the new U.S.-Mexican border. He would have learned that San Juan Bautista Bay had not been included in the Gadsden Purchase. Therefore, either Mexico south to the bay would have to be annexed to the United States, or any railroad line built to the bay would have to run through northern Mexico and thus be subject to Mexican government control. Second, Poston knew that Gray and his Texas Western Railroad survey had preceded him through the Yuma crossing by just a day or two.[40] Having shadowed Gray through northern Sonora, Poston knew that Gray had not found any new port site on the gulf coast and that he would likely recommend that the Texas Western company build a railroad to the crossing. And Poston was right. In his 1855 report on the survey, Gray laid out a railroad route from El Paso through the Yuma crossing to San Diego and declared a spot near Colorado City "the only site adapted for a railroad crossing of the Colorado below the Gila, on this route."[41] Just as in Sonora Poston had tied his speculative strategy to what he believed was the Texas Western Railroad's, here at the Yuma crossing he did the same, declaring that the transcontinental railroad would cross the Colorado River at Fort Yuma and that Colorado City would be a profitable commercial site.[42] But Poston's intent was quite different from Gray's. It was for the syndicate to gain legal title to the lands at the Yuma crossing and then force the Texas Western Railroad to pay a high price for the land it needed.[43]

Heintzelman's July 11 journal entry shows that he was immediately interested in Colorado City and thought to invest in it with Jaeger and Ankrim but wanted Jaeger's advice first. Heintzelman talked with Jaeger about the town site the next day. And on July 14, Poston and Ehrenberg took a sketch from Heintzelman's own survey of the Fort Yuma military reservation and used it to guide them in planning Colorado City.[44] The sketch would have shown them which lands at the crossing were part of the reservation and thus not available for private development. Exactly when Colorado City was surveyed is not known, but it probably was sometime between July 14 and July 25, after which Poston and Ehrenberg left Fort Yuma for San Diego.[45]

Poston's method of procuring investment for Colorado City was different than the approach he had used in Mexico. In Sonora, Poston had acquired legal power of attorney for a group of wealthy Mexicans to negotiate a deal with American investors and the Texas Western Railroad to develop the San Juan Bautista Bay port site. The Sonorans would, presumably, work to clear the way politically for the success of the project, even to the extent of contriving the secession of Sonora from Mexico. At the Yuma crossing, Poston persuaded investors to file claims on tracts of land along the Colorado River and then cede legal control of their claims to the syndicate, represented by the trustees of Colorado City—Poston, Ehrenberg, and McLemore. The syndicate would, then, as in the San Juan Bautista Bay agreement, undertake to persuade the Texas Western Railroad to build a line to the site (which they already seemed disposed to do) and develop a port site for the railroad.

The area that Ehrenberg surveyed included tracts for seven investors: George F. Hooper, George A. Johnson, Louis J. F. Jaeger, Henry Burch, James Porter, Isaac E. Lanier, and Julius Sacharznoski. The tracts extended from the junction of the Gila and Colorado rivers, west for about three miles along the Colorado, between the southern bank of the river and the U.S.-Mexican border. The tracts ranged in size from 70 acres for Hooper to 160 acres for Burch, Porter, and Lanier. The size of the largest parcels suggests that the legal foundation of this strategy was the U.S. Preemption Act of 1841, under which individuals occupying federally owned land could purchase up to 160 acres at a low price by claiming the land as their property.[46] The tracts' dimensions were recorded in a document of "indenture," signed on August 3, 1854, in San Diego and transferring ownership of the tracts to the trustees of the "Colorado Company"—John C. McLemore, Herman Ehrenberg, and Charles D. Poston—for the sum of one dollar paid to each of the original owners.[47]

Heintzelman had been relieved of command at Fort Yuma in June. His replacement, Major George H. Thomas, arrived with troops on July 14 and assumed command the following day. That same day, Heintzelman left for San Diego and arrived by July 22. But although Heintzelman wrote on July 14 that Poston and Ehrenberg would follow "in a day or two," Poston remained at Fort Yuma, probably until late July, attempting to interest other investors in Colorado City.[48] The evidence for the delay, Goodale says, is the preemption notices taken out by the original Colorado City landowners on their tracts within the Colorado City plat. These documents were dated Fort Yuma, July 25, 1854, and were recorded in San Diego.[49] In addition, the August 3 indenture transferring ownership of these tracts to the Colorado Company trustees was signed in San Diego by Hooper, Jaeger, Porter, Lanier, and Sacharznoski. It makes sense that these men would have traveled to San Diego with Poston and Ehrenberg; and if they did, their party would not have left Fort Yuma until at least July 25, the date of the preemption notices.

Poston says little about the journey to California—only that his party traveled 218 miles from Fort Yuma to San Diego and that they "made the journey on mules with extraordinary discomfort."[50] Mileages on Ehrenberg's 1854 "Map of the Gadsden Purchase" indicate that they followed Cooke's Road, across the Colorado Desert and the coastal mountains of California to the Pacific. This was the route to California pioneered by Kearny and Cooke in 1846–47 and used by most California emigrants who took the southwestern route in the years immediately following. It was known to these early travelers as an extremely difficult and dangerous route, more trying even than the Gila Trail to the Colorado and probably the most hazardous part of the entire emigrant trail to California.

From Fort Yuma, the trail led west along the southern bank of the Colorado and south into Mexico, passing through a sand desert about fifty miles wide and containing huge, shifting dunes.[51] After fifteen miles, travelers would come to "Cooke's Wells," two wells dug by Kearny's and Cooke's men that contained limited amounts of water and repeatedly filled with sand so that they had to be reexcavated by each group of travelers that used them.

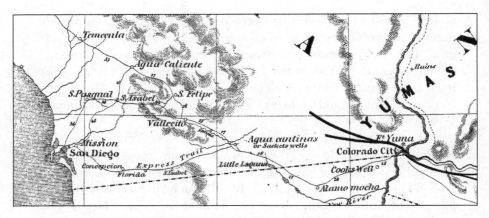

Figure 15. Section of Ehrenberg's 1854 "Map of the Gadsden Purchase," showing Poston's route to San Diego. Courtesy of the Arizona Historical Society, Tucson.

There was no food to be found along this part of the route, and both men and animals in Kearny's and Cooke's parties survived on mesquite beans.[52]

The trail then proceeded to Alamo Mocho and another two wells used by Kearny and Cooke, then over a dry lake bed to the well at Pozo Hondo. From there, travelers would continue to Carrizo Springs, then down a deep-sand road, through a grove of palm trees and some small springs (called "Palm Springs" by the soldiers) to Vallecito, a valley a mile or more in length that contained grass. From here, the trail crossed the coastal Sierra range, past the deserted Indian village of San Felipe, then through mountain forests to Warner's Ranch (called "Agua Caliente" on Ehrenberg's map, after a hot spring nearby).[53] From here, Poston's party followed a route taken by Kearny in 1847, southwest to the village of San Isabel, west to San Pasqual, and then southwest again to San Diego.[54] The point-to-point distances for this route on Ehrenberg's map total exactly 218 miles, the same distance that Poston reported in the "Reconnoisance."[55]

In San Diego, on July 31, Heintzelman received word that Poston and Ehrenberg had arrived from Yuma and that they had with them a map of Colorado City, showing the claims filed by investors. Heintzelman owned a one-twentieth share in Colorado City but was not a landholder. Also, he had left Fort Yuma before all the Colorado City tracts had been sold, so he had not seen the final distribution of claims. Now, in San Diego, he got his first look at the layout of Colorado City, and he did not like what he saw. First of all, the tracts were obviously unequal in size; yet each investor

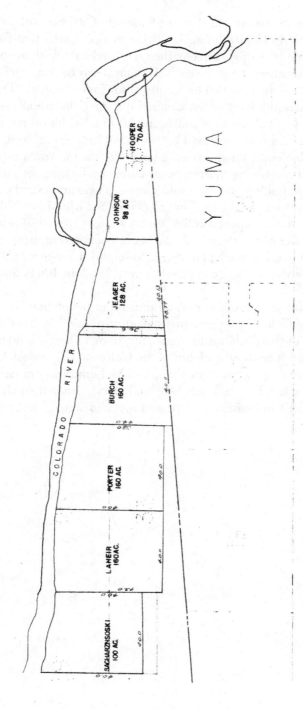

Figure 16. Colorado City diagram. Courtesy of the Arizona Historical Society, Tempe.

got the same one-twentieth share in Colorado City. Second, for reasons unfathomable to Heintzelman, Louis Jaeger had agreed that Jaeger and Ankrim would get a single tract for their ferry and a single share for the two of them rather than one share each. Perhaps it was because Heintzelman was a partner in the ferry that he felt this arrangement unjust. "This side of the river [the south bank of the Colorado] is ours," he complained in his journal, "& I will object to any division of it into lots for others, or shares. . . . I don't like the arrangement & would not have agreed to it." Finally, even though Heintzelman was not a landholder at the Yuma crossing but still owned a one-twentieth share in the company, he thought it wrong that other nonlandholders had been sold shares: "There are several persons on the river who have not the shadow of a claim [and who] have 20ths." Most aggravating in this respect was the "Great Western" (Sarah Bowman), the famous frontier prostitute, who had a "house of entertainment" and store at the Yuma crossing and had managed to acquire a one-twentieth share in Colorado City and win the contract to provide adobe bricks for the city's construction.[56]

Despite his private objections, there is no evidence that Heintzelman ever expressed his disagreements to Poston or tried to alter Colorado City's land- or shareholding arrangements. In San Diego on August 3, the preemption notices for the claims of the Colorado City investors and the indenture naming Poston, Ehrenberg, and McLemore as trustees for these claims were filed. Poston, Ehrenberg, and Heintzelman then all departed San Diego for San Francisco on the steamer *Southerner*.[57] They arrived on August 7.[58]

CHAPTER TEN

Deals and Disappointments

Events in San Francisco at first seemed to predict success for both the San Juan Bautista Bay port site and Colorado City. A letter from Asa Dean in El Monte, Sonora, published in the *Daily Alta California* on August 8, 1854, reported that Sonorans were disenchanted with their government and the Gadsden Treaty, and that at least some were eager for American occupation. Already in July a group of San Diegans had proposed to form the San Diego and Gila Southern Pacific and Atlantic Railroad Company and to survey a route that would cross southern California past Fort Yuma (the site of Colorado City) and along the Gila to the Rio Grande River, where it would connect with the Texas Western Railroad and the commercial centers of the South.[1]

On August 21, several notices favorable to Colorado City appeared in the *Daily Alta California*. A letter from Sen. Thomas J. Rusk of Texas declared that plans for constructing a transcontinental railroad over the southern route were now a "fait accompli," since the railroad had already been begun on the eastern end. "Its connection with San Diego," Rusk said, "is no longer considered problematical, as the route will intersect the Colorado River 200 miles distant from this town" (the approximate location of Colorado City). Rusk announced that "such a road will be promptly constructed," that "companies have been formed" and were now "constructing roads from the mouth of the Ohio River, Vicksburg, and New Orleans to the Texas line." Moreover, the Texas legislature had voted to give 10,240,000 acres to the construction of a railroad line to El Paso. The work was to be contracted on August 1 (three weeks earlier), and three different companies had already filed bids.

95

In the same issue, an article by "P" exaggerated Poston's explorations and reflected his dismissal of San Juan Bautista Bay as a port site, but gave a good indication of how Poston and Heintzelman thought to develop Colorado City:

> A company has been formed for the purpose of taking up land and establishing settlements on the line of the road through the Gila country. Some of the agents of the country, with their surveyors, arrived in this place last week from the Colorado [Poston, Ehrenberg, and Heintzelman had arrived in San Francisco on August 7], having thoroughly explored that river and the Gulf of California as far south as Guaymas. They report no available harbor or bay on the Gulf, and selected a site on the east bank of the Colorado, near Fort Yuma, as the only eligible position near that river for a settlement. This location is within the present limits of the United States and the State of California. The new treaty [the Gadsden Treaty] does not embrace any more valuable land in that vicinity for the required purposes.

A third article on the same page gave ample publicity to Colorado City and showed the scope of Poston's dream of becoming an influential commercial force in San Francisco and the Gadsden Purchase:

> We understand that there are several companies forming here for the purpose of developing the resources of the Gila Territory, lately purchased from Mexico, and that some of the first men are engaged in it. [One] formed about a month ago, is the Colorado company, owners of the new city of Colorada [sic] near Fort Yuma. Their object is a magnificent one, and should they succeed as they expect, a new era for the San Francisco merchants will begin. They propose to open steam navigation on the upper Colorado, approach the Mormon settlements towards Salt Lake to the nearest point, and thus open the trade with about one hundred thousand people, who now draw their powerful supplies from St. Louis, Mo. Their place, they say, will also be the post for the new territory, the country between the Gila and Colorada Rivers, and the Northern States of Mexico.

According to Heintzelman's journal, on August 12 and 13, he, Poston, and John McLemore met with "various men" about Colorado City, including a Lieutenant Stevens of the U.S. Navy, who became a shareholder in the company.[2] A few days later, on August 16, Heintzelman left San Francisco for the East, arriving in New York on September 11. The very next day, he set out to locate officials of the Atlantic & Pacific (A & P) Railroad Company, which had recently purchased the Texas Western Railroad and would take over that company's effort to build a transcontinental railroad across Texas to the Pacific. He was unsuccessful; but later that day, and the next, he met with Andrew Gray, who was also in New York. Gray, who may have been a stockholder in the A & P Company, knew just the people Heintzelman wanted to see. On September 13, he invited Heintzelman to dinner and introduced him to Robert J. Walker and Thomas Butler King, the president and vice president, respectively, of the A & P Company. But according to Heintzelman, they did not discuss business at all—neither the transcontinental railroad nor Colorado City.[3]

In the months following, Heintzelman spent time in New York, Philadelphia, and Washington, as well as Carlisle Barracks, Pennsylvania, where he had two brief tours, and Buffalo, where his wife and children were living.[4] In Washington, he mostly attended to army business—visiting old military comrades and officials at the War Department, settling financial accounts relating to his Fort Yuma command, and politicking for a new posting. He remained interested in the affairs of Colorado City, referring to it in his journal as "our city," but he seems to have done nothing to advance its prospects as a port or railroad terminus. That project was left, mainly, to Poston.

At this task, Poston was not idle. In San Francisco on August 15, he was issued a stock certificate for Colorado City worth a one-twentieth share in the company.[5] He later said that the remainder of the shares were sold in San Francisco at one thousand dollars each.[6] On August 30, 1854, he saw the Colorado Company incorporated with a capital stock of five hundred thousand dollars in shares of one hundred dollars, making Poston's and Heintzelman's interests worth at least twenty-five thousand dollars each. The incorporation document was signed by the three trustees of the company—McLemore, Ehrenberg, and Poston.[7]

Of course, the main business Poston had in San Francisco was to report to the syndicate on his expedition and to explain the projects he was proposing at San Juan Bautista Bay and Colorado City. The "Reconnoisance in Sonora," dated September 15, may have been that report. Poston says that he "laid the result of the reconnaissance (which was not much) before the syndicate."[8] Goodale says that in this statement Poston treated his report "cavalierly."[9] But Poston's dismissive statement was made in 1894 and was likely motivated by the syndicate's failure to adopt either of his projects.

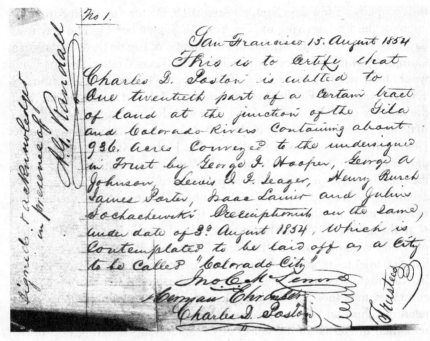

Figure 17. Copy of Charles D. Poston's Colorado City stock certificate. Courtesy of the Arizona Historical Society, Tempe.

Poston had not abandoned the idea of locating a port at San Juan Bautista Bay, as evidenced by his including the proposal in the "Reconnoisance." But San Juan Bautista Bay, which had not been included in the Gadsden Purchase, was now less interesting to American investors than sites in U.S. territory. And since Poston was now a trustee of Colorado City, he could expect a larger profit if a railroad line built by the Atlantic & Pacific Company extended to the Yuma crossing. Therefore, Poston emphasizes in the "Reconnoisance" his preference for Colorado City as both a port and a crossing point for the transcontinental railroad: "Having now made a reconnoisance of the coast from the mouth to the head of the Gulf of California and a large portion of both the Gila and Colorado Rivers I freely offer Colorado City as the best and only point suitable for the location of a city in the Territory of the U.S. in this vicinity and capable of becoming the point of supply for the extensive territories of Utah and New Mexico portions of Sonora Chihuahua & California."[10]

To support his case, Poston adds that "it has been fully ascertained by recent surveys that a route for a railroad [from Yuma to San Diego] can be procured in a distance of 180 miles." In fact, Poston was so far committed to Colorado City that he says he had organized in San Diego a company "for the purpose of constructing a Railroad from San Diego to the Colorado, the subscribers being wealthy citizens of San Diego Co." who had offered to "mortgage one half of their individual property to secure means necessary for the construction of the road."[11]

However, despite Poston's arguments, the syndicate proposed only to "explore," not settle or develop, the Colorado River region, and only if the federal government would provide financial and military support. "It was decided," Poston says, "that I should proceed to Washington, for the purpose of soliciting assistance of the Federal Government in opening the new Territory for settlement."[12]

This was a very restrictive response to Poston's proposals—practically speaking, a rejection of them—and Poston must have been bitterly disappointed. It was as much an embarrassment as his Kentucky failures—in fact, more so because he had traveled hundreds of miles and literally risked his life to propose these projects to investors whom he thought would be daring enough to pursue them. But Poston's schemes were simply not practical from a business standpoint, and his potential investors were in no hurry to involve themselves in either of them.

At the start of their venture, the syndicate and Poston may have shared the expansionist views expressed in the "Reconnoisance," but in the end the Sonoran port project was simply too risky for the syndicate to pursue. Implementing it would have involved not only enormous amounts of capital but impossibly complex and risky annexation politics. As for Colorado City, it, too, would have taken a massive amount of capital to develop. And in fall 1854 the Atlantic & Pacific Company could not raise the money even to build a railroad across Texas, much less one to the Colorado River.[13] The syndicate probably doubted that the A & P, or any eastern railroad, would build a line to remote Fort Yuma. Moreover, frauds perpetrated by eastern railroad companies were all too common in the 1850s.[14] Railroad speculators such as Walker and King often made brave starts with much fanfare, then went bankrupt when they were unable to raise enough capital to develop their plans. Thus, from the syndicate's viewpoint, they could easily have invested a large amount of money in Colorado City and lost everything. To Poston, both of his projects glittered with promise. But to his San Francisco backers, they were loaded with risk. Nevertheless, Poston went ahead with preparations for his Washington trip, meeting with General Wool, commander of the U.S. Army's Pacific Division, and persuading him to recommend to the secretary of war that the War Department support further exploration of the Colorado River region.[15]

Meanwhile, in fall 1854 news concerning a transcontinental railroad seemed to offer cause for both optimism and pessimism. An article in the November 28 *Daily Alta California* proclaimed that the San Diego Gila Railroad had been chartered in Sacramento and that when completed it would run from San Diego to the Gila River and would be part of "the Great Atlantic & Pacific Road now in course of construction through the state of Texas." However, a December 10 article in the same publication announced, "The 'Moonlight Railroad' scheme of Robert J. Walker & Company [the A & P Company] has met with a sudden ending."

Walker and King's dealings are worth summarizing, since, ultimately, they had a decisive impact on the fate of Colorado City and were typical of the financial machinations practiced by some mid-nineteenth-century railroad speculators. The Texas Western Railroad had been chartered by the Texas legislature in 1852 as part of the ongoing effort by Southern politicians and businessmen to build a transcontinental railroad across Texas, along the southern route. But the Atlantic & Pacific Railroad, organized in New York in 1852 and led by Walker and King, wanted to acquire the sole franchise for the transcontinental railroad. To this end, in 1854 Walker and King raised six hundred thousand dollars to buy the Texas Western charter. They then bid to the State of Texas to build a railroad across the state to El Paso. They were the only bidders, but under Texas law they had to put up three hundred thousand dollars in gold as bond. They were unable to do so and tried, instead, offering stock in a Memphis bank. When this stock was rejected, they offered stock in the Sussex Iron Company of New Jersey, which they had purchased with six million dollars' worth of Texas Western stock. This, too, was rejected. Walker then reorganized the A & P Railroad under the charter of the Texas Western Railroad and filed in Texas's General Land Office a claim for a railroad line along a route already approved by the Texas legislature. When the governor of Texas called for bids on this line, and no other companies bid, the legislature passed a bill throwing the land open to settlement. Walker and King, now without resources to continue, did not contest this. The Texas Western Railroad was able to continue after renewing its charter in 1856 and changing its name to the Southern Pacific Railroad.[16] However, by the end of 1854, as the *Alta California* indicated, Walker and King had exhausted themselves in twisted legal maneuvers and questionable financial dealings. The *Alta California* went on to assert that most Californians would now agree that the most practical route for a railroad through California would be the "central route," favoring San Francisco as a terminus rather than San Diego.

Despite having received his marching orders from the syndicate, Poston seems not to have left California for some time. In one of his journals, Poston says, "At this time I received a letter from my father in law and the friend of my youth, Samuel Haycroft [sic] calling me home on account of the immanent [sic] danger of my wife's death. Returned by way of the Isthmus of Nicaragua to New Orleans and there by rail through the Southern States to Kentucky where I arrived the latter part of the year 1854."[17] However, elsewhere Poston contradicts this timeline. In his 1895 speech he says, "The Christmas of 1854 was passed in San Francisco with the friends of my youth, when I sailed for New York and Washington."[18] Also, Goodale shows that Poston completed two significant real estate deals in San Francisco in November 1854. In the first, thirteen lots were transferred to Poston from his attorney, William H. Tiffany, for $1,500 on November 7, and in the second, Poston sold property to Moses and Miller Sturdevant on November 24.[19] Poston's 1895 speech suggests that he departed San Francisco shortly after Christmas, but exactly when he left is unknown.

Whenever Poston returned to Kentucky, Margaret had recovered by the time he arrived, and Samuel Haycraft says that Poston passed 1855 "in the seclusion of his early home with his family."[20] However, Poston says that he spent 1855 "in the Atlantic cities and Christmas 1855 in Washington endeavoring to assuage the thirst of the desert by libations containing less alkali than abounds in Arizona."[21] This admission suggests that Haycraft's portrayal of Poston as the dedicated husband and father, spending all of 1855 with his family in Elizabethtown, is inaccurate and conceals a very different sort of behavior. The lure of the eastern cities for Poston, of course, was that there was still a chance that he might find support for Colorado City there. And so from San Francisco he was off to Washington to speak with government officials about his project.

Heintzelman says that Poston arrived in Washington on January 28 and that the major received a letter from him ten days later. The timing suggests that Poston may have gone to Washington before he visited Elizabethtown.[22] According to Heintzelman, Poston energetically pursued the business of Colorado City in Washington, while McLemore, General Hitchcock, who had become an investor in Colorado City, and Ankrim had charge of the company's interests in San Francisco. Ehrenberg "was to go to the Colorado," although for what purpose Heintzelman does not say.[23] Poston himself says that while in Washington, he "met in society with many senators and members of the government who were at that time interesting themselves in a trans-continental railway."[24] And he seems to have made some headway at the War Department, since Heintzelman wrote that the secretary of war had promised, if a bill supporting a southern route for the transcontinental railroad failed, to establish a line of forts from El Paso to the Colorado. Poston also called upon the government to make Colorado City a U.S. port of entry. He was not successful.

Nevertheless, Colorado City seemed to be progressing. Even before Poston left San Francisco for Washington, George Hooper had established a store in the house of Sarah and Albert Bowman, which he purchased in 1854, and built a warehouse.[25] Steamboat owner and captain George A. Johnson erected a house and buildings for his Colorado Steam Navigation Company. The house was also used as a customs station.[26] Heintzelman learned of these developments in Washington and wrote in his journal, "The Gadsden Purchase is rapidly filling with emigrants."[27] A post office was built and a postmaster appointed for Colorado City on March 17, 1858.[28] Heintzelman adds that the syndicate's modest goal for the Colorado River region was achieved, though not by Poston, and in San Francisco, not in Washington: "The Mormons called on General Hitchcock & he promised this month to explore the Colorado."[29]

However, two weeks later, Colorado City's prospects began to fade. Heintzelman's journal entries on the topic are vague, but Poston told Heintzelman that some Colorado City investors were threatening to "break up" the company, and he urged Heintzelman to write a letter that would dissuade them.[30] Five days later, the picture became clearer. Heintzelman noted that Walker and King's maneuverings with the Atlantic & Pacific Railroad had destroyed investor confidence in the company and, with it, the prospects of building a transcontinental railroad to Colorado City. At the same time, Heintzelman learned from Poston that Hooper, Ankrim, Jaeger, and perhaps Johnson were "dissatisfied" with the company. It was probably they who were threatening to overturn the venture.[31]

Despite this setback, Poston's hopes for Colorado City remained alive. On March 4, he left Washington by train for New York City, and while there, he dined with Walker and King at Walker's Fifth Avenue mansion. King was Poston's former boss at the San Francisco customs house, and Poston says that they renewed acquaintance "over sparkling vintages."[32] Even as far away as San Francisco, Walker and King's manipulation of Atlantic & Pacific Company finances had been publicly discredited, and their stock offerings no longer attracted significant investment.[33] Nevertheless, Poston describes a grandiose scheme for the transcontinental railroad discussed at

Walker's dinner table, in which Walker would seek international financing in Europe, company secretary Samuel Jaudon would find financing in New York and the "Atlantic cities," Cincinnati merchant Edgar Conkling would be the railroad's agent in the Mississippi Valley, King would fulfill the same role in Texas, and Poston would be in charge of "the country between the Rio Grande and the Colorado." Poston urged Walker and King to develop the railroad route through Arizona, highlighting the same feature that had originally drawn him to the region—its fabled mines: "I told them all I knew about the Territory—and a great deal more,—and enlarged upon the advantages that would accrue to the railroad company by an exploration of the new Territory and a development of its mineral resources. They inquired how much it would cost to make the exploration. I replied that I would start with a hundred thousand dollars if there was a million behind it."[34]

Walker and King's latest plan, like so many others involving the transcontinental railroad, was never implemented and so could not help Colorado City. But Poston still was able to promote his city through his establishment of the Sonora Exploring and Mining Company in Cincinnati the following year. Poston's pitch to the A & P executives concerning Arizona's mineral wealth suggests that sometime in 1855 he and Heintzelman shifted priorities away from Colorado City and toward seeking investment in southern Arizona silver mines, specifically those in the Santa Cruz valley and Santa Rita Mountains near Tubac. The SEMC's 1856 report to stockholders boasted that ore from the company's mines could be "safely shipped to the Colorado river and Fort Yuma. . . . This point has already become a trading port of considerable importance, and bears the name of Colorado City. This is destined to be at no very distant day a place of great importance."[35]

Interestingly, Poston seems to have tried to interest the Southern Pacific Railroad in Colorado City by sending Thomas Butler King a copy of the "Reconnoisance in Sonora." A note on the envelope in which the report was returned to Heintzelman reads, "From T. Butler King of Georgia. Recd. Aug. 11, 1857."[36] Heintzelman confirmed his receipt of the report in his journal the same day. However, this seems to have been the first time Heintzelman had seen the report, since he wrote the following day, "I read Mr. Poston's interesting report of his exploration from Sinaloa to Yuma. It is a magnificent project if we can carry it out."[37] It seems likely that the project Heintzelman was referring to was Colorado City, not San Juan Bautista Bay.

Despite the SEMC's promises, Colorado City did not become "a place of great importance." By 1859 a new settlement, Arizona City, had sprung up at the east end of the Colorado City plat, on what would have been Hooper's and Johnson's tracts, and it quickly outgrew Colorado City.[38] Also established at the crossing since 1852 was "Jaegerville," a collection of buildings on the California side of the Colorado at the site of Jaeger's ferry, about a mile west of Fort Yuma. The buildings consisted of Jaeger's house, the ferry office, a store, and a blacksmith shop. Jaeger later converted the ferry office into a stagecoach station for the Butterfield Overland Mail and used part of his house as a hotel.[39]

An article in the *Daily Alta California* for July 27, 1859, describes all three settlements—Arizona City, Colorado City, and Jaegerville—existing together at the Yuma crossing. Arizona City sat in the angle south of the Colorado and west of the Gila River, across from Fort Yuma. Colorado City was about a mile west, on the southern bank of the Colorado, on what would have been Jaeger's tract, and across the river from Jaegerville.[40] Jaegerville is described as having two stores, buildings for the Overland Mail, two blacksmith shops, several houses, and Jaeger's house and hotel. Arizona City had six adobe houses, two more under construction, and was "flourishing." But Colorado City had only one building and was destined to be "of no more importance than at present." When Poston and his friend, Santa Rita mine engineer Raphael Pumpelly, traveled from Arizona to California in summer 1861, they stopped at Colorado City, which, Pumpelly says, consisted of just one house, Sarah Bowman's; and the three of them (Poston, Pumpelly, and Bowman) constituted the entire population of the "city."[41] The 1860 census for Arizona listed Arizona City as having eighty-five residents but did not list Colorado City at all.[42]

Why Arizona City sprang up is not known. Its beginning may have been related to the "dissatisfaction" Heintzelman noted among Colorado City investors with Poston and the project's development. Perhaps Hooper and Johnson, impatient with Poston's failure to bring the Atlantic & Pacific Railroad to the site, decided to develop their properties on their own. There also were potent entrepreneurial rivalries at the crossing.[43] Arizona City may have represented Hooper's and Johnson's efforts to declare their independence not only of failed Colorado City but of Jaeger, who was by far the most successful merchant at the crossing and dominated trade in the region.

Any commercial rivalries that may have existed at the crossing were suspended on January 20–23, 1862, when massive flooding of the Colorado and Gila rivers devastated the entire area. Jaegerville was swept away; but Jaeger's house and personal property were untouched, and he continued in business.[44] Hooper's buildings at Arizona City were destroyed and Johnson's damaged, but the town survived. Colorado City did not. It was destroyed, and the army moved its quartermaster depot to the site to make it easier for steamboats to load and unload.[45]

It was Arizona City that became the boomtown Poston had envisioned at the Yuma crossing and, in the 1860s, a major port for freight moving inland and up the Colorado by steamboat.[46] On January 28, 1873, the Arizona territorial legislature changed the town's name to Yuma.[47] Of the original Colorado City investors, Louis Jaeger and George Hooper became wealthy merchants in Arizona City, and George Johnson monopolized steamboat trade along the Colorado until 1864 and dominated it through the end of the decade.[48]

Poston's adventure in Sonora and the Gadsden Purchase ended, finally, in the eastern cities of the United States in 1855, where he was unable to obtain government support or private investment for Colorado City. However, the story of the expedition lingered on as Poston revised and retold it repeatedly in subsequent years, reinventing the experience as his literary persona changed—from the young frontier entrepreneur and adventurer exploring the deserts of Mexico and Arizona to the aging pioneer, reminiscing about his youthful experiences.

CHAPTER ELEVEN

Stories of the Sonoran Expedition

Poston's stories about his expedition reflect what David Wrobel describes as two different ways of writing about the frontier West in the nineteenth century: the literature of frontier promotion and that of pioneer reminiscence. Wrobel says that frontier promoters, or "imaginers," wrote about the possibilities of life on the frontier, diminishing the hazards and discomforts of that life, while pioneer "rememberers" told of the dangers of exploring and settling the frontier, contrasting that life with the relative ease and comfort of present-day existence.[1] Poston played both roles while telling of his frontier experiences. And while he can hardly be said to have overlooked the hardships of frontier life in the "Reconnoisance," his promotional arguments in that document stand in contrast to the dramatic and humorous tales he later told of his 1854 experiences in Sonora and Arizona.

The first of these retellings was in the chapter entitled "Poston's Narrative" in J. Ross Browne's *Adventures in the Apache Country*, published in 1869. Browne says that the account was from a "journal" that Poston gave him of his experiences in Mexico and the Gadsden Purchase.[2] Much of the text in the "Narrative" is identical with that in the "Reconnoisance," and it is possible that what Poston gave Browne was a copy of the earlier document. But the "Narrative" contains enough significant differences from the "Reconnoisance" to suggest that the former was an entirely different text, based on the "Reconnoisance" but written separately.[3]

For example, the "Reconnoisance" says nothing about preparations for the expedition or the circumstances that inspired it. However, in the "Narrative" Poston says that powerful motives for the expedition were the

Figure 18. Charles D. Poston in old age. Photo courtesy of the Arizona Historical Society, Tucson.

ratification of the Gadsden Treaty and the opportunities the treaty afforded for building a transcontinental railroad and exploiting the mines of northern Mexico. Poston also cites in the "Narrative" the exploits of Raousset de Boulbon as an inspiration to him in conceiving the expedition.[4]

One of the significant features of Poston's later expedition stories is the variation in his dates for the journey. In the "Narrative" Poston says that his party left San Francisco on February 20, 1854, rather than on February 19 as reported in the "Reconnoisance" and the *Daily Alta California*.[5] Concerning the journey to Mexico, Poston repeats the "Reconnoisance" story that the *Zoraida* stranded while trying to enter Navachiste harbor. But in the "Narrative" Poston says that the slow-sailing *Zoraida* took thirty-two days to reach Navachiste rather than the eighteen that it actually took. And in the later work, the stranding becomes a full-fledged shipwreck, to which Poston cannot resist adding melodramatic details, for example, that "keen-scented sharks gathered around the doomed ship by the hundreds" and that "the passengers looked over the sides with some forebodings that they would soon be food for the monsters of the deep."[6] When the ship's mainmast was sprung, Poston says, the ship began to leak. A few boats were loaded with baggage, arms, and food; and the passengers made for a beach a few miles away. The boats ran in on the tide, landed high on the beach, and at sundown the passengers found themselves on a "lonely barren island [Macapule], and the roaring of the waves and the breaking up of the ship did not add any thing to the cheerfulness of our landing." On Macapule, Poston says, the shipwrecked passengers found wild cattle and fruit trees and dined on roast beef, honey, and wild fruits. They also found springs of sweet water, saw wild cotton, and ate oysters they found attached to the jungle-like shrubbery along an estuary leading to the mainland. Poston quips, "This is the only place where oysters are known to grow upon trees."[7]

The "Narrative" follows closely the "Reconnoisance" account of the expedition's progress through Sinaloa and Sonora, the explorations of land and silver mines, and the trek from Sonoita to Adair Bay and back. However, the "Narrative" fundamentally alters Poston's "Reconnoisance" portrayal of his experiences after Adair Bay. In the "Narrative" Poston says that from Sonoita he journeyed not to the Gila River and the Yuma crossing, but eastward to the Santa Cruz Valley south of Tucson, where he prospected for silver and established the Sonora Exploring and Mining Company at Tubac.[8] The known dates of Poston's travel—leaving Sonoita in late June, spending July 4 at Sauceda, then arriving at Fort Yuma on July 11—show that he could not have gone as far east as the Santa Cruz valley. Instead, after a long and difficult journey through Sonora, including the harrowing trip to Adair Bay, he took the shortest route he could back home, down the Gila River to Fort Yuma and on to San Diego and San Francisco.[9]

The difference in Poston's stories highlights the difference in the purposes of his narratives—one emphasizing the difficulty of the desert country he had to traverse in 1854 and the extremity to which his expedition was brought, the other presenting for public acclaim his accomplishments as an Arizona mine developer. The latter made a far better pioneer narrative, since it omitted the failures of San Juan Bautista Bay and Colorado City and told, instead, a story of the triumph of American capital and technology, and of civilization brought to the frontier.

A similar merging of stories occurs in Poston's "Building a State in Apache Land II: Early Mining and Filibustering," published in the *Overland Monthly Magazine* in August 1894 and later collected with Poston's other three "Building a State" articles in the 1963 *Building a State in Apache Land*. In "Building a State II," Poston conflates accounts of his March 1855 meeting with Walker and King in New York and the founding of the Sonora Exploring and Mining Company in March 1856, as if the two had happened at the same time. Immediately after describing his discussion with Atlantic & Pacific Railroad officials about Arizona, Poston says, "A company was organized with a capital of two million dollars, and shares sold at an average of fifty dollars. General Heintzelman was appointed president, and I was appointed 'manager and commandant.' The office was located in Cincinnati, for the convenience of General Heintzelman, who was stationed at Newport Barracks, Ky. William Wrightson was appointed secretary." All of these details describe the founding of the Sonora Exploring and Mining Company in Cincinnati, on March 24, 1856, right down to the company's capitalization at two million dollars.[10] The combination of stories serves a similar purpose as that of the merged expedition narratives, in this case eliminating a gap in Poston's career in which nothing important happened and transforming the failed Colorado City scheme into the founding of a successful mining company.

Poston's "Building a State" series also provides a later account of the Sonoran expedition in "Building a State in Apache Land I: How the Territory Was Acquired," published in the *Overland Monthly* in July 1894. Actually, most of what is known about the circumstances leading to the Sonoran expedition and Poston's preparations for it comes from this article, including the discussions at the Government Boarding House, the influence of the Gadsden negotiations, Poston's stagnation at the customs house, the spark to action provided by the Iturbide Grant, and the formation of the San Francisco syndicate. None of this information is provided in the

"Reconnoisance" or in "Poston's Narrative." A significant detail Poston adds in this account is that the syndicate sent a former member of Congress who lived at the boardinghouse to Mexico City to obtain permission for Poston's party to enter Mexico. But Poston never identifies who this person was or what documents, if any, he brought back from the Mexican capital.[11]

"Building a State I" continues Poston's variations on expedition dates, since he says in the article that he registered at the U.S. consulate in Guaymas on January 14, 1854.[12] Since Poston's expedition did not leave San Francisco until February 19 and arrived at Navachiste Bay on March 9, the January 14 date cannot be correct. More significant, in "Building a State I" Poston abandons the fiction of the "Narrative" that he had prospected for silver in the Santa Cruz valley in 1854. Perhaps recalling the awful trek to and from Adair Bay and the desert crossing from Sonoita to the Gila River, Poston says in "Building a State I" that by the time he reached the Gila, he realized that he and his men could not survive in "a country destitute of sustenance; so we followed the Gila River down to its junction with the Colorado."[13] Unfortunately, the popularity of Browne's *Adventures* overwhelmed Poston's later correction, and Arizona historians have continued to repeat the story from the *Adventures* that Poston went prospecting to the east and found rich silver mines.[14]

In a speech the following year, 1895, Poston told a new story about his voyage on the *Zoraida*, but one just as dramatic as that in the "Narrative." In the speech, Poston gives his earliest departure date for the expedition, declaring that it left San Francisco on December 23, 1853. However, the *Zoraida*, he says, was blown "a thousand miles out into the Pacific" and then becalmed before southwest winds drove it back into the Mexican coast. The *Zoraida*'s eighteen-day sailing time from San Francisco to Navachiste suggests that this story is inaccurate. But in the speech, Poston seems to have been determined to make his adventure sound as dangerous as possible. By the end of his party's expedition, he adds, they had been put to such an extremity that their return to San Francisco in August "was considered a miracle."[15]

A lighter story that Poston told in the same speech demonstrates that at least some ordinary Mexicans were happy to see Americans in their country and that the expedition was not all hardship and privation. In the Sonoran city of Alamos, a "shoemaker" came to the house that Poston and his men had rented, offering a basket of "ladies' slippers" for sale. When Poston naïvely asked what they were to do with the slippers, the man told him that "the ladies for whom they had been made to measure would call for them during the evening." Poston says that they paid five dollars a pair for the footwear (rather a high price for shoes in 1854), "and the slippers were gone in the morning."[16] The story may help to explain Poston's lament in an 1892 newspaper article, "Diary of a Pioneer," that because of "the attraction of the fair señoritas in Sinaloa and Sonora," many of his men had drifted away from the expedition by the time he was ready to enter the Gadsden Purchase.[17]

One of the more notorious stories of the expedition that emerged after 1854 was that Poston and Ehrenberg had laid out Colorado City in order to pay Louis Jaeger for their ferry passage across the Colorado River. Actually, it appears that Poston himself concocted this tale. In an 1891 article Poston mentions the story and slyly deflects authorship onto some nameless others: "It has been said that we had to stop and locate a city to pay for our ferry across the Colorado River."[18] Raphael Pumpelly repeated the story in 1918, saying that he had heard it from Poston. Having no money to pay their passage, Pumpelly says, Poston

> hit upon the expedient of paying the ferriage in city lots. Setting Ehrenberg, the engineer of the party, and under him the whole force, at work with the instruments, amid a great display of signal stakes, they soon had the city laid out in squares and streets, and represented in due form on a sketch, not forgetting water lots and a steam ferry. Meanwhile Jaeger sat smoking his pipe in front of his cabin on the opposite shore, and, watching the unusual proceeding, his curiosity led him to cross the river. He began to question the busy surveyors, by whom he was referred to my friend [Poston]. On learning from that gentleman that a city was being founded so near to his own land the German became interested, and, as the great future of the place was unfolded in glowing terms, and the necessity of a steam ferry for the increasing trade dwelt upon as well as the coming of a transcontinental railway, he became enthusiastic, and began negotiations for several lots. The result was the sale of a small part of the embryo city, and the transportation of the whole party over in part payment for one lot.[19]

Like the story of Poston's prospecting Arizona silver mines in 1854, this story has been repeated by several historians.[20] However, it is misleading to write about Colorado City as if it were some sort of scam or practical joke. Poston told the story again in 1894, in the *Overland Monthly*, and said nothing about Colorado City's being a ruse contrived to pay a ferrying charge.[21] In fact, it is evident from the "Reconnoisance" that, rather than being a spur-of-the-moment affair, Colorado City was planned beforehand,

and Heintzelman's journal entry for July 11, 1854, makes it clear that Poston talked with Jaeger and Heintzelman about Colorado City *before* he had Ehrenberg survey the site, not after. There are other problems with Pumpelly's tale. Although Pumpelly says that Jaeger negotiated for "several lots" at Colorado City, Heintzelman, in his journal, repeatedly takes Jaeger to task for purchasing only one lot for the ferry. And Pumpelly himself says that however the project began, Poston "afterward did all that could be done to forward the growth of the place."[22] Poston's subsequent actions in San Diego and San Francisco verify that he did try to develop the town site, and expected it to become a crossing point for the transcontinental railroad. Why Poston invented the ferry-passage story is unclear. It may have been to hide the embarrassment of Colorado City's failure as a business venture.

In "Diary of a Pioneer," Poston tells an entertaining story of what happened when his party, crossing the desert between Sonoita and the Gila River, arrived at the Sauceda villages on July 3, 1854, and decided to have a "feast" the next day celebrating the Fourth of July. They bought a steer from the Tohono O'odham who inhabited the villages, slaughtered it, and hung it overnight. The next morning, they barbecued the meat in a pit. They also purchased several jars of milk cooling in a springhouse, which the Indians sold for a dollar each. Poston paid the Indians to pick some saguaro fruit, which, when mixed with the milk, provided dessert; and Poston topped off the feast by passing around a gallon of "the finest Baccanori Mescal, seven years old" that he had been keeping in a leather case. Poston says that they omitted the customary patriotic speeches after dinner and, instead, concluded the feast by smoking "killikinick" (also known as kinnikinnick, a mixture of the dried leaves and bark of assorted plants, often smoked by the Indians), taking care to share with their hosts.

A final accomplishment Poston claimed in these later tales was his discovery of copper ore at the famous Ajo mines in southern Arizona and his subsequent involvement in developing the mines. Poston says that while he was resting in Sonoita, some Sonorans returning from California arrived and reported finding rich ore to the north. Ehrenberg assayed their samples and found them to contain 50 percent copper with traces of gold. Poston says that on his journey north to the Gila, he stopped at the site of the Ajo mines, collected his own ore specimens, and then "carried [the samples] to San Francisco for the organization of the first mining company under the American occupation."[23] The company he refers to is the Arizona Mining and Trading Company, which developed the Ajo mines in the late 1850s. However, despite this claim, Poston makes no mention of the Ajo mines in the "Reconnoisance," and it seems unlikely that had the mines shown promise and been available for investment, Poston would have neglected to mention them to his San Francisco backers.

The copper mines at Ajo had been worked by Spaniards and Mexicans as early as 1750. The mines had been visited before Poston arrived by Peter R. Brady, a member of Gray's Texas Western Railroad survey. Brady had prospected the mines with Tom Childs Jr. in 1850. When Gray's expedition arrived in Sonoita, not long before Poston's, Brady journeyed to Ajo, where he obtained samples of copper ore. Back in California, Brady went to San Francisco and persuaded several businessmen there to invest in the mines. They formed the Arizona Mining and Trading Company, and Brady joined an expedition that left Los Angeles in October 1854 to take possession of, and develop, the Ajo Copper Mine.[24]

Poston may have visited the Ajo mines on his journey to the Gila River. But contrary to his claims, he had no involvement with the Arizona Mining Company. This may have been because when he arrived in San Francisco in August 1854, he found that the company was already capitalized and planning their expedition to the mines. Brady does not mention Poston as an investor. The omission is not surprising. The company already had Brady's ore samples and did not need Poston's. And Poston, who by his own testimony had spent most of his money on his own expedition, had little or nothing to invest. As happened on other occasions in his life, Poston just missed the connection that would have brought him the wealth he sought.[25]

Notably absent from any of these later stories of the Poston expedition is any mention of the San Juan Bautista Bay land deal, perhaps too controversial to bring to light later in the century because of its annexationist elements. Barely mentioned is the near-fatal trip to Adair Bay, and not at all the starvation march down the Gila River and the journey across the Colorado Desert. The failed Colorado City project Poston mentioned only to suggest that it had been a joke. In an oblique reference to his transcontinental railroad hopes, Poston did boast, in a reminiscence article on Andrew Gray, that "but for the Civil War the trans-continental railway would probably have passed through Arizona twenty years ago, and Col. Andrew B. Gray would have been chief engineer."[26] In 1895 Poston hinted that others had become rich from his early explorations while he had gotten nothing: "The men who had accompanied me on the previous espeditions [sic] and shared the dangers and hardships got all the money and my fortune was at the end of the rainbow."[27] But he named no names, did not say what expeditions he meant, and was not specific about how much money others had made.

It is not surprising that Poston viewed his Sonora–Gadsden Purchase venture with some embarrassment. Measured by its practical accomplishments, it had little significance. Goodale argues that Gray's and Bartlett's surveys were of greater scope and had greater impact. And Poston's inexperience in financial matters and the complex, overheated politics of the transcontinental railroad and U.S.-Mexican relations condemned both Colorado City and San Juan Bautista Bay to failure.[28] In fact, the list of failures in Poston's expedition includes nearly all the objectives he had aimed at. He did not locate the Iturbide Grant or acquire any of the famed silver mines of Sonora. He was unable to locate a new port site on the Gulf of California or develop Colorado City. When it came to large-scale financial investment and coordinating the resources that could develop cities and open mines, Poston, particularly in 1854, lacked the business acumen and the financial and political connections to make these kinds of projects work.

Sadly, Poston also failed to win the fortune that would have carried him out of debt and allowed him to return to Kentucky and his family with his reputation restored. Given the collapse of Poston's schemes in California, his reluctance to revisit Kentucky is not surprising. He had left his family and spent four years hoping to establish himself in California. After three of those years, he had quit his job and risked his life and what little money he had on a six-month expedition in Mexico and Arizona that he thought would make his fortune. Yet he was now no better off than when he had left Kentucky in 1850. He had large debts, little money, no occupation, and no prospects. He was still a "failure."

Nevertheless, despite the disappointment of this ending, Poston, as was characteristic of him, hardly lacked for optimism and ambition as he moved forward enthusiastically into other ventures, in mining, politics, land speculation, government service, and foreign travel, all of which contributed to his story—and his reputation as a leader in the settlement of the American Southwest.

Postscript

Poston's Story

Charles Poston's life after 1855 recapitulated the themes of his youth: the ever-present optimism, the appetite for travel and adventure, the quest for wealth, and the repeated attempts to join himself to power and influence. Poston's fortunes after San Francisco and Washington at first remained tied to those of Samuel Peter Heintzelman, who, having spent four hard years at the desert outpost of Fort Yuma, was given a more comfortable posting in 1855, at Newport Barracks, Kentucky, across the Ohio River from Cincinnati. A year later, in March 1856, he invited Poston to come to Cincinnati to meet businessmen who were interested in investing in mining opportunities in southern Arizona. Poston did, and from those meetings, the Sonora Exploring and Mining Company was born on March 26, 1856. Heintzelman was named president. Edgar Conkling was chosen as secretary. Other major investors included William and Thomas Wrightson, editors of the *Railroad Record*, a Cincinnati journal promoting railroad development and the southern transcontinental route.

Poston was designated "Commandant and Managing Agent" for the company at its mines near Tubac.[1] As soon as he could arrange for supplies, he was off to Texas, where he led an expedition from San Antonio across New Mexico to Tucson, arriving late in August. He was met in Tucson by Herman Ehrenberg, who had remained in San Francisco when Poston and Heintzelman went east, and subsequently went to Arizona to look for gold and silver mines. He pointed Poston and Heintzelman to the Santa Cruz valley, south of Tucson.[2]

Poston established headquarters at the deserted Spanish presidio of Tubac on the Santa Cruz River and purchased the nearby Arivaca Ranch for the SEMC from the brothers Tomás and Ignacio Ortiz for ten thousand dollars. He and his three German mining engineers—Ehrenberg, Frederick Brunkow, and Charles Schuchard—then proceeded to locate and reopen old silver mines in the area, the most promising of which was the Cerro Colorado, or "Heintzelman Mine." They also discovered a vein of silver in the Santa Rita Mountains, east of Tubac. That discovery became the Salero Mine, the principal property of the Santa Rita Mining Company, an SEMC subsidiary.[3] The mines were an international enterprise, with Mexican laborers working under the direction of the German engineers. However, the mines of the SEMC and Santa Rita company were not as profitable as Poston had predicted, and Poston was not a skillful mine superintendent.

Puzzled at the mines' inability to make money and suspicious of Poston's management, Heintzelman took a leave of absence from the army in summer 1857 in order to raise capital for the SEMC and supervise operations more closely. In summer 1858 he went to Arizona to take over operation of the mines, arriving on August 17. He found the mines ten thousand dollars in debt and the ore not as rich as Poston had reported. Poston, it appeared, had spent too much money in running his Tubac headquarters. A promised amalgamation works at Arivaca had not been built, the engineers were mismanaging the Mexican workers, and more laborers were needed, although there was no cash to pay them. Heintzelman reorganized company operations, cut unnecessary expenses, and put money into building new furnaces and purchasing new machinery.[4]

However, despite Heintzelman's efforts, the company's financial problems persisted. In December 1858, in an effort to obtain more capital, Heintzelman sold five hundred shares of company stock to the Connecticut arms manufacturer Samuel Colt, with an option to purchase five thousand more shares within a year.[5] Colt must have done so, because by April 1859 he was the SEMC's largest stockholder, and the company's executive committee made him president, replacing Heintzelman. The SEMC's new board of directors was stacked with Colt's associates, Poston was made a director of the company, and Heintzelman was out of company management. On February 9, 1860, the company was reincorporated in New York.[6] But even Colt could not make the company profitable, calling it "a hole to bury money in."[7] If the remoteness of the mines, the difficulty of transportation, and the scarcity of cash were not problems enough, incessant Apache raiding made supplying and operating the mines impossible. In 1861 the raids and the withdrawal of the army from Arizona at the start of the Civil War forced the abandonment of the mines, and Poston and Santa Rita mine engineer Raphael Pumpelly fled Arizona for California.[8]

Colt died in 1862, and the following year his associates formed the Arizona Mining Company and purchased the property of the SEMC with stock in the new company. In the exchange of Arizona Mining Company shares for SEMC stock, Poston emerged as the new company's third largest stockholder, with 1,692 shares. But the Arizona Mining Company, too, was unable to make the mines pay. So in January 1870 they deeded the company's property to Poston, and the founder and former superintendent of the Sonora Exploring and Mining Company found himself sole owner of his former company's property.[9] He would spend many more years trying to make it yield the fortune he had expected from it.

In 1862 Poston returned to Washington, D.C., and, with Heintzelman and William Wrightson, lobbied for the passage of an act making Arizona a U.S. territory.[10] They finally achieved that goal when President Abraham Lincoln signed the territorial act into law at the end of 1863.[11] Poston was appointed Arizona's first superintendent of Indian affairs and traveled to San Francisco and Arizona to take up his duties. He was accompanied from San Francisco by J. Ross Browne, who described their tour of the new territory in *Adventures in the Apache Country*.

Poston was a conscientious advocate for the peaceful Arizona Indian tribes, but what he really wanted was to be Arizona's first territorial delegate to Congress. He won election to this post in 1864 and went immediately to Washington to join the Thirty-Eighth Congress. Poston worked hard as a delegate, placing four bills and nine resolutions from the territorial legislature before the House of Representatives in a short, three-and-a-half-month session.[12] None of the measures he offered passed, but he gained the respect of House members for his only speech before that body, on March 2, 1865, in which he advocated a reservation for Indians along the Colorado River, with farmland that would be made productive by irrigation.[13] The speech led him to be considered as something of an expert on agricultural irrigation.

Poston wanted to be reelected territorial delegate but was defeated in 1865 by Arizona governor John N. Goodwin and again in 1866 by Coles Bashford, a former governor of Wisconsin. After the 1865 contest, he joined Judge Clancey T. Botts in the practice of law in Washington, D.C., with an office at the corner of 15th Street and New York Avenue.[14]

Poston's reputation as an irrigation expert did pay off when his friend Ross Browne was appointed minister to China in 1868 and managed to get Poston an appointment as envoy to Asia, charged with studying Asian irrigation methods and matters involving immigration. Poston was also given the task of conveying a copy of the recently approved Burlingame Treaty to the emperor of China. The treaty granted "most favored nation" trade status to China. Poston traveled with Browne to China, delivered the treaty, and then traveled through Asia, the Middle East, and Europe, settling finally in London, where he stayed for the next six years.[15]

In London, Poston styled himself a "Councillor at Law (United States)."[16] But his practice was mostly brokering investments in Arizona land and mining properties. He represented the Santa Rita Mining Company in its transfer to a British firm on January 13, 1870.[17] And he promoted the Tumacacori Mining and Land Company, in which he managed to interest noted British investment broker William Blackmore to the extent of two thousand shares.[18] Poston never gave up trying to attract investors to his Arivaca and Cerro Colorado mining properties, and the Tumacacori company was probably a repackaging of the old SEMC–Arizona Mining Company claims.

In London, Poston also began a career as a popular writer, working as assistant editor of a London magazine and writing numerous newspaper and magazine articles. He authored a two-volume work, *The Parsees* (1872) and *The Sun-Worshippers of Asia* (1877), on the Zoroastrian religion, in which he had become interested while visiting India.[19]

Poston said that his time in London was "one of the happiest" of his life and but for "national and family ties at home" he would have remained in England for the rest of his life.[20] Those ties may have helped bring him back to the United States in 1876, but in his journal Poston pointed to another, more practical, motive. While in Europe, he had made friends with Mrs. John Bigelow, wife of the former U.S. minister to France and current secretary of state of New York. The Bigelows were prominent Democrats, and Mrs. Bigelow persuaded Poston to work in the 1876 presidential campaign of Democrat Samuel J. Tilden, promising Poston the position of U.S. consul general in London if Tilden won. When Poston returned to the States, he escorted Mrs. Bigelow through the Philadelphia Centennial Exposition and worked for the Tilden campaign as a "secret agent" in Washington, reporting on happenings that might be of interest to the campaign.[21] His behavior was typically pragmatic. Poston's political sympathies and associations from his youth had been Whig and Republican. Thus, when Tilden lost to Republican Rutherford B. Hayes, Poston may have been deflated, but he quickly accepted an appointment from outgoing president Ulysses S. Grant (a Republican) as registrar for the U.S. government land office in Florence, Arizona. The position paid only five hundred dollars a year and was hardly the London consulship, but it was a paying job, and Poston returned to Arizona in the spring of 1877.[22]

Poston was right in judging his London years as a high point in his life. He spent most of the rest of his life subsisting on minor political patronage appointments and seeking—unsuccessfully—to revive the speculative opportunities of his past. In Florence, he engaged once again in land sales, but this time of U.S. government property, not private claims. He resigned his position in 1879 and in 1884 obtained appointment as consular agent in the border town of Nogales, Arizona. He was only there a short time before he accepted a position as military agent of the U.S. government in El Paso, Texas, advising the U.S. and Mexican military on troop movements along the border that would avoid troublesome clashes between the two forces.

Although the status of Poston's positions had diminished, his ambitions had not. Four times—in 1884, 1889, 1892, and 1895—he applied to the president of the United States to be named governor of Arizona in recognition for services rendered the territory. He was denied all four times. He had served the territory it was true—decades ago. But he had no current credentials for the governorship and no longer any political influence that might move an American president to grant his requests.

In 1890 Poston was appointed a statistical agent of the U.S. Agriculture Department in Phoenix at fifty dollars a month. He was told that he could have the position for life. But in 1892, after applying to President Cleveland for appointment as Arizona governor, he was not only denied the governorship but dismissed from his job as agent. In January 1895 Arizona governor Louis C. Hughes placed Poston in charge of an agricultural experimental station maintained by the University of Arizona near Phoenix. Poston was to do research and help farmers improve their agricultural practices. But on June 1 university president Theodore Comstock dismissed Poston because he feared that Poston, who was living at the station, would file a preemption claim on the property.[23] It was Poston's last government appointment.

For years, Poston had clung to the notion that his old SEMC properties would yet make him wealthy. He had tried promoting investment in the properties in both Europe and the United States, sometimes under different corporate names but, apparently, was never able to attract enough capital to reopen the mines.[24] Finally, in the 1880s, he gave up. In 1882 he won a court judgment for $266,238 against a Tucson merchant, Charles H. Lord, who had attempted to seize the abandoned Arivaca Ranch.[25] Poston's claim to the property came from his purchase of it from the Ortiz family for the SEMC in 1856, the Arizona Mining Company's having taken it over in 1863 and then having deeded it to Poston in 1870.[26] But to collect his judgment, Poston had to prove that his claim to Arivaca was legitimate, and he could not. A federal judge in Tucson ruled that his title was invalid. Two years later, Poston expressed his bitterness in a letter to a Tucson newspaper: "The decision in the Arivaca case was the most infamous I ever heard pronounced from a judicial tribunal.... Everybody in Arivaca is a thief. Nobody has paid anything for his possessions, save the undersigned; and he is the rightful owner."[27] Disgusted with the outcome of his suit, on November 21, 1882, Poston sold the Arivaca Ranch to the Arivaca Land and Cattle Company, which also was unsuccessful in having its claim validated.[28]

In a final attempt to glean something from his Arizona mining properties, Poston filed a claim for $1,279,750 with the House Committee on Claims on February 16, 1888, for Indian depredations on the property of the Arizona Mining Company. Poston's argument was that Apache raids had forced abandonment of the mines in 1861, when they had belonged to the SEMC. As in the Arivaca case, his claim was based on his ownership of the former Arizona Mining Company properties. The case went to the U.S. Court of Claims on September 10, 1891. It was heard in Phoenix in January 1898 and seems to have been unsuccessful.[29]

Poston also pursued new schemes reminiscent of his Sonoran and Gadsden Purchase ventures. In July 1887 he opened an office in Chicago as secretary of the Sierra Madre Mining Company of Sonora, Mexico, and sold shares in the company. There is no evidence that the company ever made money. In 1892 he filed a claim on a piece of land northwest of Phoenix called "Hole in the Rock" that he planned to develop as a resort, with a reservoir, hotel, and electric tram connecting the site with Phoenix. But he never completed the legal requirements for ownership and abandoned the scheme.[30] In 1893 he launched a project with Charles T. Hayden to build a toll road between Tempe and Globe, Arizona, but their financial backers defaulted—even as Poston and Hayden were in the field surveying the road.[31] Of Poston's commercial ventures late in life, Benjamin Sacks says, "Some ... were rashly conceived, some were grandiose, others premature; none was successful."[32]

Early in 1884 Poston received word from his daughter that his wife, Margaret, was gravely ill. A month later, he was told that Margaret had died in Washington, D.C., and would be buried at Elizabethtown. Poston did not attend the funeral. But he and Margaret had been married for thirty-five years, and he felt the loss keenly. "My wife had been paralysed on the 21, February 1851," he wrote in his journal, "making thirty-three years ... suffering with this incurable affliction; which she endured with patience, fortitude, and even cheerfulness—It had been the *Sorrow of my life* —as we had grown up from children together and were most affectionately attached to each other."[33] Poston moved on—or tried to. On September 3, 1885, he married Mattie Tucker, a teacher, typesetter, and clerk in the territorial legislature. However, the great difference in their ages (Poston was 63; she was 28) and the fact that Poston was used to living alone and going his own way probably doomed the relationship. Mattie left her husband soon after the marriage. Thus, Poston's second marriage quickly fell into the pattern of his first. He and Mattie remained married, but they lived apart.[34]

As his fortunes declined, Poston needed a way to earn income and, as he had in England, took up writing. In the 1870s in Florence he had written a long narrative poem entitled "Apache-Land" about the creation of the Arizona Territory.[35] In the 1880s he frequently wrote articles for the *Arizona Star*, particularly pieces attacking the Democratic Party; "tribute" articles about old pioneer friends, such as Ehrenberg, Heintzelman, and Gray; and sketches of famous British personalities he had met in London.[36] In 1886 he wrote a "history of the Apaches" that went unpublished.[37] And in 1894 he wrote his four "Building a State in Apache Land" articles for the *Overland Monthly*, about the exploration and creation of Arizona Territory. Poston also was a good speaker and was in demand in Phoenix in the 1880s as a lecturer and toastmaster at dinners.[38]

Mostly, in his last years Poston struggled to live on a fifty-dollar quarterly pension from the U.S. government and a twenty-five-dollar monthly pension awarded him in 1899 by the Arizona legislature for his service to the territory.[39] In 1897 he was living in two rooms of an adobe building at 137 East Monroe Street in Phoenix and was said to be drinking heavily. The rooms, reportedly, were "full of dirt, old newspapers and articles of wearing apparel."[40] Former *New York Tribune* editor and U.S. ambassador to France Whitelaw Reid visited and called Poston's dwelling a "wretched adobe hut."[41]

On the afternoon of June 24, 1902, Poston was found lying dead in the doorway between the two rooms he occupied. In the words of the *Tucson Daily Citizen*, he appeared to have "simply dropped dead."[42] He was seventy-seven years old. No coroner's jury was convened to determine the cause of death. Poston was indigent, and the *Arizona Republican*, in announcing his death, made it clear that unless funds could be raised, he would be buried in a potter's field. Various citizens contributed, and Poston was buried on June 28 in Phoenix's Porter Cemetery. On April 26, 1925, he was reinterred on Primrose Hill, land he had purchased years before near Florence.[43] A final notation in his journal, recorded anonymously by someone else, read: "He died alone in abject poverty and squalor."[44] Not surprisingly, Poston's Haycraft and Pope relatives knew nothing of his death, his whereabouts, or his condition. His grandson Gustavus Pope said, "He must have deliberately kept my mother (Sarah Lee Poston Pope) in ignorance of his real financial condition or she would have forced him to accept an annuity from her."[45] Desperate as Poston was for money, it was probably the last thing he would have wanted.

Such a disappointing end was a far remove from the optimism and excitement of Poston's 1854 expedition, but much of it was prefigured in elements of his early life—his broken family relationships, his quest for wealth and power, his fascination with travel and adventure, and his early business failures—all of which seem to have driven him to a life of exploration and speculation. This peculiar form of ambition set him on a lifelong quest for the "big strike" and seems to have convinced him that he could not live a settled life until he had achieved it. But it was this same powerful appetite for adventure and risk that made California in the 1850s and Arizona in the 1860s the right places for him. In the end, the story of Poston's Sonoran expedition reveals a Charles Poston many people may not have known, a daring adventurer and ambitious speculator, who would not find the fortune he sought, but achieved, instead, a different sort of success—his iconic stature as an Arizona pioneer.

APPENDIX

Charles D. Poston, "Reconnoisance in Sonora"

An original copy of the "Reconnoisance in Sonora," in Charles D. Poston's handwriting and dated 15 September, 1854, is located in the William Blackmore Collection, Box 2, Folder 1, in the Fray Angélico Chavez History Library, New Mexico History Museum, The Palace of the Governors, Santa Fe, New Mexico.[1] The document is written on lined paper, eight-and-a-half by twelve inches in size. Poston folded the left sides of the pages in order to create a one-and-three-quarter-inch margin in which he wrote section heads. The text occupies the remainder of each page. The pages are bound with a red ribbon run through holes punched at the top of the document and tied at the middle.

Accompanying the "Reconnoisance" is an envelope in which the document was sent. A title on the back reads, "Charles D. Poston's Reconnoisance in Sonora." This title is written in large, bold cursive over fainter cursive that reads, "Major Heintzleman [sic] care of W. Wrightson Esquire, Rail Road Record Office, Cincinnati, Ohio." On the left end of the envelope, a note by Heintzelman reads "From T. Butler King of Georgia. Recd. Aug. 11, 1857."

In August 1857 Poston was superintending operations of the Sonora Exploring and Mining Company in Tubac. Heintzelman was the company's president. King was general superintendent and land commissioner of the Southern Pacific Railroad Company. King had been a stockholder in

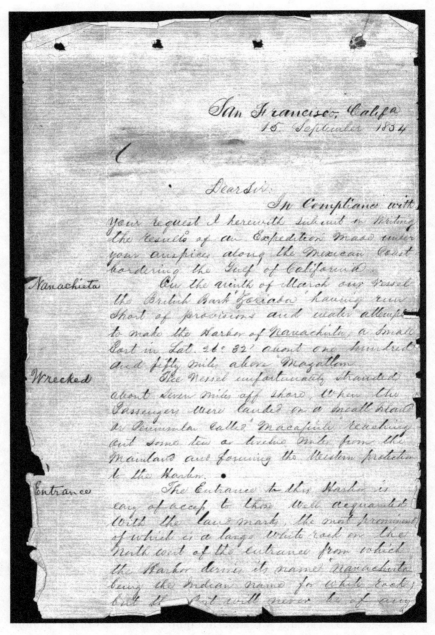

Figure 19. "Reconnoisance in Sonora" first page. Photo courtesy of the Fray Angélico Chavez History Library, Santa Fe.

Figure 20. "Reconnoisance in Sonora" envelope. Photo courtesy of the Fray Angélico Chavez History Library, Santa Fe.

the Sonora Exploring and Mining Company and Poston's former boss as collector of customs at the San Francisco Customs House.[2]

The four different texts of the "Reconnoisance"—the title on the envelope, the address to Heintzelman, the receipt, and the "Reconnoisance" itself—appear to be in four different hands. Something was written on the first page of the "Reconnoisance" below the date and above the salutation, but it is now too faint to read. Sacks speculates that it may have been the name of John C. McLemore, a supporter of Poston's expedition to whom the "Reconnoisance" was addressed, and that McLemore's name was erased when the report was sent to someone else.[3]

Poston was a fair speller, but he capitalized arbitrarily and punctuated only sporadically, including omitting periods at the ends of sentences. Since Poston's capitalization of common nouns and adjectives can be distracting and has no significance in determining the meaning of the text, I have normalized capitalization in this transcript. I also have inserted periods at the ends of sentences where there is no other end punctuation (Poston sometimes ended sentences with dashes). However, I have not added other punctuation, and I have preserved Poston's spelling. Like many writers, Poston tended to misspell the same words repeatedly. The designation *sic* is used for the first such misspelling but is not repeated for subsequent ones. Expressions underlined in Poston's text appear here in italics.

Poston guided "Reconnoisance" readers by using numerous topic headings in the left margin of his report. He "boldfaced" these headings by tracing over them and repeated the headings when a section ran over onto a new page. In this transcript, the headings are run into the text. Headings that repeat a previous heading without starting a new section have been deleted. Where Poston placed a heading in mid-paragraph, that heading appears boldfaced in parentheses, ( ), in the text. Numbers that appear in brackets, [ ], indicate the beginnings of pages in Poston's manuscript.

Reconnoisance in Sonora

San Francisco, Calif[a]

15 September 1854

Dear Sir:

In compliance with your request I herewith submit in writing the results of an expedition made under your auspices along the Mexican coast bordering the Gulf of California.[4]

Navachista

On the ninth of March our vessel the British bark *Zoriada* [sic], having run short of provisions and water attempted to make the harbor of *Navachista* [sic], a small port in Lat. 26° 32" about one hundred and fifty miles above Mazatlan.[5]

Wrecked

The vessel unfortunately stranded about seven miles off shore, when the passengers were landed on a small island or peninsula called *Macapule* reaching out some ten or twelve miles from the mainland and forming the western protection to the harbor.[6]

Entrance

The entrance to this harbor is easy of access to those well acquainted with the landmarks, the most prominent of which is a large white rock on the north west of the entrance from which the harbor derives its name *Navachista*, being the Indian name for *white rock*; but this port will never be of any [2] consequence except as a suitable place for contraband trade, small coasting business or oyster gathering.

Harbor of Navachista

It is sufficiently commodious for schooners of one hundred tons and affords sample protection for hundreds of this class of vessels so much used and so well suited for coasting in the Gulf.

Estuary Oysters Turtle Fish Game

The estuary of the harbor reaching about eight miles in the interior abounds in oysters, turtle and fish. The oysters are of good size and excellent flavor and literally grown on the trees, (i.e.) there is a jungle or marsh of scrubby undergrowth to which they attach themselves. The natives gather them by pulling them from the bushes or cutting off limbs to which the oysters are attached and carrying them home in this convenient fashion.

Adjacent Country

The surrounding country is rich bottom land and produces a considerable quantity of corn beans cheese stock & poultry for exportation to California.

Port of Navachista

This port is the principal shipping point for the towns in the northernpart [sic] of the state of Sinaloa the principal of which is the city of Culiacan where there is a branch mint in operation under prevalege [sic] from the Mexican govt. and where large amounts of coin are annually shipped principally via Navachista to avoid the export duties.

[3] Landing

We were detained here nearly two weeks in landing ourselves and baggage from the island to the mainland and preparing for a journey on muleback through the interior of the country to our destination at Guaymas some six hundred and fifty miles distant by land; but thanks to the friendly aid and attention of a Mexican gentleman of Culiacan who was our fellow passenger we at last procured a sufficient number of mules from a neighboring hacienda and prepared to commence our journey.[7]

Proprietor

The owner of the land hereabouts was an old Spaniard who had moved here from Manilla [sic] and had no doubt conveyed many a cargo into the interior in greater haste than we required.[8]

Journey by Land

He drove up several hundred mules from which we picked out about twenty five of the best looking and saddled and packed for the journey.

Mayo Country

Our trail after a few days led through the country of the Mayo Indians generally over good soil sufficiently timbered and well watered.

Timber & Soil

The timber along the Mayo River is much larger than I expected to find and the soil rich enough to produce cotton or sugar equal to Alabama or Louisianne.

Mayo Indians

The Indians have well regulated pueblas [sic] and have regular alcaldes &c. in imitation of the Mexican system.

[4] Villa del Fuerta

At *"Villa del Fuerta"* a small town on the Fuerta River where the same is crossed by the *"Camino Nacional"* or Great Mexican Road leading to California we found the first Mexican authorities and having presented our passports and caused the usual hubbub we received permission to pass on through the country.

Rio del Fuerta

The Fuerta River is said by travelers in Mexico to be the most beautiful stream in the republic, having a gravelly bed and clear fresh stream of water.

Land

The land along the banks is very productive and in a highly creditable state of improvement and cultivation.

Alamos

The next town of any importance we reached was the *"old city of Alamos"* or *"Real de Alamos"* which had been a very rich and prosperous mining town in the days of the monarchy, but has decayed and crumbled into ruins like everything else under the mismanagement of the republic so that it is now a fair representation of a "dried up old Spanish town" with nothing but its former wealth and pride to feed upon.

Silver Mines

There are some fifty or sixty rich silver mines in the vicinity of this city from which they formerly derived an immense revenue, but very few of them are worked now.

The *"new mines"* near the road are now worked by one of the families of Alamos who have preserved some of the original enterprize—about one hundred [5] were employed in getting out ore and working the rude machinery of the country. The yield was said to be about two ounces or thirty two dollars to the cargo (or mule load) of about 250 lbs. of ore. They abandon working a mine which yields less than one marco or about eight dollars to the cargo of ore.

Mayo River

The most convenient port for this city of Alamos and the surrounding country is at the mouth of the Mayo River called Santa Cruz but as there is no harbor of sufficient capacity and no settlement of any consequence there the port is very seldom resorted to except for fish oysters etc.

Yaqui River

We next struck the Yaqui River—a large bold stream rising near El Paso in Chihuahua and emptying into the Gulf of Calif[a] about sixty miles below Guaymas.

Harbor

The entrance to this river forms a good harbor for small vessels and the river could be navigated by steamboats about one hundred miles.

Land

The Yaqui bottom is the most extensive and valuable body of land in Sonora being fully fifty miles wide and extending one hundred and fifty miles up the river. The soil is equal to any on the Mississippi or Missouri and produces spontaneously wild cotton and cane with a variety of native fruits. It is inhabited exclusively by the Yaqui Indians who have always [6] maintained their ancient possessions against the Spanish or Mexican government and guard them with a very jealous eye, not allowing the least intrusion.

Indian Pueblos

Their pueblos are well regulated and governed by an alcalde elected annually by the "popular suffrages."

Tariff

They levy a tax on all vessels entering or navigating the river and exact duties upon all imports and exports, but their tariff is very simple and easily settled.

Road

We travelled along the banks of this river nearly to its mouth when we took the coast road to Guaymas. This led through a desert sandy country containing very little water or grass partaking of the nature of the sea coast with occasional beds of sand and sea shells.

Guaymas

Guaymas is a miserable Mexican seaport town of about three thousand five hundred inhabitants (such as they are) shut in from the gulf as well as the winds by high rugged hills of black trap rock entirely destitute of vegetation and reflecting the intense rays of the sun until the place seems like a huge bake-oven. — (June) — [9]

Land Breeze

The sea breeze from the gulf usually sets in late in the evening and usually raises clouds of dust and drives the inhabitants to the interior of the houses at the very time in the evening when they most need exercise and fresh air.

Harbor

The harbor of Guaymas is good and entirely safe; very much the shape [7] of the harbor of Acapulco and about one third the size, the soundings around the mole are two to three fathoms but increase in the middle of the bay to five, six and seven fathoms; but the area of deep water is very small and distant from the shore.[10]

Adjacent Country

The country around Guaymas for a semicircle of one hundred miles is a blasted barren desert entirely destitute of wood water and grass, producing only cacti and a stunted growth of mesquit [sic].

Water

The water used at Guaymas is all procured from wells and has a brackish unpleasant taste and generally causes temporary disease with strangers unaccustomed to its use.

Hermosillo (Beautiful)

From Guaymas we passed over this hard barren country one hundred and ten miles to *Hermosillo* the principal town of Sonora and one of the most beautiful cities in the northern states of Mexico.

Location

This city is located on the Sonora River in the Valley of Horcasitas about sixty miles from the Gulf of Calif[a].

Valley of Horcasitas

The Valley of Horcasitas is about four miles wide at this place and continues in a southwestern direction to the gulf. The soil is very rich and near the city highly cultivated and very productive. The principal crop is wheat of which this valley produces annually about eighty thousand bushels.

Productions

There is a great abundance of fruit here such as grapes melons oranges figs [8] limes, lemons, citrons, peaches, pomegranates bananas and dates. The vineyards are extensive and beautiful, producing about twenty five hundred barrels of brandy per annum. Cotton and sugar have also been cultivated here with considerable success, but their culture is now abandoned for lack of any protection from the government or enterprize in its citizens.

Fertility

The fertility of this valley is indeed extraordinary and with the aid of irrigation at any time it may be needed in this salubrious climate and rich soil, the rich productions of a tropical climate are procured in abundance with very little labor.

River of Hermosillo

The *Petic River* formed from the confluence of the *Sonora* and *San Miguel* rivers flows through this entire valley watering invigorating and refreshing everything in its vicinity. This river is very much exhausted by the quantity of water used in the valley for purposes of irrigation in the summer, but in the winter is a strong bold stream and empties into the gulf opposite the Island of Tiburon.

Architecture

The City of Hermosillo contains many large and costly houses constructed of stone brick and adobes well finished and furnished in the interior with the best and most costly European furniture.

Commerce

It has a large trade with the northern part of the state and is the principal [9] depot and distributing point for the northern portion of the state, and part of Chihuahua. The forwarding and shipping business is done from Guaymas but all the wealth and fashion of the state seem to be concentrated at *Hermosillo*.

Population

The population in 1845 was estimated by the then secretary of the state at nearly eighteen thousand but this has since been reduced by emigration to California, Apache incursions, and dissatisfaction with the government to about twelve thousand inhabitants.

Climate

The climate is dry and warm. The mercury ranging from 80 to 100° but the location is considered very healthy and is usually free from any epidemic diseases.

Water

The conveniences for bathing and sanitary regulation of the city are excellent and may conduce materially to the general health of the city.

Canals and Irrigation

There is a dam across the river a short distance above the city for the purpose of turning the water into various acequias (canals) for the purpose of training the water through the streets gardens and houses of the city affording an abundant supply of clear fresh water for all necessary purposes to all the inhabitants of the city of whatever grade or class.

Ornamental Scenery

The city is ornamented in the usual Spanish style with a beautiful [10] (**Alameda**)[11] alameda and well shaded plaza where the whole population congregate at pleasure for recreation and amusement.

Scenery

A beautiful view of the city of *Hermosillo* and surrounding country may be obtained from the top of a large mountain of marble on its southern side. The city lays spread out at your feet the bare stone walls of the mansion houses relieved by courtyards blooming with orange trees and tropical flowers. The vineyards orchards and wheatfields stretch off to the west following the course of the invigorating stream, dotted along the banks with beautiful villas surrounded with ornamental shrubbery blooming with their delicate productions and loading the atmosphere with the sweetest perfume.

From the city of *Hermosillo* to the *Gulf of California* opposite the Island of *Tiburon* the distance is about sixty miles over a level valley through which the river flows.[12]

Island of Tiburons (Sharks) & Bay of San Juan Bautista

The Island of Tiburon is about fifty miles long by twenty-five miles wide and forms the western protection of the *"Bay of San Juan Bautista"* the largest and best harbor in the Gulf of California and as much superior to Guaymas as San Francisco is to Monterey.[13]

Entrance

The entrance to this harbor [11] is formed by the proximity of the northern end of the Island of Tiburon to a point of the mainland making out southeast and called on the maps Seargents [sic] Point leaving a channel one mile or a mile and a half wide.

Harbor

The *Bay* then makes around this point northwardly from two to three miles, being skirted by a ridge on the west protecting the anchorage from the winds of the gulf, there is also a growth of mesquit trees along the western side of this ridge or spur from the mountains at the north which afford a protecting and agreeable shade. The bay meanders around eastwardly when a smaller bay or estuary makes in to the north east, of sufficient capacity for small boats, called *Cockle Harbor*.

Capacity

The bay is here about four miles wide has the appearance of deep water and is well protected and sheltered on all sides so as to be a safe anchorage.

It continues southwest the whole length of the Island of *Tiburon* forming a sound from two to ten miles wide and near fifty miles in length.[14]

The depth of the water at the southern part of the island or near the mouth of the Petic River is not so great, as the sand and drift from that river has practically filled up the channel.

Mainland

It would be entirely practicable to connect the *island* with the *mainland* here by a *pier or breakwater* which [12] would also tend to increase the depth of the water above by impeding the flow of water through this channel.

Island

The island seems placed there by nature as a protection to the harbor and mainland against the storms and inclement weather of the gulf, and could be easily made a useful naval station and impregnable fortress.

Capacity

Its usefulness and adaptability for *commercial purposes*—ie [sic], the island—is doubtful on account of its isolated position but it has several good harbors and an abundant supply of running water which would be very convenient for supplying vessels going to sea.

Condition

The *island* and adjacent *mainland* remains in nearly the same condition as when originally discovered by the Spaniards as it has up to the present time been inhabited by a savage and sanguinary tribe of Indians who have resisted all the attempts of the Spanish or Mexican governments at conquest or extermination.

Ceris Indians

This tribe is called the Ceris and are supposed by the Spanish and Mexican writers to be of Asiatic origin and probably descendants of the Turks as their idiom is said to resemble that language. They live on fish game oysters and such sustenance as they can gather around the island and sea shore as they never venture into [13] the interior except when compelled by hunger when they make the most savage inroads upon the ranches on the Petic River murdering the men and taking the women captive.

It is believed that they have several captives on the island at the present time.

Expedition against the Ceris

The Mexican authorities at Guaymas and Hermosillo have made several expeditions against these savages both by land and sea from their respective places and have killed great numbers of both men women and children so that the tribe could not now number over fifty warriors. This remnant of the tribe is not always to be found in one place, sometimes living on the mainland near the mouth of the river sometimes on the island and sometimes along the sea shore to the north.

They are disposed to be friendly with English or Americans but are deadly in their hostility towards Mexicans.

In a late expedition the Mexicans captured the wife of the principal chief and sent her to Mazatlan to be placed in servitude out of their reach.

They are very miserable and offer their services in gathering fish oysters &c in return for shirts whiskey knives &c. But they are entirely ignorant of the use of firearms, their bows and arrows being sufficiently destructive.

Their bows are made of the [14] mesquit or cedar and are very elastic.

Ceris Indians

Their arrows are straight and tipped with feathers painted and ornamented with considerable taste. (**Poisoned Arrows**) The material is cane and the points fishbone dipped in deadly poison. This is prepared by holding the liver of some animal to the bite of a rattlesnake until the item becomes saturated with poison when the points of the arrows are dipped and twisted in the poisonous mass and then dried in the sun.

The poisoned arrow point is reversed in the hollow cane arrow until needed for use when the least scratch of the poisoned barb is considered certain death.

The Mexicans near Hermosillo live in continual dread of these inhuman and remorseless savages from whom they have no protection whatever.

Spences [sic] Report

A more lengthy and accurate description of the *Island of Tiburon* and *Bay of San Juan Bautista* will be found in the report of Señor Don Tomas Spence a captain in the Mexican Navy accompanying this report which is entitled to full credit as he is a very intelligent and worthy gentleman who commanded the naval expedition against the Ceris Indians.[15]

Survey of San Juan Bautista

The *Bay of San Juan Bautista* has never been surveyed by the Spanish or Mexican government, consequently no accurate information could be

[15] obtained of its capacity or soundings. The unsettled condition of the government in Sonora and the continual fear of filibusters making a landing on their land rendered it impossible to procure liberty to cruize [sic] in the gulf at this time and an especial order of the government made it a capital offense for any foreigners to be caught prowling about the coast or harbors.

Visited by Lt. Hardy Br. Navy Lt. Stanley U.S. Navy

Lieut. Hardy of the British Navy visited this harbor during a cruise in the Gulf of Calif^a in the years 1825–6.

Lt. Stanley in command of the American sloop of war "St. Marys" [sic] cruising in the Gulf during the war with Mexico visited this harbor for the purpose of sending a force in the interior but for some cause abandoned the enterprize.

Anchorage

He found good safe anchorage and an abundant supply of fresh water of which he replenished his casks.

Report

This officer was so much pleased with the location of the *Island of Tiburon* and adjacent harbor that he prepared maps of the vicinity and made a report to the secretary of the navy of the nature and advantages of the island and bay in case the country should be secured by the United States.

The information was appreciated [16] (**Maps of Tiburon &c.**) and favorably acknowledged by the department in reply.

Lt. Stanley favored me with a sketch of the locality before leaving Calif^a and gave much valuable information of the island and vicinity. He is probably the first American officer who has ever visited this part of the Gulf of California.

Smuggling at San Juan Bautista

I was informed by merchants of Sonora and the fact is well known by Genl Valleja and other Mexicans of Calif^a that this harbor has been frequently used for landing contraband goods and that large vessels from England, South America and China had often landed cargoes of goods there and taken away silver and copper without the knowledge or interference of the officers of the government.

There is no port of entry north of Guaymas as under the Mexican government in Calif^a there was no port of entry north of Monterey.

Oysters, Fish & Game

The harbor abounds in oysters and fish. The island and shores of the bay have swarms of seafowl ducks geese &c.

Building Materials

There is a sufficient quantity of stone, water, and other necessary building materials in the immediate vicinity for the construction of houses roads and all the necessary improvements for a large settlement.

[17] Water

If necessary for purposes of irrigation or other uses the Petic River could be conducted by a canal to any given point on the bay.

Soil

The mainland is a rich sandy loam well sprinkled with a growth of the evergreen mesquit.

Interior

The interior country is the rich and prolific valley of the Petic River extending to the head waters of the branche [sic], draining as they do nearly the whole northern part of Sonora along which the principal estates of the country are located and a large majority of the towns and villages are situated including Hermosillo the principal city and *Ures* the capital of the state and reaching north to Arispe and the vicinity of the valley of the Santa Cruz.

Site for a City and Terminus for a Railroad

The land immediately on the Bay of San Juan Bautista forming an eligible site for a large city belongs to an intelligent and liberal minded gentleman of Hermosillo who holds the same under a grant made by His Excellency Manuel Maria Gándara Governor of the State of Sonora in November 1851 with conditions of colonization &c in the following boundaries,

Boundary

"Commencing at a black and white rock in the Sea of Cortez on a point known as *Sargeants* [sic] *Point* [18] opposite the northern end of the Island of Tiburon, thence north three leagues, east five leagues, south to the water and thence northwesterly along the line of high water mark to the place of beginning. Containing about seven leagues.[16]

Proprietor

The owner of this land was very far superior to his countrymen in intelligence and education having practiced law in the City of Mexico some eight or ten years but is now living upon his paternal estate near Hermosillo in the enjoyment of an immense income and every refinement and luxury that can be introduced into that remote province.

Purchase

After an acquaintance of two or three weeks and the examination of the proper testimonials from Mexicans in Calif[a] this gentleman entered into an arrangement proposed by me for the purpose of building a large city on his land by opening negotiations with the company projecting the continental railroad through Texas to make this point the western terminus.[17]

Agreement

An agreement to this effect was drawn up together with an irrevocable power of attorney in my name on the following terms. The original grantee and such Mexicans as he may interest in the scheme to have one undivided half of the proceeds and such Americans as become interested with me to have the other undivided half.[18]

[19] Power of Attorney

The property to remain undivided and all contracts regarding the same to be made under the power of attorney until the same can be vested in a board of trustees or corporation for the benefit of those having interest in the same.

Owners

The Mexican parties interested number five and are the principal men of Sonora including Gándara then governor of the state.[19] They are all well established in the country being worth in the aggregate over a million of dollars at present value of property and have sufficient social and political influence to control the destinies of the state.

Project

To carry out the intention of the parties and meet the expectations of Mexicans in good faith it is necessary that the Americans to become interested must have sufficient influence and ability to produce the results anticipated viz. the location of the western terminus of the continental railroad at this point the establishment of a port of entry and the building of a city at this place and the consequent and necessary transfer of the sovereignty of the country to the United States.

Annexation

The Mexicans interested in this scheme as well as a large majority of the influential citizens of Sonora are *"annexationists"* or in favor of annexation to the United States.

[20] Consequences

This is an undertaking which might well make the boldest operators and most ambitious speculators pause and reflect before embarking on the enterprize; but when we consider the immense and beneficial results which will follow at its consummation, the great and profitable ends to be accomplished seem much more worthy of the expenditure of time and money than most of the more ordinary pursuits of life.

Railroad

It is generally conceded that El Paso on the Rio Grande forms one of the natural depressions in the Rocky Mountains or branch of the Cordilleras which necessarily makes that the convergence point for any railroad projected across the southern portion of the continent.

Route

The most practicable route then runs south-westerly passing through the Guadalupe Cañon and thence to the Valley of the Santa Cruz where it crosses the head waters of the rivers emptying into the Gulf of California.

Gray and Bartlett

The route projected by Gray and Bartlett thence continues northwesterly to the junction of the Gila and Colorado Rivers and thence to San Diego and San Francisco on the Pacific Ocean.

Gadsden's Purchase

The purchase of the new territory known generally as Gadsden's Purchase was made (ostensibly at least) for the purpose of securing the right of way for a railroad as a commercial barrier against the Indians [21] and indeed it seems as necessary to the United States as the defenseless Mexicans as the practicality of a route through the desert between Salt Lake City and the Sierra Nevada is extremely doubtful and the possibility of constructing a road over those mountains is far from being fully established. It is not however necessary to canvass that subject as our business is entirely with the southern route.

Texas Road

The roads projected from the Mississippi all converge toward the level plains of Texas where they hope to make a united effort to reach the Pacific Ocean, to grasp the gold of Calif[a], to reap the long sought trade of the Indies and China, to gather the fruits and spices of the South Pacific islands, and to coin the silver from the western coast of Mexico and South America—in short to revolutionise the commerce of the world.

Route to Gulf of California

The route usually traveled and called the *"Emigrant Trail"* as before remarked passes through the Guadalupe Cañon and strikes the headwaters of the Rio Grande de Sonora and Rio San Miguel the principal tributaries of the Petic River which empties into the Gulf of Calif[a] opposite the Island of Tiburon; therefore it is reasonable to conclude that this is the best natural course for the road to follow to the ocean.

Wagon Road

The road now used from Santa Cruz [22] to Hermosillo is one of the best wagon roads in the country and has been regularly used since the occupation of the country by the Spaniards.

Military Road

It was the old military road from Guaymas and Hermosillo by El Paso to Santa Fe and other parts of New Mexico and has been always used for transporting goods to the interior and for bringing the produce and manufactures of establishments in the north to a market on the sea coast.

Boundary Com[n]

The United States Boundary Commission with a carriage and several wagons descended the valley of this river to Ures and Hermosillo in 1851.

Santa Cruz Road

The road from Hermosillo to Santa Cruz passes through the largest towns and most densely populated valleys in Sonora capable with good cultivation of producing immense quantities of corn grain cotton sugar and fruit, everything in fact necessary for subsistence or valuable for exportation.

Minerals & Precious Stones

The mountains on each side these valleys contain probably the richest mineral deposits of any mineral region in Mexico and are considered inexhaustible in mines of gold, silver, copper, quicksilver, and precious stones.

Gándara's Views

It is the opinion of Gándara as well as several other intelligent Mexicans and Americans that this region of country would surpass the wonderful [23] productions of California if the mines could be worked with the same freedom and facilities and it is admitted by all that much more confidence would be felt in the permanence of the silver and copper mines of Sonora than in the placeres of California.

Advantages

It is unnecessary to enter into a detail of the superior advantages this road would possess over any other route projected at the present time — Its main advantage is that it shortens space, a great desideratum! —

Santa Cruz to the Gulf of California

The distance from the Valley of *Santa Cruz* to the *Bay of San Juan Bautista* will not exceed two hundred miles and will pass through a country affording many of the necessary materials for the construction of a road, whilst the distance from Santa Cruz to San Diego via the Gila and Colorado will be fully five hundred miles and from the same point to San Francisco more than a thousand miles.

Economy

This saving of expense in the construction of a road, and time in the transportation of freight over the same would always enable a road terminating in the Gulf of Calif[a] to do business proportionably cheaper and sooner than a road terminating at San Francisco or on the Pacific; or in doing business at the same rate enable the Sonora road to make a proportionately [24] larger profit on the amount of business done, not to say anything of the possibility of making a road only two hundred miles long instead of five hundred or a thousand, which at an estimated cost of thirty thousand dollars per mile will be a matter worthy of the careful consideration of the projectors of the road.

Terminus

The terminus proposed to be located on the Bay of San Juan Bautista is nearer the line of navigation to China the Pacific islands, Australia and the western coast of Mexico & South America than even the magnificent bay of San Francisco!!!

Freight & Passengers

The road is projected for the transportation of merchandise & passengers *across the continent* and not from San Francisco, San Diego or any other particular point, and in this view it would seem good policy to select the shortest route.

Corporation

The road is being constructed by an associated company of individuals who will of course accept the best terms that may be offered for for [sic] their corporate and individual benefit.

Texas Grant

The grant of land already made by the State of Texas will insure the construction of the road as far west as El Paso on the Rio Grande.

[25] Mexican Interest in the Railroad

Citizens of Sonora and northern Mexico must look with an envious eye at the construction of a great national road skirting their boundary but confering [sic] upon them no benefits and the dissatisfaction thus engendered can be easily used to induce them to take any steps that may be necessary to secure to the United States the right of way for the road, the opening of ports or in fact the *sovereignty of the country* by cession or annexation.

Terminus

The terminus of the road on the Gulf of California has already been secured, it combines everything necessary for a great city in natural advantages materiel and location, and seems by its very position to invite occupation and commerce.

Independence of Sonora Advantages

In case of the people of the State of Sonora declaring their independence of the Mexican government any grant of lands mines or commercial privaleges [sic] that might be desired by the projectors of the road to aid in its construction could be easily obtained.

Ways & Means

This result could be obtained by offering the use of the necessary means and facilities to prominent citizens of Sonora several of whom are already interested in this scheme. A corporation of such magnitude as the Texas Railroad Co. could afford to favor such an [26] enterprize from benefits which would ultimately accrue to them from its success.

Consideration of Texas Institutions

The Texas road will never terminate in California if a more southern route can be secured, the institutions of the two states are uncongenial and it would seem to one a breach of faith to that great state which by her generous confidence and princely liberality has breathed this magnificent enterprize into existence to make a western terminus in a state having different institutions and antagonistic principles.

Southern Measure

The project is essentially a Southern measure fostered by Southern liberality and the legitimate offspring of Southern enterprize.

Conclusion

It is unnecessary to discuss the subject further at present.

I place the matter in your hands for the purpose of making two parties beside yourself interested in the grant of land at San Juan Bautista.

Future Operations

To secure other concessions for aid in constructing the road will require more mature deliberation and another interview with the Mexican parties as well as some concerted course of action by some corporate body having control of both financial and political power.

[27] Negotiations

The projectors of the Texas Railroad are the proper persons to approach on this subject as I feel confident their views will coincide to some extent with those already expressed in the foregoing condensed statement.

Hermosillo Again

After returning to Hermosillo I made an excursion, occupying nearly a month, to the northeastern portion of the state for the purpose of collecting some information in regard to the silver mines and other resources of the state in that direction.[20]

Silver Mines

Many of the silver mines are very rich and will someday be worked with good machinery and yield a remunerating and permanent income on capital and labor invested.

Value

Interests of one undivided half were frequently offered at nominal prices in consideration of furnishing the machinery necessary to work them with success.

Importance

I am satisfied that the silver mines of Sonora would prove a more regular and permanent source of wealth than the placeres of Calif^a but this is a subject of too much importance to be spoken of here and needs the care and consideration of a second report which will in due time be prepared.[21]

[28] Hermosillo Again

I returned to Hermosillo the 1 of June having now been in the country three months traveling at a considerable expense in the outfit and sustenance of myself and company. No reliable news of the conclusion of a treaty defining the limits of the Gadsden Purchase had been received and no consul of the United States having arrived in the country the prospects of consummating any arrangements in a satisfactory and legal manner were considerably embarrassed.

Col. Gray Survey of Texas R.R. Co.

It was reported at this time that Col. Andrew B. Gray Surveyor of the Texas Railroad Company had arrived on the frontier and that a part of his company headed by himself had come down to Altar in Sonora for the purpose of exploring the Gulf of California for a port suitable for the terminus of the railroad projected across the continent.

Organize a Company to Explore the Gulf

Fearing that my design would be superseded by the discovery of a port above Tiburon on the Gulf as there were vague rumors of a port called "Adair's Bay" I immediately organized a company for the purpose of exploring the Gulf of California by land in search of such a port and a proper site for a town hoping the same would fall within [29] the limit of the treaty then pending.

Departure

I accordingly started from Hermosillo with a company of fifteen men and twenty two animals well-armed and provisioned for the exploration.

Altar

On our arrival at Altar in Lat 30° 45', we learned that Col. Gray had been there and made sundry inquiries about the coast and determined the latitude of Altar which convinced him that this place as well as any port near it on the Gulf must fall below the line of 31 N. latitude which was then regarded as the line of the treaty extending to the gulf.

Lobos

There is a port on the gulf about sixty miles south west of Altar called the "Ensenada de Lobos" located by Spence in Lat 30° 15' 23" Longitude 112° 30' but for the purposes of sheltering vessels this port is little better than an open roadstead protected slightly on the northwest by a sandspit making out into the gulf. It is approached on a desert sandbeach and can never become a place of very great importance.

Reconnoisance

A reconnoisance of this port for the purpose of determining its capacity as a harbor was made by Capt. Tomas Spence by order of the [30] local government of Sonora in the year 1853 a copy of which was kindly furnished me by Gov. Gándara previous to setting out a translation of which is hereto appended to which reference is made for the full and accurate particulars concerning the "Ensenada de Lobos."

Sonoita

Col. Gray having gone on to Sonoita the extreme northern post of Mexican settlement near the gulf we continued our journey and upon reaching Sonoita learned that he had concluded his reconnoisance of the gulf and gone to join his party at Fort Yuma.

Pinacate Mountains—an Extinct Volcano

We followed Gray's trail down to the coast a distance by the windings of the path of about sixty miles crossing a coast range of mountains called the Pinacates (black beetles) and then through about fifteen or twenty miles of sand hills to the beach.

Sand Desert

We found here nothing but desolation, neither water grass wood or any kind of vegetation for our animals, nothing but a desert of sand as far as the eye could reach up and down the coast, extending at least two hundred and fifty miles by a width of twenty five to thirty.

[31] Adairs [sic] Bay

There is no vestage [sic] of a port or harbor for any kind of vessels. The channel of the gulf is on the west or lower Calif^a side and vessels never run near this coast on steering for the mouth of the Colorado.

Attempt to Reach the Colorado

We traveled along this *miserable* shore, over these *interminable* sandhills without grass or fresh water as long as *human patience* or *mule endurance* could stand the privation and hardship consequent upon our situation.—
We were endeavoring to reach the mouth of the Colorado River in the hope of finding a resting spot or oasis near its mouth but found it impossible. The mules became wearied with sinking knee deep in the sand every step, and enervated with drinking brackish water, and eating the leaves of the dwarf mesquit which was the only living sprig which prevailed here. The men were discouraged with the prospect of finding a *"Port on the Gulf"* worn out with heat and fatigue and irritated by the constant and excessive use of salty water procured by digging wells in the sand wherever we halted at noon or night.

Take Observations

From a prominent *sandhill* we took an observation of our locality and found ourselves

[32] Famished in the Sand

some forty or fifty miles distant from the mouth of the Colorado without the hope of reaching it with our broken down animals and even that accomplished it would have been impossible to proceed along its banks as the whole country for ten to fourteen miles around is cut up with sloughs and back water rendering the country impassable and the water unfit for use.

The whole country for sixty miles up the river is subject to overflow and consequently can never form the site for a town or commercial city.

Character of the Colorado

The same character of soil prevails until within five or ten miles of the confluence of the Gila River being frequently overflows [sic] and consequently sandy and barren, especially on the southern or eastern banks.

"Turn Back"

In this view of the case it was impossible to continue the exploration. Consequently we turned back and with much difficulty and suffering reached the water tank in the Pinicate Mountains and finally the California road, which we followed to Sonoita where we remained sometime [sic] recruiting both men and animals as both had suffered severely in this horrible expedition.

[33] Disband

The exploring company was here disbanded, the citizens of Sonora returning home and others scattering about the country leaving only five of the original company to continue the exploration.

Recruit and Start Again with Only Four Men

After recruiting a week this remnant of the company started for Fort Yuma at the junction of the Gila & Colorado Rivers taking a track to the eastward through the country of the (**Papagos Indians**) Papagos Indians passing the Son Saida villages and striking the Gila River about one hundred and thirty miles above the confluence of the rivers and following the road or regular emigrant trail to the junction, thus making a circuit through the new territory of about three hundred miles.

"Jornada"

The last part of this journey was performed without any provisions and the party were obliged to subsist principally upon *mesquit*

Mesquit Beans

beans; and as this valuable esculent contributed so much to our safety if not entire preservation not only here but in other parts of Sonora it would seem only a spontaneous note of gratitude so to notice this valuable and staple product of the whole state of Sonora and along the Gila & Colorado rivers.

Mesquit Tree

The tree is an evergreen acacia [34] resembling in size and appearance the walnut of the Mississippi Valley and bearing a prolific crop of beans resembling the ordinary garden beans in hull and shape but much larger and growing without cultivation tough and hard, each bean in a well grown shell being as large as a grain of corn and containing equally as much if not more sustenance.

Mesquit Beans

The mesquit tree in full growth yields about *ten bushels of beans* which ripen during the summer and having fully matured by the months of September or October fall off and yield an easy harvest to the animals, stock, and the aborigines of the country.

Mesquit Beverage Panole Panoche & Atole

The beans contain nearly as much spirit as corn which the Indians extract for a kind of beverage. They also contain a quantity of saccharine matter which gives them a very sweet taste especially when pulverized and boiled down to the consistency of mush called by the Mexicans atóle——

Indian Food

These beans form the principle [sic] article of food for the Indians in this vicinity who gather them in large baskets and put them up in great granaries for the exigencies of the winter season——

[35] Fort Yuma

We finally came in sight of Fort Yuma at the junction of the Gila and Colorado rivers and were delighted with the *"mess fare"* and hospitable reception given to us by its gallant and intelligent commander Major Heintzelman, which seemed the more grateful [sic] after a long absence from home and a journey of two months without any intercourse with the precincts of civilization.[22]

Encamp

We encamped immediately here at the junction of the rivers on the southern bank of the Colorado within the boundary line of the United States under the treaty of 1848.[23]——This is an elevated plot of ground protected from overflow and having solid banks covered with a thick growth of sycamore, willow and the everlasting mesquit. The undergrowth is so thick that it is impenetrable except preceded by the axe and the large sycamores and evergreen mesquits yield a pleasant shade.

Boundary Line

Mr. Commissioner Bartlett in running the boundary line of the United States particularly mentioned this plot of ground in congratulating the citizens of the United States upon the acquisition of both sides of the Colorado River at this point as necessary for commercial purposes.[24]

[36] Fort Yuma

He says "Fort Yuma stands upon a rocky hill at the junction of the Gila and Colorado Rivers and on the northwest angle of the bank of the united stream.[25]

Colorado and Gila Rivers

"The Colorado comes from the north and where it receives the Gila is about 500 yards wide.

"A bend which the Gila takes about fifteen miles from its mouth makes it come from the south to join the Colorado. The united stream first takes a westerly course forcing itself through a cañon in a chain of rocky hills seventy feet high and about 350 yds. in length.

"After sweeping around some seven or eight miles it again assumes a southerly direction; and after a very tortuous course of about 130 miles empties into the Gulf of California.

"The singular bend which the Colorado takes after it receives the Gila gives to the United States both of its banks for the distance of seven miles from the junction or to the point where it resumes it [sic] southerly course.

"This arises from the stipulation of the fifth article of the treaty with Mexico defining the boundary line which says,

'A straight line shall be [37] drawn from the middle of the Rio Gila where it unites with the Colorado to a point on the Coast of the Pacific Ocean one marine league south of the Bay of San Diego.'[26]

Commercial Point

"The land on the southern bank of the Colorado which we thereby obtained is of little value for agricultural purposes but should a considerable town be built where Fort Yuma presently stands *which is altogether probable* if a railway should ever pass here it will be an advantage to the United States to possess both banks of the river for so long a distance."

Discovery of the Colorado River

Fernando Alarchon [sic] a Spanish navigator discovered and entered the Colorado in 1542. He states that he went up the river 85 leagues (255) miles——As far as he went he found the natives cultivating maize——They brought him cakes of maize and loaves of mesquit. He found cotton growing but nowhere saw any fabrics of it——

Missionary Exploration and Improvements

Father Kino next to Alarchon followed the Colorado beyond its confluence with the Gila and was the first to preach the Gospel among the Indians. He established a mission at the mouth of the Gila above the junction, the remains of which can be seen here now——It existed as late as 1776 when it was destroyed by Indians.

[38] Exploration of the Colorado

Major Heintzelman commander at Fort Yuma has explored the Colorado about eighty miles above the fort and is fully convinced of the practicality of navigating the Colorado to the vicinity of the Mormon settlements. He is confidently of the opinion that the Colorado affords equal facilities for navigation with the Ohio or Missouri and has on each bank large tracts of arable land capable of producing cotton and sugar.

Temperature

The thermometer kept at Fort Yuma makes the mean temperature 82° Far. for May and June.

Depth of Water

The depth of water below the junction is usually from twenty to twenty five feet and the (**Velocity**) velocity of the stream something more than five miles an hour.

Indians

The Indians in the vicinity of Fort Yuma are completely subdued and under good subjection.

Steamboats on the Colorado

The steamer "*Genl. Jesup*" is now plying on the Colorado from the head of the Gulf of California to Fort Yuma engaged principally in transporting government stores but carrying a considerable quantity of Mdse for distribution in the northern portions of Sonora Chihuahua & New Mexico.[27]

[39] Resources of the Colorado

In view of the settlement of the territory acquired by the Gadsden Purchase, the opening of mines in Sonora and New Mexico, the opening of navigation to the vicinity of the Mormon settlements, and the location of the continental railroad to cross at this place this seems to be a point of sufficient local and geographic importance to justify the location of a commercial point.

Colorado City Located

Accordingly a sufficient amount of land was located immediately below the junction of the rivers containing about one thousand acres and a city laid out and called "Colorado City."[28]

Great Crossing

This has always been a great crossing place from Texas the southern states and the northern part of Mexico to Calif[a].

Emigrants

The emigration across here in 1849 numbered ninety thousand in 1850 sixty thousand and since that year from thirty five to fifty thousand persons a year with large numbers of wagons and immense droves of stock.

Ferries

This yields a large income to three ferries which are established here and would pay a very handsome dividend upon the cost of constructing a bridge ——

[40] Great Western Turned up at Colorado City

A house of entertainment and supply is kept just outside of the line of the new city in the recently acquired territory by the *"Great Western"* who distinguished herself by her humanity and hospitality in the Mexican War.[29]

Stores

A store has also been started in the new city by Col. Hooper the sutler of the fort, and large quantities of goods are being disposed of for consumption in the vicinity and in the northern portions of Sonora & Chihuahua.

Title

The title papers of the land located for a town site are on record in San Diego County vesting the title to the property in yourself (Jno. C. McLemore) Charles D. Poston and Herman Ehrenberg (Surveyor) as trustees for those who may become interested in the property—

Conclusion of Reconnoisance

Having now made a reconnoisance of the coast from the mouth to the head of the Gulf of California and a large portion of both the Gila and Colorado Rivers I freely offer Colorado City as the best and only point suitable for the location of a city in the Territory of the U.S. [41] in this vicinity and capable of becoming the point of supply for the extensive territories of Utah and New Mexico portions of Sonora Chihuahua & California.

Cross the Desert to San Diego

We now crossed the desert to San Diego a distance by the trail we followed 218 two hundred and eighteen miles but it has been fully ascertained by recent surveys that a route for a railroad can be procured in a distance of 180 miles.

San Diego & Colorado Railroad

During our stay at San Diego a company was organized for the purpose of constructing a railroad from San Diego to the Colorado, the subscribers being wealthy citizens of San Diego Co. and offering to mortgage one half of their individual property to secure means necessary for the construction of the road.

San Diego

The commanding importance of the bay of San Diego will not be overlooked by any corporation engaged in constructing a railroad across the continent and the appreciation of real estate here consequent upon the location of the terminus of the railroad at this point will be a matter [42] well worthy of the attention of speculators and capitalists.

Omission Mineral Statistics

You will observe that I have omitted in this report any account of the mineral resources of the State of Sonora and the new territory as they would only distract the mind from the subject at issue viz. the opening of ports and building of towns for the purpose of affording facilities for the opening of trade and development of the rich mineral and agricultural resources of the country—

References

The books maps and papers refered to or necessary to confirm and substantiate the foregoing statements will be placed in your possession for the purpose of enabling you to assist in consummating the crude projects indicted in this imperfect report.

I remain very respectfully
Your friend
And obt. sert.[30]

Charles D. Poston

Notes

Introduction

1. Poston may first have been called "Father of Arizona" in a March 15, 1899, act of the Arizona legislature awarding him a pension of twenty-five dollars a month for services rendered to the territory. Gressinger, *Poston: Sunland Seer*, 188–89.

2. "Locating" the grant meant identifying the lands that the Iturbide family could claim from the Mexican government.

3. Browne, *Adventures in the Apache Country*, 235–54.

4. The four articles were "Building a State in Apache Land I"; "Building a State in Apache Land II"; "Building a State in Apache Land III: War Time in Arizona," *Overland Monthly Magazine* 24 (September 1894): 291–97; and "Building a State in Apache Land IV: Arizona a Territory at Last," *Overland Monthly Magazine* 24 (October 1894): 404–8. All four articles were later gathered and published in 1963 as *Building a State in Apache Land*.

5. The spelling "Reconnoisance," although not standard today, was accepted at the time Poston wrote his report.

6. Robinson, "Arizona in 1861," 70n14.

Chapter 1

1. Gustavus D. Pope to Major George H. Kelly, April 13, 1925, SCAW, Box 24, Folder 4. The Debrille name also was spelled "Dibrell" (Sacks, "Poston: Prince of Arizona Pioneers," 3), "Dibrelle," or "Debrelle." Charles preferred the spelling "Debrille" (Goff, *Charles D. Poston*, 1).

2. Goff, *Charles D. Poston*, 2.

3. Ibid., 2–3; Haycraft, *History of Elizabethtown*, 158. Goff says that Poston's apprenticeship started on July 17, 1847, but Haycraft says that it began in January of that year.

4. Goff, *Charles D. Poston*, 2.

5. Ibid., 3–4.
6. Goff, *Charles D. Poston*, 3. Poston's qualifications to practice law are unclear. His biographer A. W. Gressinger says that Poston studied law with Clark in Tennessee and was admitted to practice there (*Poston: Sunland Seer*, 2). But Poston does not say that he ever practiced law in Tennessee, Kentucky, California, or Arizona. He does say that he practiced law in Washington, D.C. (Poston, "Southwestern Chronicle" II, 258). But neither Poston nor his biographers say anything about his having passed the bar or being licensed to practice law there. In London, Poston styled himself a "Councillor at Law (United States)" and said that the "law business . . . was fairly good; as there was no other American law office in London" (ibid., 259, 259n15). But while there, he seems to have limited himself mostly to brokering investment in Arizona land and mining properties.
7. Myers, Preface, 14.
8. Goodale, "Poston Manuscript," 38.
9. Poston, Journal 1847–1850, SCAW, Box 23, Folder 1; Goff, *Charles D. Poston*, 3–4.
10. Poston, Journal 1847–1850.
11. Haycraft, *History of Elizabethtown*, 159.
12. Goodale, "Poston Manuscript," 26–28.
13. Ibid., 41.
14. Haycraft, *History of Elizabethtown*, 159.
15. Colonel Benjamin H. Pope to Miss Toohey, July 12, 1935, SCAW, Box 24, Folder 4.
16. Dick Taylor, *Louisville Sunday Courier*, n.d., SCAW, Box 24, Folder 4.
17. Gustavus Pope to Kelly (cited in n. 1 above).
18. Poston, "Southwestern Chronicle" II, 256.
19. Ibid., 257; Gustavus Pope to Kelly.
20. Poston, "Southwestern Chronicle," 153.
21. Charles D. Poston to William H. Seward, SCAW, Box 23, Folder 3.
22. Goodale, "Poston Manuscript," 41–42, 42n48.

Chapter 2

1. Poston, "Southwestern Chronicle II," 252.
2. Bancroft, *California Inter Pocula*, 261.
3. Goodale, "Poston Manuscript," 67.
4. Goff, *Charles D. Poston*, 6; Gressinger, *Poston: Sunland Seer*, 3; Steel, *T. Butler King*, 85. A copy of Poston's oath of office, signed by him on February 17, 1851, is in SCAW, Box 23, Folder 1.
5. Goodale, "Poston Manuscript," 73.
6. Myers, Preface, 15. Without actually seeing Poston's recommendation letters, we cannot know if they were intended specifically to get him a position at the customs house. If so, why he waited a month before starting there is puzzling.
7. Goodale, "Poston Manuscript," 74, 127–28.
8. Ibid., 74–75, 79.

9. Hopkins, "California Recollections Continued," 336, 337. Hopkins's own career provides good examples of the favoritism he describes. He first got a job as an inspector of customs through the influence of a cousin, Sheldon U. Hopkins, who was King's deputy collector. However, Caspar soon lost his position when King was ordered by Washington to reduce his customs house staff. In the meantime, Hopkins had accepted an assignment as San Francisco correspondent for the *New York Courier and Enquirer*. He obtained this position through another family member, his brother Clement, who was an editor for the paper. When Caspar lost his customs house job, his cousin suggested that Caspar write to King, tell him about his connection with the paper, and ask if Caspar could "be of any use to him in that capacity." Hopkins did so, and King, still pursuing a political career and delighted to have a public forum for his ideas, allowed Caspar to interview him for publication. In return, King fired a clerk from the customs house and appointed Caspar in his place. He also ordered that Caspar be the only official allowed to write up claims against the government for duties illegally charged under the previous collector. King advised Caspar to charge 10 percent for this service. The claims were many and brought Hopkins an income of three to four thousand dollars a year in addition to his clerk's salary. Poston only made thirty-six hundred dollars a year as a chief clerk, which shows how much Hopkins benefited from his exchange of favors with King. Ibid., 332–34.

10. Poston, "Southwestern Chronicle" II, 253.

11. Sally Louise Morton and Betsy Ross Morton Johns, "Excerpts and Notes from Haycraft Family Journal," 196, Film Reel 2, M-690, Haycraft Family Papers, Margaret I. King Library, University of Kentucky, Lexington, cited in Goodale, "Poston Manuscript," 80 and 80n44; Goff, *Charles D. Poston*, 4; Myers, Preface, 15–16.

12. Goodale, "Poston Manuscript," 88, 88-89n62.

13. Hopkins, "California Recollections," 105.

14. Soulé, Gihon, and Nisbet, *Annals of San Francisco*, 254. A vara was an old Spanish measure of distance, whose precise definition changed with time and place. In California, a vara was about thirty-three inches, but it is not known if the fifty-vara figure the authors refer to is a square (area) or linear measure.

15. Ibid., 498, 500.

16. Poston, "Southwestern Chronicle" II, 253.

17. Hopkins, "California Recollections," 108.

18. Goodale, "Poston Manuscript," 99.

19. Ibid., 100–103. Copies of Van Voorhies's June 10, 1853, letter to Treasury Secretary James Guthrie reporting the demotion; Poston's letter to Guthrie, June 10, 1853, protesting the demotion; Poston's June 10, 1853, letter to Eastland; and Eastland's July 23 letter to Guthrie supporting Poston are in SCAW, Box 23, Folder 1.

Chapter 3

1. Poston, *Building a State in Apache Land*, 41. Poston first describes a "member of Congress and his wife" as residents at the boardinghouse then later refers to "the ex-member of Congress" (47–48).

2. Ibid., 42.

3. Ibid., 45.

4. "Treaty of Guadalupe Hidalgo," 23–24; Faulk, *Too Far North*, 32n20. Under Spanish and Mexican rule, "Upper California" was known as "Alta California." "Lower California" was, and still is, "Baja California."

5. "Treaty of Guadalupe Hidalgo," 25.

6. Ibid., 24.

7. Ibid.; Faulk, *Too Far North*, 58–59; Del Castillo, *Treaty of Guadalupe Hidalgo*, 55–57; Kiser, *Turmoil on the Rio Grande*, 48–49.

8. Faulk, *Too Far North*, 62.

9. Del Castillo, *Treaty of Guadalupe Hidalgo*, 57; Garber, *Gadsden Treaty*, 16.

10. Del Castillo, *Treaty of Guadalupe Hidalgo*, 57; Faulk, *Too Far North*, 63.

11. Faulk, *Too Far North*, 63–64, 70–76; Garber, *Gadsden Treaty*, 13–14.

12. Faulk, *Too Far North*, 76–77, 81; Garber, *Gadsden Treaty*, 14.

13. Faulk, *Too Far North*, 105; Garber, *Gadsden Treaty*, 15–16.

14. Faulk, *Too Far North*, 105–6; Del Castillo, *Treaty of Guadalupe Hidalgo*, 57.

15. McKay, "Texas and the Southern Pacific Railroad," 15.

16. Gray, *Report*, xiv.

17. Faulk, *Too Far North*, 106–7; Del Castillo, *Treaty of Guadalupe Hidalgo*, 57; Garber, *Gadsden Treaty*, 16.

18. Faulk, *Too Far North*, 124.

19. Garber, *Gadsden Treaty*, 18; Rippy, *United States and Mexico*, 127.

20. To complicate matters, the border dispute in the Mesilla Valley had created a nasty conflict among Mexican and American settlers who had moved into the region after the 1846–47 war. Americans had settled near the town of Doña Ana on the east bank of the Rio Grande, displacing Mexicans who had been living there. The Mexicans, wanting to avoid conflict, had moved to the west bank, establishing the town of Mesilla, which they believed to be in Mexico. The governors of New Mexico and the Mexican state of Chihuahua both claimed jurisdiction over the Mesilla Valley, and both gathered military forces to send into the area, raising the threat of a new war between Mexico and the United States. Since neither government could muster the finances or political support for another war, the conflict between Mexican and American settlers became another compelling reason for negotiating a new boundary through the disputed territory. Faulk, *Too Far North*, 118–24; Kiser, *Turmoil on the Rio Grande*, 37–40, 72–81.

21. Garber, *Gadsden Treaty*, 85; Kiser, *Turmoil on the Rio Grande*, 81–82; Rippy, *United States and Mexico*, 129, 138.

22. Stout, *Liberators*, 16–17.

23. Vasquez and Meyer, *United States and Mexico*, 61.

24. Garber, *Gadsden Treaty*, 100–101, 139; Kiser, *Turmoil on the Rio Grande*, 84. A revolution against Santa Anna's government was brewing in 1853 in Guerrero Province and was proclaimed, eventually, in the March 1, 1854, Plan of Ayutla that reestablished republican government in Mexico and eventually brought Benito Juárez to the presidency.

25. Garber, *Gadsden Treaty*, 91–92. Garber and Kiser (*Turmoil on the Rio Grande*, 85) say that Gadsden was given six possible boundary lines to negotiate. Garber

includes a map following p. 92 that shows all six lines, as well as the line negotiated by Gadsden, a line proposed by the U.S. Senate in a failed amendment to the treaty, and the final boundary agreed upon by both countries. Pahissa ("Mesilla Treaty," 11); Rippy (*United States and Mexico*, 138), and Trimble (*Arizona: A Cavalcade of History*, 89) say that Gadsden was given five possible lines to negotiate.

26. Garber, *Gadsden Treaty*, 91–92, 118–21.

27. The *Alta California* was not consistent in its proannexation position. On June 13 and December 28, 1853, the paper printed articles opposing annexation of Mexican territory, on both occasions because Mexicans were inferior to Americans and could not, as voting U.S. citizens, be entrusted with the country's governance. On December 28, the paper argued that Sonora or Chihuahua should not be annexed, since if these territories were brought into the United States, Southerners would demand that they be admitted as slave states, Northern politicians would refuse, and civil war would become more likely. Thus, while increasing U.S. territory was desirable, the threat of "disunion" made the prospect of Mexican annexation less attractive.

28. Goodale, "Poston Manuscript," 111.

29. An American transcontinental railroad, of course, had to run on American soil; and American farms, ranches, and mines had to be within U.S. boundaries in order to avoid interference by the Mexican government in the form of property taxes and labor regulation.

30. Poston, *Building a State in Apache Land*, 44.

31. Dobie, *Coronado's Children*, xix; Acuña, *Occupied America*, 73–74.

32. Mexal, *Reading for Liberalism*, 76–77; Slotkin, *The Fatal Environment*, 11–12.

33. Garate, *Juan Bautista de Anza*, 157–83, 193–98; Garate, "Who Named Arizona?," 55–59; Polzer, "Legends of Lost Missions," 177. The Spanish crown collected a 20 percent tax on all mined minerals (the "king's fifth"), but if the property was declared a buried treasure or clandestine smelting operation, the crown claimed 100 percent. In time, Anza's reference to the "Arizona" ranch gave a name to the territory of Arizona, even though the site of the great silver find was well south of today's international border.

34. Nentvig, *Rudo Ensayo*, 3, 100.

35. Anza, "Complete Diary, 1774," 5, 7.

36. Ward, *Mexico in 1827*, 136.

37. Gray, *Report*, 215.

38. Nentvig's *Rudo Ensayo* was published in 1863, Anza's diary in 1966, and Gray's report in 1856.

39. "Sonora—and the Value of its Silver Mines," 7.

40. Humboldt, *Political Essay*, 288.

41. Pratt, *Imperial Eyes*, 147. Historian David Weber says that even before the Mexican War, many North Americans were "contemptuous of Mexican government and of Catholicism, and they viewed Mexicans as indolent, ignorant, bigoted, cheating, dirty, bloodthirsty, cowardly half-breeds." They believed Mexico "deserved to be conquered because it was less industrious and efficient than the United States" (*Foreigners in Their Native Land*, 60, 61).

42. Humboldt, *Political Essay*, 333.

43. Ward, *Mexico in 1827*, 311–12, 318.
44. Officer, "Mining in Hispanic Arizona," 9.
45. Gray, *Report*, 218–19.
46. Hardy, *Travels in the Interior of Mexico*, 413, 430.
47. Stout, *Liberators*, 51. Southwest historian Howard Lamar says that after the Gadsden Purchase was completed, mining promoters spread stories of the region's mineral wealth, recycling the traditional tales of the Sonoran silver mines and feeding rumors that the area might become the site of a "second California gold rush" (*The Far Southwest*, 363).
48. A popular saying of the time held, "It takes a gold mine to work a silver mine."
49. Poston, *Building a State in Apache Land*, 45.
50. Ibid., 46–47.
51. Ibid., 47.

Chapter 4

1. Brack, *Mexico Views Manifest Destiny*, 16, 25, 56–57; Bauer, *Mexican War, 1846–1848*, 3–4; Knapp, "Mexican Fear of Manifest Destiny"; Christensen and Christensen, *U.S.-Mexican War*, 221.
2. Brack, *Mexico Views Manifest Destiny*, 63; *The Other Side*, 4.
3. O'Sullivan, "Annexation," 5.
4. The historian Frederick Merk cautions that the philosophy of Manifest Destiny, though ardently espoused by some, did not have broad support: "From the outset Manifest Destiny—vast in program, in its sense of continentalism—was slight in support. It lacked national, sectional, or party following commensurate with its bigness.... The thesis that it embodied nationalism, found in much historical writing, is backed by little real supporting evidence" (*Manifest Destiny and Mission*, 216).
5. Limerick, *Legacy of Conquest*, 231. On the influence of racism on American expansionism, see also Hietala, *Manifest Design*, 171–72.
6. Brack, *Mexico Views Manifest Destiny*, 170–71. Limerick also describes the American stereotype of the "lazy" Mexican (*Legacy of Conquest*, 240–41).
7. *The Other Side*, 3–4, 37; Christensen and Christensen, *U.S.-Mexican War*, 233.
8. In the nineteenth century the Mexican government used the term "filibusters" to refer to all individuals who aimed to invade Mexico in armed groups. The term comes from the Dutch *vribuiter*, meaning "freebooter" or "pirate" (Stout, *Schemers & Dreamers*, x).
9. Stout, *Schemers & Dreamers*, xiv.
10. Ibid.; Stout, "Post-War Filibustering," 194.
11. Stout, *Schemers & Dreamers*, xiv; Martinez, "Filibustering and Racism," 46; Stout, "Post-War Filibustering," 193–94.
12. Stout, "Post-War Filibustering," 192–93, Stout, *Liberators*, 13–14.
13. Stout, *Liberators*, 50.
14. After the war with the United States, three Mexican political leaders—Secretary of War Mariano Arista (1848), Representative Mariano Paredes (1850), and Senator Juan Nepomuceno Almonte (1852)—proposed that laws be passed allowing

foreign immigrants to settle near the northern border with the United States. Their aims were to improve the economy of a sparsely populated region, protect the northern states from Apache raids, and discourage Americans from settling in Mexican territory and then accepting annexation to the United States, as had happened in Texas and California. Most of the proposals specified that Mexico would accept only European settlers and that colonists would be expected to become Mexican citizens exclusively. Faulk, "A Colonization Plan for Northern Sonora," 293–95, 306; Scroggs, *Filibusters and Financiers*, 21; Stout, "Post-War Filibustering," 193–94; Stout, *Schemers & Dreamers*, 11. These plans were rejected by the Mexican Congress, but some Mexican leaders, such as Santa Anna, liked the idea of immigrant settlement and did what they could to support it. Santa Anna, for example, supported French immigration into Sonora, while Sonoran governor Manuel María Gándara supported settlement by German immigrants in his state. Scroggs, *Filibusters and Financiers*, 55–56; *Daily Alta California*, November 20, 1853; January 3, 1854; March 25, 1854.

15. Stout, *Liberators*, 51–57; Stout, *Schemers & Dreamers*, 24–26.

16. Stout, *Liberators*, 59–77, 103–20; Stout, *Schemers & Dreamers*, 26–32.

17. Stout, *Liberators*, 81–95, 98–101. Another informative resource on the Walker filibuster is Wyllys, "Republic of Lower California."

18. Browne, *Adventures in the Apache Country*, 237.

19. Rippy, *United States and Mexico*, 104–5.

20. Wyllys, *Arizona*, 111–12; Vasquez and Meyer, *The United States and Mexico*, 54. The law stated that "any person that shall within the territory of jurisdiction of the United States, begin or set foot, or provide or prepare the means for, any military expedition or enterprise to be carried on from thence against the territory or dominion of any foreign prince or state, colony, district, or people with whom the United States are at peace, every such person so offending, shall be declared guilty of a high misdemeanor and shall be fined not exceeding three thousand dollars, and imprisoned not more than three years."

21. Stout, *Schemers & Dreamers*, xiii.

22. Fillmore sent Hitchcock to California with orders to stop any filibustering expeditions leaving California. Pierce later sent Wool to replace Hitchcock, armed with a proclamation ordering all military officers to arrest violators of the neutrality law. Brown, *Agents of Manifest Destiny*, 193–94, 209–10. However, even allowing that these efforts were sincere, they were, mostly, ineffective. Pindray's expedition and Raousset's first filibuster began as legitimate colonizing efforts approved by the Mexican government. Walker's expedition was undisguised filibustering, but Hitchcock was unable to stop it. Wool attempted to stop Raousset's second filibuster but failed. The neutrality statute itself was vaguely worded and nearly impossible to enforce, since it did not precisely define a violation. And California officials charged with prosecuting those arrested were sympathetic to the filibusters and disinclined to prosecute. Their lack of motivation was inspired by California citizens, who, by and large, supported the filibusters and, when constituted as juries, were unlikely to find them guilty. Rippy, *United States and Mexico*, 97–101.

23. Stout, *Liberators*, 88–89.

24. *Daily Alta California*, November 23, 1853.

25. Stout, *Liberators*, 94.
26. *Daily Alta California*, January 3, 1854.
27. Ibid.; Stout, *Liberators*, 91–92.
28. *Daily Alta California*, January 3, 1854.

Chapter 5

1. Poston, *Building a State in Apache Land*, 47.
2. Sacks, "Charles Debrille Poston," 4.
3. Poston confirmed these objectives years later in two sources: the "Memorial of Charles D. Poston Addressed to the Joint Commission of the U.S.A. and United States of Mexico Appointed Under the Convention of July 4, 1868," 1870, SCAW, Box 24, Folder 3; and *Letter from the Secretary of the Interior*.
4. Poston, *Building a State in Apache Land*, 47.
5. Goodale, "Poston Manuscript," 103–4, 104n82.
6. Ibid., 125.
7. Poston's departure from the customs house is reported in a letter from Van Voorhies to Treasury Secretary James Guthrie, SCAW, Box 23, Folder 1.
8. Poston, *Building a State in Apache Land*, 48.
9. Ornish, *Ehrenberg*, 3–41; Browne, *Adventures in the Apache Country*, 237–38; Goodale, "Poston Manuscript," 116.
10. Goodale, "Poston Manuscript," 116–17n96.
11. The *Alta California* notice was inaccurate. The *Zoraida* did not sail until February 19.
12. SCAW, Box 23, Folder 1.

Chapter 6

1. "Reconnoisance in Sonora," 127. All page references are from this book.
2. Ibid., 137.
3. Ibid., 128.
4. Goodale, "Poston Manuscript," 135.
5. "Reconnoisance in Sonora," 127.
6. Voss, *On the Periphery*, 78, 102.
7. "Reconnoisance in Sonora," 128–29.
8. Browne, *Adventures in the Apache Country*, 241.
9. Voss, *On the Periphery*, 77–78, 83–84, 123–28.
10. "Reconnoisance in Sonora," 129. Poston spells both the town and the river "Fuerta." Poston does not describe specifically his routes to the Sonoran cities he visited, so it is impossible to say precisely how he arrived at each one.
11. "Reconnoisance in Sonora," 128–29.
12. Ibid., 129; Browne, *Adventures in the Apache Country*, 243.
13. Browne, *Adventures in the Apache Country*, 243.
14. *Notables of the West*, 225; Voss, *On the Periphery*, 39.
15. Voss, *On the Periphery*, 38.

16. "Reconnoisance in Sonora," 130.
17. Browne, *Adventures in the Apache Country*, 243.
18. Hardy, *Travels in the Interior of Mexico*, 110.
19. Browne, *Adventures in the Apache Country*, 243. In an 1895 speech, Poston says that he and his men were arrested "on the charge of having landed without a license" but that he had "taken the precaution to procure passports before leaving San Francisco which together with some letters of introduction, an explanation of the cause of our involuntary landing satisfied the Prefect that we were not dangerous characters, and we were released on parole not to upset the Mexican government, and treated with every kindness" (SCAW, Box 24, Folder 3).
20. "Reconnoisance in Sonora," 130.
21. Hu-DeHart, *Yaqui Resistance*, 16, 20–47; Spicer, *Yaquis*, 43, 50–53.
22. "Reconnoisance in Sonora," 130–31.
23. Browne, *Adventures in the Apache Country*, 243–44.
24. The historian Cynthia Radding says that armed rebellions by Mexican native peoples usually emerged from a "context of ongoing resistance" and usually only after negotiation had failed (*Wandering Peoples*, 13, 299).
25. Spicer, *Yaquis*, 54–55; Hu-DeHart, *Yaqui Resistance*, 4–5. The eight Yaqui towns were, from west to east along the Yaqui River, Belem, Hiurivis, Rahum, Pótam, Vicam, Tórim, Bácum, and Cócorit (Spicer, *Yaquis*, 226).
26. Deeds, "Indigenous Rebellions," 47.
27. Spicer, *Cycles of Conquest*, 57.
28. Voss, *On the Periphery*, 41.
29. Hu-DeHart, *Yaqui Resistance*, 55.
30. Spicer, *Yaquis*, 56–57; Spicer, *Cycles of Conquest*, 58–59; Radding, *Wandering Peoples*, 9–10. Radding argues that political relations between Indians and Spanish and Mexican authorities were guided by a "colonial pact" in which Indians accepted some accommodation to Spanish and Mexican rule (providing labor for mines and ranches and serving as auxiliary forces in military campaigns) in return for political autonomy and the protection of their lands. The pact was tacit (not codified in any law or treaty), varied over time, and was not consistently followed. But when Indians perceived that it was not being honored, and negotiation failed to resolve the issue, armed rebellion could occur ("Colonial Pact," 52–53; *Wandering Peoples*, 12–13).
31. Poston, *Building a State in Apache Land*, 48.
32. "Gadsden Treaty," 39–40.
33. "Reconnoisance in Sonora," 131. Poston's dismissal of Guaymas is surprising, since throughout the nineteenth century Guaymas was widely considered one of the finest ports on the Pacific coast (Acuña, *Occupied America*, 75). Probably, Poston criticized Guaymas in order to promote his own choice of San Juan Bautista Bay as a gulf port site.
34. "Reconnoisance in Sonora," 132–33.

Chapter 7

1. Bolton, *Rim of Christendom*, 203, 203n3.
2. "Reconnoisance in Sonora," 134–35.

3. Ibid., 136–37.
4. Poston spelled the Indians' name "Ceri."
5. Radding, *Wandering Peoples*, 7.
6. Sheridan, *Empire of Sand*, 3–5.
7. "Reconnoisance in Sonora," 135.
8. Sheridan, *Empire of Sand*, 461.
9. "Reconnoisance in Sonora," 136.
10. Ibid., 138.
11. Ibid., 138–39. In "Poston's Narrative," Poston spelled Astiarazán's name as "Artiasarana" (Browne, *Adventures in the Apache Country*, 250) but then corrected the spelling to "Astiazaran" in his 1881 U.S. Court of Claims testimony. In that testimony, Poston said that Joaquin Astiazarán was a "judge in one of the courts" (*Letter from the Secretary of the Interior*, 53).
12. "Reconnoisance in Sonora," 139.
13. Voss, *On the Periphery*, 41–42.
14. Hardy, *Travels in the Interior of Mexico*, 109–10.
15. Ward, *Mexico in 1827*, 2:446.
16. "Reconnoisance in Sonora," 138.
17. Radding, *Wandering Peoples*, 175; Sheridan, *Landscapes of Fraud*, 94.
18. Sheridan, *Landscapes of Fraud*, 102; Mattison, "Early Spanish and Mexican Settlements," 282–83, 287.
19. "Reconnoisance in Sonora," 139.
20. Love, "Poston and the Birth of Yuma," 409.
21. Voss, *On the Periphery*, xiii–xv, 24–25; Balmori, Voss, and Wortman, *Notable Family Networks*, 2.
22. Balmori, Voss, and Wortman, *Notable Family Networks*, 15–17.
23. Ibid., 16.
24. Ibid., 99–100; Voss, *On the Periphery*, 83.
25. Acuña, *Sonoran Strongman*, 16–17; Voss, *On the Periphery*, 92, 95–97.
26. Voss, *On the Periphery*, 93; Balmori, Voss, and Wortman, *Notable Family Networks*, 91.
27. Voss, *On the Periphery*, 41; Mattison, "Early Spanish and Mexican Settlements," 300–301; Sheridan, *Landscapes of Fraud*, 98–99; Wagoner, *Early Arizona*, 214–15.
28. "Reconnoisance in Sonora," 139, 144.
29. "Reconnoisance in Sonora," 139.
30. In 1881 Poston gave a hint as to who, besides Joaquin Astiazarán and Gándara, might have been in the group with whom he negotiated. In testimony before U.S. Surveyor General John Wasson concerning ownership of the Sopori land grant in Arizona, Poston said that Joaquin was not at La Labor when Poston went there in 1854 but that he met Fernando Astiazarán there and Joaquin's brother-in-law, Fernando Cubillas, who also was part of the Gándara-Iñigo-Aguilar network. Cubillas had been a state judge and, in 1853, interim governor of Sonora. He also was the son-in-law and business partner of Guaymas merchant Manuel Iñigo. *Letter from the Secretary of the Interior*, 67; Balmori, Voss, and Wortman, *Notable Family Networks*, 91, 103; Acuña, *Sonoran Strongman*, 71; Bancroft, *History of the North Mexican States*, 681n30.

Notes to Pages 66–73 • 165

31. Cline, *United States and Mexico*, 41–45.
32. Acuña, *Sonoran Strongman*, 17.
33. Bancroft, *History of the North Mexican States*, 681; Voss, *On the Periphery*, 99, 136.
34. Bancroft, *History of the North Mexican States*, 693–94; Calvo Berber, *Nociones de historia de Sonora*, 187; Villa, *Compendio de historia del estado de Sonora*, 265; Voss, *On the Periphery*, 136.
35. Poston, *Building a State in Apache Land*, 84.
36. "N's" letter to the *Daily Alta California*, January 3, 1854, reported that, with letters of introduction to pave the way, he was hospitably treated by wealthy Mexicans in the Sonoran cities of Hermosillo, Ures, and Arispe.
37. Voss, *On the Periphery*, 115.
38. "Reconnoisance in Sonora," 139–40.
39. Goodale, "Poston Manuscript," 147.
40. "Reconnoisance in Sonora," 140.
41. Ibid. In Poston's view, as in that of many Americans, the southern route had a redemptive purpose for Mexicans as well as Americans, although what a "commercial barrier against the Indians" might have been is unknown. The argument that the railroad would make such a barrier was frequently heard in discussions of the southern route. But there is no evidence that the Apaches, who raided wagon trains, ranches, farms, and small villages, would have recognized any such barrier.
42. Ibid., 141.
43. Ibid., 142.
44. Ibid.
45. Hietala, *Manifest Design*, 59.
46. *The Other Side*, 3.
47. Hietala, *Manifest Design*, 21, 24.
48. Goodale, "Poston Manuscript," 149.
49. "Reconnoisance in Sonora," 143–44.
50. Ibid., 144. Although headquartered in New York City, the Texas Western Railroad was chartered by the Texas legislature and funded by a grant from the state.
51. Ibid.
52. Ibid.

Chapter 8

1. "Reconnoisance in Sonora," 145.
2. Browne, *Adventures in the Apache Country*, 247.
3. "Reconnoisance in Sonora," 145. The term *placeres* is Spanish, a plural of *placer*, a common type of gold mining, in which miners take gold "dust" or small nuggets from streams by panning.
4. Ibid.
5. Garber, *Gadsden Treaty*, 131, 145.
6. Ibid., 83.
7. *Report of the Secretary of the Interior*, 27–29.

8. Ibid., 32, 34.
9. Ibid., 30–31.
10. Ibid., 32. Poston made substantially the same argument about a transcontinental railroad route to the gulf sixteen months later, in the "Reconnoisance."
11. Gray, *Report*, xiv–xv, 7–8.
12. Ibid., 83–85.
13. "Reconnoisance in Sonora," 146. Poston makes clear that this was a new expedition, suggesting that his original party had disbanded.
14. Love, "Poston and the Birth of Yuma," 411.
15. "Reconnoisance in Sonora," 146–47.
16. Hartmann, *Desert Heart*, 7, 11; Lumholtz, *New Trails in Mexico*, 225–26.
17. Poston and his contemporaries, like the Spanish and Mexican explorers and settlers before them, referred to all of the O'odham as "Papagos." The Hia C-ed O'odham were also known as "Areneños," "Sand Pimas," or "Sand Papagos."
18. Kino, *Historical Memoir*, 187, 187n, 283.
19. Bolton, *Rim of Christendom*, 456.
20. Ives, *Land of Lava*, 48, 50, 69–70.
21. Gray, *Report*, 88, 220; "Reconnoisance in Sonora," 147.
22. "Reconnoisance in Sonora," 147.
23. Hartmann, *Desert Heart*, 37, 85.
24. Gray, *Report*, 88.
25. "Reconnoisance in Sonora," 147; Ehrenberg, "Map of the Gadsden Purchase."
26. Gray, *Report*, 217.
27. "Reconnoisance in Sonora," 147.
28. Ibid., 147–48.
29. Ives, *Land of Lava*, 36.
30. Bolton, *Rim of Christendom*, 481.
31. Hardy, *Travels in the Interior of Mexico*, 330–31.
32. Michler, "Report," 103, 113.
33. "Reconnoisance in Sonora," 148.
34. Bolton, *Rim of Christendom*, 482–83.
35. Gray, *Report*, 220.
36. "Reconnoisance in Sonora," 148. Poston's early and later accounts differ concerning the size of the group that continued north from Sonoita. In the "Reconnoisance," Poston says that "five of the original company" went north, which might be taken to mean Poston, Ehrenberg, and three others. The "Reconnoisance" suggests that Poston's expedition was reconstituted several times and at times probably included Mexicans and Tohono O'odham guides, as well as Americans.

Chapter 9

1. Goodale, "Poston Manuscript," 157–58.
2. "Reconnoisance in Sonora," 148.
3. Ibid.; Poston, "Diary of a Pioneer"; Poston, "In Memoriam" [Ehrenberg]; Ives, *Land of Lava*, 229n33.

4. Poston, "Diary of a Pioneer"; Poston, "In Memoriam" [Ehrenberg]. Ehrenberg's 1854 map shows a route leading from Sonoita ninety-five miles through the mountains, past "Savette," and twenty-five to thirty miles west of the "Sierra del Ajo Copper Ms." to the vicinity of Gila Bend. Ehrenberg does not say that he and Poston traveled that road, but it seems a likely route. Arizona historian Ralph Moody says that northern Sonora (southern Arizona) was crisscrossed with traditional Native American trails, some of which had been used for as long as five hundred years before Europeans arrived and eight hundred years before Poston's expedition (*Old Trails West*, 26). Poston and other explorers before him were not wandering through a "trackless wilderness."

5. "Reconnoisance in Sonora," 148.

6. Clark and Clark, *Oatman Story*, 96.

7. Bieber, *Southern Trails to California*, 56. The "Pimas" were the Akimel O'odham, or "River People," who lived in the vicinity of the Gila River and were hospitable to Americans; without their help, thousands of travelers on their way to California would have perished.

8. Hague, *Road to California*, 21; Etter, *To California on the Southern Route*, 35.

9. Manje, *Unknown Arizona and Sonora*, 72–74, 111–15; Hague, *Road to California*, 45, 70–71; Bolton, *Spanish Exploration in the Southwest*, 429; Bolton, map, "Pima Land 1687–1711," *Rim of Christendom*, after 594; Anza, "Complete Diary, 1774," 37, 43–45; Pourade, *Anza Conquers the Desert*, 63–64, 101–56; Anza, "Diary of the Second Anza Expedition," 13–51; Font, "Diary of an Expedition to Monterey," 42–174; Garcés, "Diary from Tubac to San Gabriel," 309–24; Faulk, *Destiny Road*, 14.

10. Hague, *Road to California*, 21–22; Forbes, "Development of the Yuma Route," 102.

11. Hague, *Road to California*, 110–11, 124–26; Hanchett, *Crossing Arizona*, 43–49; Faulk, *Destiny Road*, 17; Bean and Mason, *Diaries and Accounts of the Romero Expeditions*, 14–24; Fages, "The Colorado River Campaign."

12. Hague, *Road to California*, 140, 172, 198–99; Forbes, "Development of the Yuma Route," 110–12; Pattie, *Personal Narrative*, 174–208.

13. Hague, *Road to California*, 251; Cooke, "Journal of the March of the Mormon Battalion," 27.

14. Couts, *Hepah, California!*

15. Faulk, *Destiny Road*, 44.

16. Hague, *Road to California*, 21, 293; Etter, *To California on the Southern Route*, 35.

17. Bieber, *Southern Trails to California*, 56; Etter, *To California on the Southern Route*, 51.

18. Eccleston, *Overland to California*, vi; Etter, *To California on the Southern Route*, 36; Hague, *Road to California*, 292.

19. Young, *West of Philip St. George Cooke*, 216.

20. Cooke, "Journal of the March of the Mormon Battalion," 178, 180, 182–84; Eccleston, *Overland to California*, 218, 219, 223.

21. Bieber, *Southern Trails to California*, 60–61; Eccleston, *Overland to California*, 215–16.

22. Audubon, *Western Journal*, 162.
23. Eccleston, *Overland to California*, 215–17.
24. Ibid., 216–17; Conkling and Conkling, *Butterfield Overland Mail*, 174–75; Cox, "From Texas to California in 1849," 201–2.
25. McGinty, *Oatman Massacre*, 108; Clark and Clark, *Oatman Story*, 95–96; Stratton, *Captivity of the Oatman Girls*, 109.
26. Bartlett, *Personal Narrative*, 2:203; Clark and Clark, *Oatman Story*, 95–96.
27. Browne, *Adventures in the Apache Country*, 86.
28. "Reconnoisance in Sonora," 148; Cooke, "Journal of the March of the Mormon Battalion," 204; Cox, "From Texas to California in 1849," 146; Trafzer, *Yuma*, 37–38.
29. Heintzelman, Journal, July 11, 1854.
30. "Reconnoisance in Sonora," 151–52.
31. Hargett, "Pioneering at Yuma Crossing, 331–32.
32. Faulk, *Destiny Road*, 124–25; Martin, *Yuma Crossing*, 178.
33. Trafzer, *Yuma*, 79; Browne, *Adventures in the Apache Country*, 282.
34. Trafzer, *Yuma*, 51.
35. Thompson, *Civil War to the Bloody End*, 37, 39. Arizona military historian Ray Brandes says that the U.S. Army first established a post at the Yuma crossing in 1849 under the name "Camp Calhoun." The post Heintzelman established in 1850 was known as "Camp Independence." When it moved in 1851, it was renamed "Camp Yuma." Camp Yuma did not officially become "Fort Yuma" until 1861 (*Frontier Military Posts of Arizona*, 81–84). However, since Poston, Heintzelman, Gray, Bartlett, Emory, Michler, Whipple, and others who traveled through the region in the 1850s all called the post "Fort Yuma," this book does the same.
36. Thompson, *Civil War to the Bloody End*, 61.
37. Hargett, "Pioneering at Yuma Crossing," 333.
38. "Reconnoisance in Sonora," 152.
39. Heintzelman, Journal, July 11, 1854.
40. Ibid.
41. Gray, *Report*, 99.
42. When the Southern Pacific Railroad was finally built from California to Arizona in 1877, it crossed the Colorado River exactly where Poston and Gray had recommended. Love, *From Brothel to Boomtown*, 15; Sheridan, *Arizona*, 123–24.
43. Love, *From Brothel to Boomtown*, 15; Love, "Poston and the Birth of Yuma," 409.
44. Heintzelman, Journal, July 14, 1854.
45. Love agrees that Colorado City was not surveyed until at least July 14 (*From Brothel to Boomtown*, 14).
46. Preemption Act of 1841, Section 10.
47. SCAW, Box 36, Folder 2. In the same location is a diagram of Colorado City that is helpful in envisioning the relative size and location of the tracts.
48. Heintzelman, Journal, July 14, 1854; Goodale, "Poston Manuscript," 178–79.
49. Goodale, "Poston Manuscript," 179n76. Goodale cites San Diego County Record Book E, p. 304.
50. "Reconnoisance in Sonora," 153; Poston, *Building a State in Apache Land*, 57.

51. Faulk, *Destiny Road*, 26.
52. Ibid.; Emory, *Notes of a Military Reconnoissance*, 100–101; Cooke, "Journal of the March of the Mormon Battalion," 204–5.
53. Cooke, "Journal of the March of the Mormon Battalion," 209–10, 209n212, 212–16, 218–19, 221–24, 227.
54. Emory, *Notes of a Military Reconnoissance*, 107–13.
55. Heintzelman's journal entries for July 15–23 indicate that he also followed this route from Fort Yuma to San Diego.
56. Heintzelman, Journal, July 31, 1854.
57. Heintzelman, Journal, August 4, 1854; Goodale, "Poston Manuscript," 182.
58. *Daily Alta California*, August 8, 1854.

Chapter 10

1. Goodale, "Poston Manuscript," 176–77.
2. Heintzelman, Journal, August 13, 1854.
3. Ibid., September 12, 13, 1854; Poston, *Building a State in Apache Land*, 62–63.
4. Thompson, *Civil War to the Bloody End*, 65.
5. A copy of the stock certificate is in SCAW, Box 23, Folder 1.
6. Poston, "Yuma City and Scaffold," *Phoenix Herald*, May 1, 1891, quoted in Gressinger, *Poston: Sunland Seer*, 18; Poston, "Southwestern Chronicle" II, 254.
7. SCAW, Box 36, Folder 2.
8. Poston, *Building a State in Apache Land*, 60. The report was addressed specifically to John C. McLemore. Poston says in the "Reconnoisance" (153) that the title papers of Colorado City were on record in San Diego County, "vesting the title to the property in yourself, Jno. C. McLemore, Charles D. Poston and Herman Ehrenberg Surveyor as Trustees." Confirming this is the fact that McLemore, Poston, and Ehrenberg are listed as the trustees of Colorado City on Poston's Colorado City stock certificate. That the "Reconnoisance" is addressed to McLemore suggests that he may have been the head of Poston's syndicate, a conclusion with which Love agrees (*From Brothel to Boomtown*, 12).
9. Goodale, "Poston Manuscript," 185.
10. "Reconnoisance in Sonora," 153.
11. Ibid. It is not known whether this effort was related to the other San Diego plan to build a railroad through the Yuma crossing to the Rio Grande, or whether it was a separate plan to build a line only to Colorado City.
12. Poston, *Building a State in Apache Land*, 60.
13. McKay, "Texas and the Southern Pacific Railroad," 24–25.
14. Reed, *History of the Texas Railroads*, 100.
15. Poston, *Building a State in Apache Land*, 60.
16. McKay, "Texas and the Southern Pacific Railroad," 24–25; Reed, *History of the Texas Railroads*, 99–101.
17. Poston, "Southwestern Chronicle" II, 254–55.
18. Poston, speech delivered in 1895, SCAW, Box 24, Folder 3.
19. Goodale, "Poston Manuscript," 201–2.

20. Haycraft, *History of Elizabethtown*, 159.
21. Poston, speech delivered in 1895, SCAW, Box 24, Folder 3.
22. Heintzelman, Journal, February 7, 1855. It took Heintzelman twenty-six days to travel from San Francisco to New York City (Journal, August 16, September 11, 1854). If Poston left San Francisco after Christmas and returned to the eastern United States by the same route as Heintzelman (Poston traveled via Nicaragua), he could have arrived at New York in late January (the destination he identified in his 1895 speech), gone immediately to Washington, and arrived at about the time Heintzelman indicates.
23. Ibid.
24. Poston, "In Memoriam: Col. Andrew B. Gray." Poston also says in this article that he saw Andrew Gray in Washington, but he does not say that Gray joined him in his lobbying efforts for Colorado City or a southern route for the transcontinental railroad.
25. "Reconnoisance in Sonora," 152; Kerckhoff, *Old Customhouse*, 4, 6, 39; Crowe and Brinckerhoff, *Early Yuma*, 41; Love, *From Brothel to Boomtown*, 8.
26. Kerckhoff, *Old Customhouse*, 4; Love, *Visitor's Guide to Historic Yuma*, 25.
27. Heintzelman, Journal, February 7, 9, 1855.
28. Barnes, *Arizona Place Names*, 104, 499.
29. Heintzelman, Journal, February 9, 1855. Mormons from southern Nevada had settled along the Colorado River north of Fort Yuma. They had to be supplied overland from St. Louis, nearly a thousand miles away. They would have welcomed military exploration that would open the river so they could be supplied by steamboat from the Gulf of California. Poston had spoken with General Wool about this in San Francisco in August 1854. Walker and Bufkin, *Historical Atlas of Arizona*, 28; Barnes, *Arizona Place Names*, 56; *Daily Alta California*, August 21, 1854; Poston, speech delivered in 1895, SCAW, Box 24, Folder 3.
30. Heintzelman, Journal, February 23, 1855.
31. Ibid., February 28, 1855.
32. Ibid., March 4, 1855; Poston, *Building a State in Apache Land*, 62–63. Poston calls the Atlantic & Pacific Company the "Texas Pacific Railroad Company."
33. Goodale, "Poston Manuscript," 187, 187n94.
34. Poston, *Building a State in Apache Land*, 63.
35. "Sonora—and the Value of its Silver Mines," 6.
36. The envelope is collected with the "Reconnoisance in Sonora" in the Fray Angélico Chavez History Library, Santa Fe.
37. Heintzelman, Journal, August 11–12, 1857.
38. *Daily Alta California*, July 27, 1859.
39. Hargett, "Pioneering at Yuma Crossing," 334, 339; Martin, *Yuma Crossing*, 170, 195–96.
40. The article was reprinted from the *Mariposa* (Calif.) *Gazette*, June 28, 1859.
41. Pumpelly, *My Reminiscences*, 258.
42. *Federal Census—Territory of New Mexico and Arizona*, 2–3.
43. Hargett, "Pioneering at Yuma Crossing," 336.
44. Ibid., 342; *Daily Alta California*, February 11, 1862.

45. McClintock, *Arizona*, 139; Crowe and Brinckerhoff, *Early Yuma*, 6. In 1865 Heintzelman sent a power of attorney to George Hooper to sell Heintzelman's interest in Colorado City (North, *Samuel Peter Heintzelman*, 17).
46. Masich, *Civil War in Arizona*, 94; Bancroft, *History of Arizona and New Mexico*, 615–16.
47. *Arizona Sentinel*, February 8, 1873.
48. Masich, *Civil War in Arizona*, 94–95.

Chapter 11

1. Wrobel, *Promised Lands*, 3–5.
2. Browne, *Adventures in the Apache Country*, 235–36. "Poston's Narrative" did not appear in any of the earlier versions of the *Adventures*. The first version was a series of ten articles published in the *San Francisco Evening Bulletin*, January–April 1864, under the title "A Trip Through Arizona." The second version was series of six articles published in *Harper's Monthly* in 1864–65 under the title "A Tour of Arizona." "Poston's Narrative" first appeared in the 1869 publication of *Adventures in the Apache Country*. Browne may have had the "Narrative" from Poston in 1864 as he says in the *Adventures*, but he did not publish it until five years later.
3. Browne himself was confused by the state of the "Narrative," calling it a "confused mass of manuscript," and it is possible that he tried to edit some of it. Near the beginning is a sentence describing Poston and Ehrenberg in the third person, something not found in other Poston writings: "Among them [the Sonoran expedition party] were two men whose names afterward became identified with its [the Gadsden Purchase's] history—they were Charles D. Poston and Herman Ehrenberg, the one a native of Kentucky and the other a German" (*Adventures in the Apache Country*, 236, 237).
4. Browne, *Adventures in the Apache Country*, 236–37. The Gadsden Treaty was not ratified until June 29, 1854, four and a half months after Poston sailed for Mexico. So while knowledge that the treaty was being negotiated could have inspired Poston's plans, ratification would have come too late to do so.
5. Ibid., 237.
6. Ibid., 238. A number of historians have repeated the story that the *Zoraida* was wrecked, including Myers, Preface, 22; Gressinger, *Poston: Sunland Seer*, 7–8; and Lockwood, *Pioneer Days in Arizona*, 131. But as a comparison of the "Reconnoisance" and the "Narrative" shows, they were misled by Poston. Even in the "Reconnoisance," Poston uses the heading "Wrecked" when describing what happened to the *Zoraida* (127).
7. Browne, *Adventures in the Apache Country*, 238–41.
8. Ibid., 252–54.
9. Goodale agrees that Poston did not travel to the Santa Cruz valley in 1854 ("Poston Manuscript," 149n37), and Love considers the Browne account "obviously in error" ("Poston and the Birth of Yuma," 405).
10. Poston, *Building a State in Apache Land*, 63–64. Compare "Possessions and Prospects of the Sonora Silver Mining Company," 2–4.

11. Poston, *Building a State in Apache Land*, 47–48.
12. Ibid., 48.
13. Ibid., 55.
14. The story of Poston's 1854 exploration of the Santa Cruz valley is repeated in Goff, *Charles D. Poston*, 10; Gressinger, *Poston: Sunland Seer*, 15; Lockwood, *Pioneer Days in Arizona*, 131; and Wyllys, *Arizona*, 118.
15. Poston, speech delivered in 1895, SCAW, Box 24, Folder 3.
16. Ibid.
17. The señoritas may have had something to do with reducing Poston's party, but mostly what caused men to leave him was the expedition's failure to make discoveries of any profit to them, combined with the hardships of the journey. Poston acknowledges that the difficulty of the Adair Bay trip, in particular, drove men away from him ("Reconnoisance in Sonora," 148).
18. Poston, "Yuma City and Scaffold," *Phoenix Herald*, May 1, 1891.
19. Pumpelly, *My Reminiscences*, 258.
20. Corle, *The Gila*, 187–92; Goff, *Charles D. Poston*, 10; Gressinger, *Poston: Sunland Seer*, 17; Hargett, "Pioneering at Yuma Crossing," 335–36; Martin, *Yuma Crossing*, 179; Myers, in Poston, *Building a State in Apache Land*, 146n23; Ornish, *Ehrenberg*, 53–54 (quotes Pumpelly's story). Love considers the Poston-Jaeger story invented (*Brothel to Boomtown*, 15; "Poston and the Birth of Yuma," 404); North considers it "legendary and questionable" (*Samuel Peter Heintzelman*, 16). Goodale is noncommittal about the story's accuracy ("Poston Manuscript," 171).
21. Poston, *Building a State in Apache Land*, 56–57.
22. Pumpelly, *My Reminiscences*, 258.
23. Poston, "Diary of a Pioneer."
24. Gilluly, *Ajo Mining District*, 98; Rose, *Ancient Mines of Ajo*, 18, 21–23; Gray, *Report*, 166; *Report of the Governor of Arizona to the Secretary of the Interior*, 48.
25. Mining historian Ira B. Joralemon says that "most of the ore [on the ground at Ajo] that looked so rich was only stained by copper carbonate, so that it assayed one or two percent copper" (*Copper*, 172–73). In other words, Poston may have discovered that the samples he collected at Ajo were worthless.
26. Poston, "In Memoriam: Col. Andrew B. Gray."
27. Poston, speech delivered in 1895, SCAW, Box 24, Folder 3.
28. Goodale, "Poston Manuscript," 202–3.

Postscript

1. North, *Samuel Peter Heintzelman*, 21–22; Poston, *Building a State in Apache Land*, 63–64; Sacks, "Charles Debrille Poston," 5–6; "Sonora—and the Value of its Silver Mines," 4.
2. "Sonora—and the Value of its Silver Mines," 41–42; Poston, "In Memoriam" [Ehrenberg]. Poston and Ehrenberg may have heard about the Santa Cruz valley silver mines from the Astiazaráns while in Sonora in 1854. Joaquin Astiazarán owned the huge Sopori land grant in the Santa Cruz valley, which was included in the Gadsden Purchase. In 1881 testimony before the U.S. surveyor general, Poston said

Notes to Pages 116–119 • 173

that he had learned about Sopori and other ranches in the Santa Cruz valley while he was in Mexico in 1854. He also said that Ehrenberg had told him about Sopori before Poston arrived in Arizona in 1856 (*Letter from the Secretary of the Interior*, 53, 67). Poston's statement confirms that Ehrenberg did visit the Santa Cruz valley before Poston reached Arizona and that he told Poston what he had found there.

3. Poston, "Southwestern Chronicle" II, 255; North, *Samuel Peter Heintzelman*, 25.
4. North, *Samuel Peter Heintzelman*, 28, 40–42.
5. Ibid., 148.
6. Ibid., 171.
7. Goff, *Charles D. Poston*, 25.
8. Poston, "Southwestern Chronicle" II, 256; Pumpelly, *My Reminiscences*, 245–66.
9. North, *Samuel Peter Heintzelman*, 175; Arizona Mining Company Reports, SCAW, Box 44, Folder 18; Poston, "The United States and Apache Indians, Indian Depredation Claim No. 3254," SCAW, Box 24, Folder 3.
10. Arizona already was a part of New Mexico Territory, but many Arizonans wanted Arizona to be a separate territory, with its own governor, legislature, and courts.
11. The political process by which Arizona became a U.S. territory and Poston's contribution to that process are admirably detailed in Sacks, *Be It Enacted*.
12. Gressinger, *Poston: Sunland Seer*, 97–99.
13. Ibid., 99–113.
14. Goff, *Charles D. Poston*, 46–48.
15. Ibid.; Gressinger, *Poston: Sunland Seer*, 118–20; Poston, "Southwestern Chronicle" II, 258–59.
16. Poston, "Southwestern Chronicle" II, 259n15.
17. Goff, *Charles D. Poston*, 51–52.
18. Brayer, *William Blackmore*, 102n12. Blackmore was among the first to employ the strategy of bringing together "pools" of investors in major land deals, rather than pursuing only wealthy individual investors. Blackmore was especially interested in American land and mining properties. When Poston met him, Blackmore had already purchased a large tract of land, the Sangre de Cristo Grant, in New Mexico and Colorado (ibid., 6–7). Sacks says that one of Poston's attempted business ventures late in his career was the promotion of a trans-Mexico railroad ("Charles Debrille Poston," 11). The fact that the manuscript of the "Reconnoisance in Sonora" is in the William Blackmore Collection at the Chavez History Library in Santa Fe suggests that Poston gave it to Blackmore, perhaps for the purpose of persuading him of the value of San Juan Bautista Bay as a port and railroad terminus.
19. Gressinger, *Poston: Sunland Seer*, 120; Goff, *Charles D. Poston*, 53.
20. Poston, "Southwestern Chronicle" II, 259.
21. Ibid., 260–61.
22. Poston, "Southwestern Chronicle" III, 353.
23. Ibid., 359, 359n21.
24. North, *Samuel Peter Heintzelman*, 175.
25. Gressinger, *Poston: Sunland Seer*, 167; Goff, *Charles D. Poston*, 56–57.

26. North, *Samuel Peter Heintzelman*, 175.
27. Goff, *Charles D. Poston*, 56; Gressinger, *Poston: Sunland Seer*, 167–68.
28. Goff, *Charles D. Poston*, 57. The Arivaca Land and Cattle Company took its claim to the U.S. Court of Private Land Claims, established by Congress in 1891. But the court decided that the description of Ortiz's original Arivaca grant was too indefinite to determine what the grant's boundaries were and thus declared the Arivaca company's title invalid.
29. Poston, "Southwestern Chronicle" III, 356; Poston, "The United States and Apache Indians, Indian Depredation Claim No. 3254," SCAW, Box 24, Folder 3.
30. Gressinger, *Poston: Sunland Seer*, 182; Goff, *Charles D. Poston*, 61.
31. Goff, *Charles D. Poston*, 61–62.
32. Sacks, "Charles Debrille Poston," 11.
33. Poston, "Southwestern Chronicle" III, 354–55.
34. Goff, *Charles D. Poston*, 58; McClintock, *Arizona*, 595–96. Mattie outlived Charles Poston but never remarried.
35. It was published in San Francisco by A. L. Bancroft & Company, Printers, 1878.
36. Goff, *Charles D. Poston*, 55–56.
37. SCAW, Box 24, Folder 2.
38. Goff, *Charles D. Poston*, 56.
39. *Tucson Daily Citizen*, June 26, 1902; Poston, "Southwestern Chronicle" III, 359; Gressinger, *Poston: Sunland Seer*, 188. The territorial pension of twenty-five dollars a month was granted on March 15, 1899. In 1901 the legislature increased the amount to thirty-five dollars a month (Gressinger, *Poston: Sunland Seer*, 190).
40. *Tucson Daily Citizen*, June 26, 1902.
41. Goff, *Charles D. Poston*, 63.
42. *Tucson Daily Citizen*, June 26, 1902.
43. Goff, *Charles D. Poston*, 63–64.
44. Poston, "Southwestern Chronicle" III, 359.
45. Gustavus Pope to Kelly, SCAW, Box 24, Folder 4. Ironically, Sarah died in March 1854, just four months before her father, although it is unlikely that Charles knew about her death. When Sarah's husband, army doctor Colonel Benjamin F. Pope, was assigned duty in Manila and died there on February 14, 1902, Sarah and her children sailed back to the United States with his body. But she died at sea of dysentery contracted before she left. Goff, *Charles D. Poston*, 63.

Appendix

1. A photocopy of the original can be found in the Poston Papers, Arizona Historical Society, Tucson.
2. North, *Samuel Peter Heintzelman*, 23.
3. Cited in Goodale, "Poston Manuscript," 112n91.
4. This appears to be the communication Poston refers to in *Building a State in Apache Land*, when he says that when he returned to San Francisco after the expedition, he "laid the result of the reconnaissance ... before the 'Syndicate'" (60).

5. Poston spells "Navachiste" as "Navachista." According to www.worldatlas.com, Navachiste Bay is at latitude N 25°27′, longitude W 108°50′. Zoraida is a character in Cervantes's *Don Quixote*. Her name, which is Arabic in origin, means "enchanting woman," an appropriate name for a ship bearing men seeking their fortune in an exotic land.

6. Macapule extends northwest and southeast, very close to the mainland, so it is understandable that Poston would be unsure on first sight whether it was an island or peninsula. His "twelve miles" seems to refer to the length of the island, extending from near the mainland at its southeastern end, out into the entrance to both the Macapule and Navachiste bays. Poston may be mistaking the small bay inside Macapule Island for Navachiste's main harbor just to the north. This would not be surprising. Navachiste is a complex of islands and lagoons close to one another.

7. The journey by land from Navachiste Bay near Macapule through the towns of Fuerta and Alamos to Guaymas would have been closer to 250 miles.

8. Poston is suggesting that the "old Spaniard" was a smuggler.

9. The significance of Poston's writing "June" here is unclear. He may be reporting what he has heard about the weather in Guaymas in June, although by his own account, Poston was not in Guaymas in June. He later says that on June 1, 1854, he was in Hermosillo and that after that he followed Colonel Andrew B. Gray's expedition to northern Sonora and Adair Bay.

10. Guaymas was Sonora's main port on the Gulf of California for most of the nineteenth and early twentieth centuries and is today the principal port of Sonora.

11. An "alameda" is a boulevard.

12. This distance might be accurate if Poston traveled to a point opposite the southern end of Tiburon. If he traveled to a point opposite the northern end of the island, at the site of his proposed port city, the distance would be closer to seventy-five miles (www.worldatlas.com).

13. The dimensions of Tiburon at its longest and widest points are about thirty-three miles long by twenty-one miles wide (www.worldatlas.com).

14. The dimensions of the bay are closer to one mile wide near the middle of the island to twenty-one miles wide at the island's southern end, and forty-five miles long from the northernmost reach of the bay at "Cockle Harbor" to the southern end of Tiburon (www.worldatlas.com).

15. No evidence exists of any attachments to Poston's report.

16. Poston places quotation marks at the beginning of this sentence, as if he is quoting a document. But he does not close the quotation or identify its source.

17. The "company" would have been the Texas Western Railroad.

18. The "original grantee" was Joaquin Astiazarán.

19. Poston is incorrect here. In March 1854 Santa Anna replaced Gándara as governor of Sonora with General Yáñez. Gándara was not returned to the governorship until 1855. Bancroft, *History of the North Mexican States*, 681; Voss, *On the Periphery*, 136.

20. Poston appears to have written "northwestern" and then revised by writing an "Ea" over the "we" to make "northeastern."

21. No evidence exists of another report.

22. Poston left Hermosillo on June 1 and arrived at Fort Yuma on July 11, so he had been away from "civilization" for a little less than six weeks.

23. The Treaty of Guadalupe Hidalgo, which ended the war between the United States and Mexico.

24. Poston refers to John Russell Bartlett, who led the U.S. Boundary Commission charged with surveying the boundary between Mexico and the United States through New Mexico Territory after the 1846–47 war.

25. From here, Poston quotes Bartlett through "for so long a distance." He does so by placing double quotation marks at the beginning of each line of the quoted text. The quotation, which includes a subquotation from the Treaty of Guadalupe Hidalgo, is not continuous in Bartlett's text but is in two separate locations. It can be found in Bartlett, *Personal Narrative*, 2:158–59, 160–61.

26. The quotation from Article V of the treaty is only approximate. The actual wording is, "And, in order to preclude all difficulty in tracing upon the ground the limit separating Upper from Lower California, it is agreed that the said limit shall consist of a straight line, drawn from the middle of the Rio Gila, where it unites with the Colorado, to a point on the Coast of the Pacific Ocean, distant one marine league due south of the southernmost point of the Port of San Diego, according to the plan of said port made in the year 1782, by Don Juan Pantoja, second Sailing-Master of the Spanish fleet, and published at Madrid in the year 1802, in the Atlas to the voyage of the schooners *Sutil* and *Mexicana*." "Treaty of Guadalupe Hidalgo," 24.

27. "Mdse." is a common abbreviation for "merchandise."

28. In *Building a State in Apache Land* (57), Poston says that the size of the Colorado City plat was 936 acres.

29. "The Great Western," whose real name was Sarah Bowman, was a well-known frontier prostitute and brothel keeper. Thompson, *Civil War to the Bloody End*, 62.

30. "Obt. sert." was a common abbreviation for "obedient servant."

Bibliography

Collections

Poston Papers, 1844–1891. Arizona Historical Society, Tucson.
Sacks Collection of the American West (SCAW). Arizona Historical Society, Tempe.

Newspapers

Daily Alta California
Sacramento Daily Union
Sacramento Transcript
San Francisco Daily Herald
Weekly Alta California

Books, Articles, Chapters, and Maps

Acuña, Rodolfo. *Occupied America: A History of Chicanos*. 2nd ed. New York: Harper & Row, 1981.
———. *Sonoran Strongman: Ignacio Pesquiera and His Times*. Tucson: University of Arizona Press, 1974.
Anza, Juan Bautista de. "Anza's Complete Diary, 1774." In *Anza's California Expeditions*, vol. 2: *Opening a Land Route to California*, translated and edited by Herbert Eugene Bolton. New York: Russell & Russell, 1966.
———. "Anza's Diary of the Second Anza Expedition." In *Anza's California Expeditions*, vol. 3: *The San Francisco Colony*, translated and edited by Herbert Eugene Bolton. New York: Russell & Russell, 1966.
Audubon, John Woodhouse. *Audubon's Western Journal, 1849–1850: Being the MS. Record of a Trip from New York to Texas, and an Overland Journey through Mexico and Arizona to the Gold-fields of California*. Edited by Frank Heywood Hodder. Glorieta, N.Mex.: Rio Grande Press, 1969.
Balmori, Diana, Stuart F. Voss, and Miles Wortman. *Notable Family Networks in Latin America*. Chicago: University of Chicago Press, 1984.

Bancroft, Hubert Howe. *California Inter Pocula*. San Francisco: The History Company, 1888.

——. *History of Arizona and New Mexico 1530–1888*. San Francisco: The History Company, 1889.

——. *History of California*. Vol. 6, 1848–1859. San Francisco: The History Company, 1888.

——. *History of the North Mexican States and Texas*. Vol. 2, 1810–1889. San Francisco: The History Company, 1889.

Barnes, Will C. *Arizona Place Names*. Tucson: University of Arizona Press, 1988.

Bartlett, John Russell. *Personal Narrative of Explorations and Incidents in Texas, New Mexico, California, Sonora, and Chihuahua*. 2 vols. New York: D. Appleton and Company, 1854. Reprint, Chicago: Rio Grande Press, 1965.

Bauer, K. Jack. *The Mexican War, 1846–1848*. Lincoln: University of Nebraska Press, 1974.

Bean, John Lowell, and William Marvin Mason, eds. *Diaries and Accounts of the Romero Expeditions in Arizona and California, 1823–1826*. Palm Springs, Calif.: Palm Springs Desert Museum, 1962.

Bieber, Ralph P., ed. *Southern Trails to California*. Glendale, Calif.: The Arthur H. Clark Company, 1937.

Bolton, Herbert Eugene. *Rim of Christendom: A Biography of Eusebio Francisco Kino, Pacific Coast Pioneer*. New York: Russell & Russell, 1960.

——. *Spanish Exploration in the Southwest, 1542–1706*. New York: Barnes & Noble, 1908.

Brack, Gene M. *Mexico Views Manifest Destiny, 1821–1846: An Essay on the Origins of the Mexican War*. Albuquerque: University of New Mexico Press, 1975.

Brandes, Ray. *Frontier Military Posts of Arizona*. Globe, Ariz.: Dale Stuart King, 1960.

Brayer, Herbert O. *William Blackmore: The Spanish-Mexican Land Grants of New Mexico and Colorado 1863–1878*. Denver: Bradford-Robinson, 1949.

Brown, Charles H. *Agents of Manifest Destiny: The Lives and Times of the Filibusters*. Chapel Hill: University of North Carolina Press, 1980.

Browne, J. Ross. *Adventures in the Apache Country: A Tour through Arizona and Sonora with Notes on the Silver Regions of Nevada*. New York: Promontory Press, 1974.

Calvo Berber, Laureano. *Nociones de historia de Sonora*. Mexico City: Librería de Manual Porrua, S.A., 1958.

Christensen, Carol, and Thomas Christensen. *The U.S.-Mexican War*. San Francisco: Bay Books, 1998.

Clark, Hal, and Doris Clark. *The Oatman Story*. Kingman, Ariz.: H & H Printers, 2002.

Cline, Howard F. *The United States and Mexico*. Cambridge: Cambridge University Press, 1953.

Conkling, Roscoe P., and Margaret B. Conkling. *The Butterfield Overland Mail, 1857–1869: Its Organization and Operation over the Southern Route to 1861*. Vol. 2. Glendale, Calif.: A. H. Clark Co., 1947.

Cooke, Philip St. George. "Cooke's Journal of the March of the Mormon Battalion, 1846–1847." In *Exploring Southwestern Trails, 1846–1854*, edited by Ralph P.

Bieber in collaboration with Averam B. Bender. Glendale, Calif.: The Arthur H. Clark Co., 1938.

Corle, Edwin. *The Gila: River of the Southwest*. New York: Rinehart & Company, 1951.

Couts, Cave Johnson. *Hepah, California! The Journal of Cave Johnson Couts from Monterey, Nuevo Leon, Mexico, to Los Angeles, California, during the Years, 1848–1849*. Edited by Henry F. Dobyns. Tucson: Arizona Pioneers' Historical Society, 1961.

Cox, C. C. "From Texas to California in 1849: The Diary of C. C. Cox." Edited by Mabelle E. Martin. *Southwestern Historical Quarterly* 29 (1925–26): 36–50, 128–46, 201–12.

Crowe, Rosalie, and Sidney B. Brinckerhoff, eds. *Early Yuma: A Graphic History of Life on the American Nile*. Yuma: Northland Press, 1976.

Deeds, Susan M. "Indigenous Rebellions on the Northern Mexican Mission Frontier." In *Contested Ground: Comparative Frontiers on the Northern and Southern Edges of the Spanish Empire*, edited by Donna J. Guy and Thomas E. Sheridan, 32–51. Tucson: University of Arizona Press, 1998.

Del Castillo, Richard Griswold. *The Treaty of Guadalupe Hidalgo: A Legacy of Conflict*. Norman: University of Oklahoma Press, 1990.

Dobie, J. Frank. *Coronado's Children: Tales of Lost Mines and Buried Treasures of the Southwest*. Dallas: The Southwest Press, 1930.

Eccleston, Robert. *Overland to California on the Southwestern Trail*. Berkeley: University of California Press, 1950.

Ehrenberg, Herman. "Map of the Gadsden Purchase: Sonora and Portions of New Mexico, Chihuahua & California by Herman Ehrenberg, from his Private Notes, & Those of Major Heintzelman, Captn. Sitgreaves, Lieut. Derby; Bartlett, Gray, Julius Froebel & Others; Lith'y by Alex Zakreski." 1854. Arizona Historical Society, Tucson.

Emory, William H. *Notes of a Military Reconnoissance*. Washington, D.C.: Wendell and Van Benthuysen, 1848.

———. *Report of the United States and Mexican Boundary Survey, Made Under the Direction of the Secretary of the Interior*. Vol. 1. Washington, D.C.: A. G. P. Nicholson, Printer, 1857.

Etter, Patricia A. *To California on the Southern Route, 1849: A History and Annotated Bibliography*. Spokane: Arthur H. Clark, 1998.

Fages, Pedro. "The Colorado River Campaign, 1781–1782: The Diary of Pedro Fages." Edited by Herbert Ingram Priestly. *Publications of the Academy of Pacific Coast History* 3 (May 1913): 133–233.

Faulk, Odie B., ed. "A Colonization Plan for Northern Sonora, 1850." *New Mexico Historical Review* 44 (October 1969): 293–314.

———. *Destiny Road: The Gila Trail and the Opening of the Southwest*. New York: Oxford University Press, 1973.

———. *Too Far North, Too Far South*. Los Angeles: Westernlore Press, 1967.

Federal Census—Territory of New Mexico and Territory of Arizona. 89th Congress, 1st Session. Senate Document No. 13. Washington, D.C.: Government Printing Office, 1965.

Font, Fr. Fray Pedro. "Diary of an Expedition to Monterey by Way of the Colorado River." In *Anza's California Expeditions*, vol. 4: *Font's Complete Diary of the Second Anza Expedition*, translated and edited by Herbert Eugene Bolton. Berkeley: University of California Press, 1930.

Forbes, Jack D. "Development of the Yuma Route before 1846." *California Historical Society Quarterly* 43 (June 1964): 99–118.

"Gadsden Treaty." In *U.S.-Mexico Borderlands: Historical and Contemporary Perspectives*, edited by Oscar J. Martinez, 38–43. Wilmington, Del.: Scholarly Resources, 1996.

Garate, Donald T. *Juan Bautista de Anza: Basque Explorer in the New World*. Reno: University of Nevada Press, 2003.

———. "Who Named Arizona? The Basque Connection." *Journal of Arizona History* 40:1 (1999): 53–82.

Garber, Paul N. *The Gadsden Treaty*. Philadelphia: University of Pennsylvania Press, 1923.

Garcés, Fr. Fray Francisco. "Garcés' Diary from Tubac to San Gabriel, 1774." In *Anza's California Expeditions*, vol. 2: *Opening a Land Route to California*, translated and edited by Herbert Eugene Bolton. New York: Russell & Russell, 1966.

Gilluly, James. *The Ajo Mining District*. Washington, D.C.: Government Printing Office, 1946.

Goff, John S. *Charles D. Poston*. Cave Creek, Ariz.: Black Mountain Press, 1995.

Goodale, Roy L. "Poston Manuscript" (1979). Roy L. Goodale Collection, Box 2, Folders 3–4, Arizona Historical Society, Tempe.

Gray, Andrew B. *The A. B. Gray Report: Survey of a Route on the 32nd Parallel for the Texas Western Railroad, 1854, and Including the Reminiscences of Peter R. Brady who Accompanied the Expedition*. Edited by L. R. Bailey. Los Angeles: Westernlore Press, 1963.

Gressinger, A. W. *Charles D. Poston: Sunland Seer*. Globe, Ariz.: Dale Stuart King 1961.

Guy, Donna J., and Thomas E. Sheridan. "On Frontiers: The Northern and Southern Edges of the Spanish Empire in the Americas." In *Contested Ground: Comparative Frontiers on the Northern and Southern Edges of the Spanish Empire*, edited by Donna J. Guy and Thomas E. Sheridan, 3–15. Tucson: University of Arizona Press, 1998.

Hague, Harlan. *The Road to California: The Search for a Southern Overland Route*. Glendale, Calif.: Arthur H. Clark Co., 1978.

Hanchett, Leland, Jr., ed. *Crossing Arizona*. Phoenix: Pine Rim Publishing, 2002.

Hardy, R. W. H. *Travels in the Interior of Mexico, in 1825, 1826, 1827 & 1828*. London: H. Colburn and R. Bentley, 1829. Reprint, Glorieta, N. Mex.: Rio Grande Press, 1977.

Hargett, Janet L. "Pioneering at Yuma Crossing: The Business Career of L. J. F. Jaeger 1850–1887." *Arizona and the West* 25:4 (Winter 1983): 329–54.

Hartmann, William K. *Desert Heart: Chronicles of the Sonoran Desert*. Tucson: Fisher Books, 1989.

Haycraft, Samuel. *A History of Elizabethtown, Kentucky and Its Surroundings*. 1869. Reprint, Elizabethtown: The Women's Club of Elizabethtown, Kentucky, 1921.

Heintzelman, Samuel Peter. Journals. Samuel Peter Heintzelman Papers, Library of Congress, Washington, D.C.

Hietala, Thomas R. *Manifest Design: Anxious Aggrandizement in Late Jacksonian America*. Ithaca: Cornell University Press, 1985.

Hopkins, Caspar T. "The California Recollections of Caspar T. Hopkins." *California Historical Society Quarterly* 25:2 (1946): 97–120.

———. "The California Recollections of Caspar T. Hopkins (Continued)." *California Historical Society Quarterly* 25:4 (1946): 325–46.

Hu-DeHart, Evelyn. *Yaqui Resistance and Survival: The Struggle for Land and Autonomy, 1821–1910*. Madison: University of Wisconsin Press, 1984.

Humboldt, Alexander Von. *Political Essay on the Kingdom of New Spain*. Vol. 3. Translated by John Black. 2nd ed. London: Longman, Hurst, Rees, Orme, and Brown; and H. Colburn, 1814.

Ives, Ronald L. *Land of Lava, Ash, and Sand: The Pinacate Region of Northwestern Mexico*. Compiled by James W. Byrkit and Karen J. Dahood. Tucson: Arizona Historical Society, 1989.

Joralemon, Ira B. *Copper: The Encompassing Story of Mankind's First Metal*. Berkeley: Howell-North Books, 1973.

Kerckhoff, Mary Ben. *The Old Customhouse (Quartermasters' Residence at Yuma Crossing)*. Yuma: Sun Printing Company, 1976.

Kino, Eusebio Francisco. *Kino's Historical Memoir of Pimería Alta: An Account of the Beginnings of California, Sonora, and Arizona*. Cleveland: The Arthur H. Clark Company, 1919. Reprint, Bedford, Mass.: Applewood Books, n.d.

Kiser, William S. *Turmoil on the Rio Grande: The Territorial History of the Mesilla Valley, 1846–1853*. College Station: Texas A & M University Press, 2011.

Knapp, Frank A., Jr. "Mexican Fear of Manifest Destiny in California." In *Essays in Mexican History*, edited by E. Cotner and Carlos E. Castañeda, 192–208. Austin: University of Texas Press, 1958.

Lamar, Howard Roberts. *The Far Southwest 1846–1912: A Territorial History*. New Haven: Yale University Press, 1966.

Letter from the Secretary of the Interior Transmitting Pursuant to Section 8 of the Act of July 22, 1854, Extended by the Sundry Civil Act of July 15, 1870, Certain Papers Relating to the Private Land Claim in the Territory of Arizona Known as El Sopori. United States Congress. 48th Congress, 1st Session. Executive Document No. 93, January 12, 1882.

Limerick, Patricia Nelson. *The Legacy of Conquest: The Unbroken Past of the American West*. New York: W. W. Norton, 1987.

Lockwood, Frank C. *Pioneer Days in Arizona*. New York: Macmillan, 1932.

Love, Frank. "Poston and the Birth of Yuma: The Father of Arizona Invents a Story." *Journal of Arizona History* 19 (Winter 1978): 403–16.

———. *From Brothel to Boomtown: Yuma's Naughty Past*. Colorado Springs: Little London Press, 1981.

———. *A Visitor's Guide to Historic Yuma*. Colorado Springs: Little London Press, 1982.

Lumholtz, Carl. *New Trails in Mexico: An Account of One Year's Exploration in North-western Sonora, Mexico, and South-western Arizona, 1909–1910*. New York: Scribner's, 1912. Reprint, Tucson: University of Arizona Press, 1990.

Manje, Juan Mateo. *Unknown Arizona and Sonora*. Translated by H. J. Karns. Tucson: Arizona Silhouettes, 1954.

Martin, Douglas D. *Yuma Crossing*. Albuquerque: University of New Mexico Press, 1954.

Martinez, Oscar J. "Filibustering and Racism in the Borderlands." In *U.S.-Mexico Borderlands: Historical and Contemporary Perspectives*, edited by Oscar J. Martinez, 46–49. Wilmington, Del.: Scholarly Resources, 1996.

Masich, Andrew E. *The Civil War in Arizona: The Story of the California Volunteers, 1861–1865*. Norman: University of Oklahoma Press, 2006.

Mattison, Ray H. "Early Spanish and Mexican Settlements in Arizona." *New Mexico Historical Review* 21:4 (1946): 273–327.

McClintock, James H. *Arizona, Prehistoric, Aboriginal, Pioneer, Modern*. Vol. 2. Chicago: S. J. Clarke Publishing Co., 1916.

McGinty, Brian. *The Oatman Massacre: A Tale of Desert Captivity and Survival*. Norman: University of Oklahoma Press, 2005.

McKay, S. S. "Texas and the Southern Pacific Railroad, 1848–1860." *Southwestern Historical Quarterly* 35 (1931): 1–27.

Merk, Frederick. *Manifest Destiny and Mission in American History: A Reinterpretation*. New York: Alfred A. Knopf, 1963.

Mexal, Stephen J. *Reading for Liberalism: The* Overland Monthly *and the Writing of the Modern American West*. Lincoln: University of Nebraska Press, 2013.

Michler, Lt. N. "Report of Lt. Michler." In William H. Emory, *Report of the United States and Mexican Boundary Survey, Made Under the Direction of the Secretary of the Interior*, 1:101-28. Washington, D.C.: A. G. P. Nicholson, Printer, 1857.

Moody, Ralph L. *Old Trails West*. New York: T. Y. Crowell, 1963.

Myers, John Myers. Preface to *Building a State in Apache Land: With a Preface and Explanatory Notes by John Myers Myers*, by Charles D. Poston, 11–38. Tempe: Aztec Press, 1963.

Nentvig, Juan. *Rudo Ensayo: A Description of Sonora and Arizona in 1764*. Translated by Alberto Francisco Pradeau and Robert R. Rasmussen. Tucson: University of Arizona Press, 1980.

North, Diane M. T. *Samuel Peter Heintzelman and the Sonora Exploring & Mining Company*. Tucson: University of Arizona Press, 1980.

Notables of the West: Being the Portraits and Biographies of the Progressive Men of the West. Vol. 2. New York: International News Service, 1915.

Officer, James E. "Mining in Hispanic Arizona: Myth and Reality." In *History of Mining in Arizona*, edited by J. Michael Canty and Michael N. Greeley, 2:1–26. Tucson: Mining Club of the Southwest Foundation, 1991.

Ornish, Natalie. *Ehrenberg: Goliad Survivor, Old West Explorer*. Dallas: Texas Heritage Press, 1997.

O'Sullivan, John L. "Annexation." *Democratic Review* 17 (July/August 1845): 5–10.

The Other Side; Or, Notes for the History of the War Between Mexico and the United States. Translated and edited by Albert C. Ramsey. New York: John Wiley, 1850. Reprint, Whitefish, Mon.: Kessinger Publishing, 2012.

Pahissa, Angela Moyano. "The Mesilla Treaty, or Gadsden Purchase." In *U.S.-Mexico Borderlands: Historical and Contemporary Perspectives*, edited by Oscar J. Martinez, 10–12. Wilmington, Del.: Scholarly Resources, 1996.

Pattie, James O. *The Personal Narrative of James O. Pattie of Kentucky*. Edited by Timothy Flint. Santa Barbara, Calif.: The Narrative Press, 2001.

Polzer, Charles W., S.J. "Legends of Lost Missions and Mines." In *Brand Book 2 of the Tucson Corral of the Westerners, A Collection of Smoke Signals*, edited by Otis H. Chidester, nos. 11–20, 1965–69, 169–83. Tucson: Tucson Corral of the Westerners, Inc., 1971.

"Possessions and Prospects of the Sonora Silver Mining Company. Report of the Sonora Exploring and Mining Co., Made to The Stockholders." September 1857. Cincinnati: Railroad Record Print, 1857.

Poston, Charles D. *Apache-Land*. San Francisco: A. L. Bancroft & Company, Printers, 1878.

———. *Building a State in Apache Land: With a Preface and Explanatory Notes by John Myers Myers*. Tempe: Aztec Press, 1963.

———. "Building a State in Apache Land I: How the Territory Was Acquired." *Overland Monthly and Out West Magazine* 24:139 (July 1894): 87–93.

———. "Building a State in Apache Land II: Early Mining and Filibustering." *Overland Monthly and Out West Magazine* 24:140 (August 1894): 203–11.

———. "Diary of a Pioneer: My First Fourth of July in the Territory of Arizona." *Graham County Bulletin*, July 15, 1992.

———. "In Memoriam" [on Herman Ehrenberg]. *Arizona Daily Star*, February 26, 1880.

———. "In Memoriam: Col. Andrew B. Gray." *Arizona Weekly Star*, March 4, 1880.

———. "Reconnoisance in Sonora." William Blackmore Collection, Box 2, Folder 1, Fray Angélico Chavez History Library, New Mexico History Museum, Palace of the Governors, Santa Fe, New Mexico.

———. "Southwestern Chronicle: The Journals of Charles D. Poston 1850–1899." Edited by Byrd Howell Granger. *Arizona Quarterly* 13:2 (Summer 1957): 152–63; part II, *Arizona Quarterly* 13:3 (Autumn 1957), 251–61; part III, *Arizona Quarterly* 13:4 (Winter 1957): 353–62.

———. "Yuma City and Scaffold." *Phoenix Herald*, May 1, 1891. Charles Debrille Poston Biofile. Arizona Historical Society, Tucson.

Pourade, Richard F. *Anza Conquers the Desert: The Anza Expeditions from Mexico to California and the Founding of San Francisco 1774 to 1776*. San Diego: Copley Books, 1971.

Pratt, Mary Louise. *Imperial Eyes: Travel Writing and Transculturation*. 2nd ed. London: Routledge, Taylor & Francis e-Library, 2007.

Preemption Act of 1841. 27th Congress, Chapter 16, 5 Stat. 453 (1841).

Pumpelly, Raphael. *My Reminiscences*. Vol. 1. New York: Henry Holt and Company, 1918.

Radding, Cynthia. "The Colonial Pact and Changing Ethnic Frontiers in Highland Sonora, 1740–1840." In *Contested Ground: Comparative Frontiers on the Northern and Southern Edges of the Spanish Empire*, edited by Donna J. Guy and Thomas E. Sheridan, 52–66. Tucson: University of Arizona Press, 1998.

———. *Wandering Peoples: Colonialism, Ethnic Spaces, and Ecological Frontiers in Northwestern Mexico, 1700–1850*. Durham: Duke University Press, 1997.

Reed, S. G. *A History of the Texas Railroads and of Transportation Conditions under Spain and Mexico and the Republic and the State*. Houston: St. Clair Publishing Company, 1941.

Report of the Governor of Arizona to the Secretary of the Interior 1899. Washington, D.C.: Government Printing Office, 1899.

Report of the Secretary of the Interior, in Compliance with a resolution of the Senate, of January 22, communicating a report and map of A. B. Gray, relative to the Mexican boundary. 32nd Congress, 2nd Session, Executive Document No. 55, February 8, 1855.

Rippy, J. Fred. *The United States and Mexico*. New York: Alfred A. Knopf, 1926.

Robinson, Samuel. "Arizona in 1861: A Contemporary Account by Samuel Robinson, with an Introduction and Annotations by Constance Wynn Altshuler." *Journal of Arizona History* 25 (Spring 1984): 21–76.

Rose, Dan. *The Ancient Mines of Ajo*. Published by author, 1936.

Sacks, Benjamin. *Be It Enacted: The Creation of the Territory of Arizona*. Phoenix: Arizona Historical Foundation, 1964.

———. "Charles Debrille Poston: Prince of Arizona Pioneers." *Smoke Signal* (publication of the Tucson Corral of the Westerners), no. 7 (Spring 1963).

Scroggs, William D. *Filibusters and Financiers: William Walker and His Associates*. New York: Macmillan and Company, 1916.

Sheridan, Thomas E. *Arizona: A History*. Rev. ed. Tucson: University of Arizona Press, 2012.

———. *Empire of Sand: The Seri Indians and the Struggle for Spanish Sonora, 1645–1803*. Tucson: University of Arizona Press, 1999.

———. *Landscapes of Fraud: Mission Tumacácori, the Baca Float, and the Betrayal of the O'odham*. Tucson: University of Arizona Press, 2006.

Slotkin, Richard. *The Fatal Environment: The Myth of the Frontier in the Age of Industrialization, 1800–1890*. Middletown, Conn.: Wesleyan University Press, 1986.

"Sonora—and the Value of its Silver Mines. Report of The Sonora Exploring and Mining Co., Made to the Stockholders. December 1856." Cincinnati: Railroad Record Print, 1856.

Soulé, Frank, John H. Gihon, M.D., and James Nisbet. *The Annals of San Francisco*. New York: D. Appleton & Company, 1855. Reprint, Berkeley: Berkeley Hills Books, 1999.

Spicer, Edward H. *Cycles of Conquest: The Impact of Spain, Mexico, and the United States on the Indians of the Southwest, 1533–1960*. Tucson: University of Arizona Press, 1962.

———. *The Yaquis: A Cultural History*. Tucson: University of Arizona Press, 1980.

Steel, Edward M. *T. Butler King of Georgia*. Athens: University of Georgia Press, 1964.

Stout, Joseph Allen, Jr. *The Liberators: Filibustering Expeditions into Mexico, 1848–1862 and the Last Thrust of Manifest Destiny.* Los Angeles: Westernlore Press, 1973.

———. "Post-War Filibustering, 1850–1865." In *The Mexican War: Changing Interpretations*, edited by Odie B. Faulk and Joseph A. Stout, 192–202. Chicago: Sage Press, 1973.

———. *Schemers & Dreamers: Filibustering in Mexico, 1848–1921.* Fort Worth: Texas Christian University Press, 2002.

Stratton, Royal B. *Captivity of the Oatman Girls: Being an Interesting Narrative of Life among the Apache and Mohave Indians.* New York: Carlton and Porter, 1859.

Thompson, Jerry. *Civil War to the Bloody End: The Life and Times of Major General Samuel P. Heintzelman.* College Station: Texas A&M University Press, 2006.

Trafzer, Clifford E. *Yuma: Frontier Crossing of the Far Southwest.* Wichita: Western Heritage Books, 1980.

"Treaty of Guadalupe Hidalgo." In *U.S.-Mexico Borderlands: Historical and Contemporary Perspectives*, edited by Oscar J. Martinez, 20–37. Wilmington, Del.: Scholarly Resources, 1996.

Trimble, Marshall. *Arizona: A Cavalcade of History.* Rev. ed. Tucson: Rio Nuevo Publishers, 2003.

———. "Charles Poston's Arizona Adventure." In *Marshall Trimble's Arizoniana: Stories from Old Arizona*, 61–71. Phoenix: Golden West Publishers, 1988, 2004.

Vasquez, Josephina Zoraida, and Lorenzo Meyer. *The United States and Mexico.* Chicago: University of Chicago Press, 1985.

Villa, Eduardo W. *Compendio de historia del estado de Sonora.* Mexico: Editorial Patria Nueva, 1937.

Voss, Stuart L. *On the Periphery of Nineteenth-Century Mexico: Sonora and Sinaloa 1810–1877.* Tucson: University of Arizona Press, 1982.

Wagoner, Jay J. *Early Arizona: Prehistory to Civil War.* Tucson: University of Arizona Press, 1985.

Walker, Henry P., and Don Bufkin. *Historical Atlas of Arizona.* Norman: University of Oklahoma Press, 1979.

Ward, H. G. *Mexico in 1827.* Vol. 2. London: Henry Colburn, 1828.

Weber, David J. *Foreigners in Their Native Land: Historical Roots of the Mexican Americans.* Albuquerque: University of New Mexico Press, 2003.

Wilson, Robert A. *Mexico and Its Religion.* New York: Harper and Brothers, 1855.

Wrobel, David M. *Promised Lands: Promotion, Memory, and the Creation of the American West.* Lawrence: University Press of Kansas, 2002.

Wyllys, Rufus K. *Arizona: The History of a Frontier State.* Phoenix: Hobson & Herr, 1950.

———. "The Republic of Lower California, 1854." *Pacific Historical Review* 2:2 (June 1933): 194–213.

Young, Otis E. *The West of Philip St. George Cooke, 1809–1895.* Glendale, Calif.: Arthur H. Clark Co., 1955.

Index

Page numbers in *italics* represent illustrations.

Adair Bay, 172n17; Gray's exploration of, 75–77; and Lieutenant Hardy, 78; and Poston, 108–9, 110, 113
Aguilar family: and control of commerce, 67; and Dolores, 63; and negotiations with Poston, 65; network of, 63; and Victor, 63
Alamos, Sonora, 52, 53, 54, 110
Almada family: and alliance by marriage with the Vega family, 53; and José, 52, 53, 55
American expansionism, 4, 99; and Manifest Destiny, 3, 7, 35–36; and northern Mexico, 26–27, 37
Ankrim, William, 86, 88, 89; and Colorado City, 90, 94, 101; and Colorado Company, 102
annexation of Mexico, 26, 35, 37, 65; and Sonora, 69; by the United States, 67–68, 89, 159n27
Anza family: and Juan Bautista de (the elder), 28; and Juan Bautista de (the younger), 28, 29, 81, 82
Arivaca Ranch, 115, 116, 118, 119–20
Arizona, 64, 85, 109, 159n33; and *Adventures in the Apache Country*, 6; and Arizona City, 103–5; and Arizonac mining site, 39; and Charles Poston, 3, 6, 88, 106, 114, 122; and commercial development, 7, 103; and Florence, AZ, 118, 119, 121; and meaning of name, 27–28, 32; mineral wealth of, 27–28, 88, 103, 116; silver mines of, 27–29, 103, 115, 116; as a U.S. territory, 117; and Yuma, 22, 86, 87, 99, 105
Astiazarán, Joaquin de, 164n30; family network, 61, 64, 65; and La Labor, 61, 64; and negotiations with Poston, 69; and San Juan Bautista land, 61, 62, 64, 65
Atlantic & Pacific Railroad Company (A&P), 97, 98, 99, 104; lack of investor confidence in, 102; and Poston's discussion about Arizona, 109; and railroad line in Texas, 100

Bartlett Boundary Commission, 22, 23, 24, 68, 72, 81, 114
Brady, Peter R., 76, 77, 113
Browne, J. Ross, 84–85, 86, 106, 118; and *Adventures in the Apache Country*, 6, 50, 117; as minister to China, 117; and "Poston's Narrative" chapter, 71, 110

California, 52, 80, 98; acquisition of, 22; American settlement of, 35, 96; and Baja area, 25, 26, 35, 40; and description of San Francisco, 15–16; as destination for Poston, 12, 13–14, 114, 122; and Fort Yuma, 87, 91; and

French immigrants, 38; and Gila Trail, 81; and gold rush, 3, 4, 76, 82; Gulf of, 6, 45, 74, 75, 96, 98, 114; and Iturbide Grant, 31–32; as productive land, 73; and prospective port, 26, 27, 56, 58, 69; and railroad route, 74, 101; and San Francisco customs house, 4, 16–18

Colorado City, 93, 95; and Charles Poston, 94, 101; and Colorado Company, 91, 96–97, 102; and copy of stock certificate, 98; failure of, 109, 112, 113, 114; flooding of, 105; and Fort Yuma, 95, 96; investors in, 90, 91, 97, 101, 102, 104; lack of government support for, 105; and Arizona City, 103–4; planning of, 111–12; and Robert Walker, 100, 102–3; and syndicate's failure to adopt project, 7, 97, 99

Cooke, Philip St. George, 84; and Cooke's Road, 81, 91–92; and Mormon Battalion, 81, 82

Ehrenberg, Herman, 49, 91, 96, 101, 115, 173n2; and articles by Poston, 121; and engineering, surveying, and mapmaking skills of, 46–47, 116; and Gila Trail, 80–81; and "Map of the Gadsden Purchase" (1854), 77, 92; and planning of Colorado City, 90, 111–12; and surveying of Colorado City, 6, 88, 90; as trustee of Colorado City, 90, 94; as trustee of Colorado Company, 91

filibusters, 45–47, 161n22; of Americans, French, and others in Mexico, 37, 41–43; and attempts of Count Gaston Raousset de Boulbon, 38–40, 41, 42, 45, 66, 108; and connections with Poston's expedition, 7, 108; and Count Charles de Pindray, 37–38; and Mexican land, 4, 52, 65; and William Walker, 40–43

Fort Yuma, 74, 75, 77, 79, 80, 86, 86, 88, 168n35; and Charles Poston, 89, 90, 91, 92, 96, 108; and Herman Ehrenberg, 90, 92; and Jaegerville, 104; and Major George Thomas, 91; and Major Samuel Heintzelman, 87, 115; as site of Colorado City, 95; and transcontinental railroad, 90, 99

Gadsden, James, 4, 158n25; and draft of treaty, 55–56; and negotiations for land in northern Mexico, 4; and negotiations for new boundary with Mexico, 21–22, 24, 25–27, 72

Gadsden Purchase, 7, 21, 45, 72, 92, 96; as body of land, 3, 6, 10, 75, 79, 81, 89, 106; and Charles Poston's expedition, 113–14; and Iturbide Grant, 4; and map of area by Herman Ehrenberg, 59; and negotiations for land in northern Mexico, 4, 27; and San Juan Bautista Bay land, 89, 98; and settlement of, 102; and transcontinental railroad, 68. *See also* Gadsden Treaty

Gadsden Treaty, 96; and Gadsden negotiations, 24–27, 42, 45, 55–56, 67, 109; ratification of, 72, 106, 108, 171n4; as reason for Poston's expedition, 106, 108; Senate debate over, 69; and sentiments of Sonorans, 95; and southern boundary of the United States, 75

Gándara, Manuel María, 61, 62, 64, 71; as governor of Sonora, 63, 64, 66; and marriage to Dolores Aguilar, 63; and removal from governorship by Santa Anna, 66; and San Juan Bautista land, 65

Gándara family: and control of commerce, 67; and Juan, 63; and negotiations with Poston, 65

Gila Trail, 80, 83, 91; and Captain José Romero, 81; and Charles Poston, 81; dangers of, 82, 84; and Father Jacobo Sedelmayr, 81, 82; and General Stephen Watts Kearny; and Gila Bend, 81, 82, 85; and Lieutenant Philip St. George Cook, 81–83; and Lieutenant Colonel William Emory, 82; and Oatman Massacre, 84–85; and trappers, 81; and use of by Spanish explorers, missionaries, native peoples,

Lieutenant Cave Johnson Couts, and Major Lawrence Graham, 81
Gray, Andrew B., 24, 29, 30, 73; and articles by Poston, 113, 121; and exploration of the Gulf of California, 75, 76; and journey in the Pinacates, 79; and *planchas de plata* (slabs of silver), 29; and promotion of Sonora as development site, 73–75; and railroad route, 89, 97; and Adair Bay, 75, 77; and survey of U.S.-Mexican border with Whipple, 81; as surveyor, 23, 114; as surveyor for Texas Western Railroad, 72, 74, 89, 113
Guaymas, Mexico, 26, 39, 42, 49, 163n33; and anti-American sentiments, 50; and Charles Poston, 44, 47, 48, 55–58, 66, 96; commerce in, 63, 67; and conditions for foreigners, 42–43, 51; and Port of Guaymas, 56, 63, 67, 175n10; and Poston's registering at the U.S. consulate, 110

Haycraft, Samuel, 10, *11*, 12; as chief clerk of the Hardin County Court, 9; and letters of introduction for Charles Poston, 13–14; and letter to Poston on imminent death of his wife, 101
Heintzelman, Major Samuel Peter, 88, 101, 104, 115, 117; and articles by Poston, 121; and Colorado City, 92, 94, 103; and Colorado City in journal of, 89, 90, 96–97, 102, 112; mining and business interests of, 87–88, 116; and position at Fort Yuma, 87, 91, 97; and *Reconnoisance in Sonora*, 123, 125; and Sonora Exploring and Mining Company, 29, 109, 123

Iñigo family: and control of commerce, 67; and Fernando Iñigo Ruiz, 63–64; and Manuel, 51; and negotiations with Poston, 65; and Sonoran treasury, 64; and success of family network, 63–64
Iturbide family, 32; and General Augustin de Iturbide, 31; and Iturbide Grant, 4, 6; and Salvador, 31

Iturbide Grant, 6, 155n2; and Gadsden Purchase, 4; location of, 31–33, 44, 45; and Poston, 109, 114

Jaeger, Louis J. F., 87, 91; and Colorado City, 90, 94, 111, 112; and establishment of a ferry business, 86, 88, 89; and Jaegerville, 104; silver mines of, 86; as successful merchant, 104, 105
Jesuit missionaries, 54–55
Johnson, George A., 86, 90, 102, 104, 105

Kearney, General Stephen Watts, 81, 82, 91–92
King, Thomas Butler, 16, 97, 99, 109, 157n9; and Atlantic & Pacific Railroad Company, 102; financial and legal dealings of, 100; and plan for transcontinental railroad, 102–3; and *Reconnoisance in Sonora*, 103, 123; and San Francisco customs house; and Southern Pacific Railroad Company, 123

"Map of the Gadsden Purchase" (Ehrenberg, 1854), 77, 78, 91, 92
McLemore, John C., 70; and Colorado City, 90, 94, 96–97, 101; and petition for appointment of Poston as U.S. Consul, 47–48; and *Reconnoisance in Sonora*, 125, 169n8; and San Francisco syndicate, 44; as trustee of Colorado Company, 91
Mexican War, 3, 25, 31, 34, 35, 36, 69, 81
Mexico, 106, 160n14; annexation of, 26, 35, 65, 67, 89; and anti-American sentiment, 42; and Catholic Church, 65, 66; and ceding of states to United States, 25; and Chihuahua, 25, 26, 97; and Coahuila, 25, 26; and conflict between liberals and conservatives, 65–66; and Disturnell's map, 22–23; economic decline of, 53; and Emigrant trail, 68; and filibusters by French and Americans, 4, 37, 38–43; and Gadsden Purchase, 21; and Gadsden Treaty, 72, 89; government of, 51, 62–63; and grant of land to

Iturbide family, 31, 44; and Guadalupe Melendrez, 40, 41; and Horcasitas valley, 57, 63; and Isthmus of Tehuantepec, 25; and Mexican revolution, 65–66, 67; and mineral wealth, 7, 21, 27, 69; mines of, 29–30, 52–53, 108, 113; native peoples of, 54–55, 59, 60, 61–62, 66; northern area of, 3, 4, 27, 28, 34, 37, 38; notable families of, 51, 62–63, 66–67; and possibilities for development, 7, 26–27; and President Anastasio Bustamante, 63; and President Antonio Lopez de Santa Anna, 25, 51; and President Arista, 39; and Santa del Cobre mines, 23; and Sonoran expedition, 48, 50–51, 105; and U.S.-Mexican boundary, 22, 24, 55–56, 89, 158n20

Navachiste Bay, 110, 175n5; and description of, 52; and port of, 49, 50–51, 108

Pierce, President Franklin, 4, 21, 47; and order to stop filibusters in Mexico, 40, 41; and possible boundary lines, 24, 25; and ratification of Gadsden Treaty, 72

Pope family: Colonel Benjamin, 12–13; Gustavus, 13, 121–22; and Sarah Lee Poston, 13, 121–22

Poston, Charles Debrille, 5, 31, 41, 73, 90, 107; and abandonment of his family, 3, 12–13, 114; and Adair Bay travels, 77–79, 108–9; and *Adventures in the Apache Country* (Browne), 6, 106; and annexation of Mexico, 67–68, 69; and Arivaca Ranch claim, 119–20; as Arizona mine developer, 109, 119, 120; and Arizona Mining and Trading Company, 112–13; as Arizona's first territorial delegate to Congress, 3, 117; as Arizona superintendent of Indian affairs, 3, 117; and articles by, 6, 109, 110, 121, 155n4; and boat voyage to Mexico, 6, 108; and career as writer, 118, 121; and Colorado City, 89–90, 91, 96, 98–99, 102, 104, 111; death of, 121; and delivery of Burlingame Treaty, 117–18; and "Diary of a Pioneer," 111, 112; and early business dealings and debts, 4, 12, 99, 114, 122; and early life in Kentucky, 4, 7, 9, 10, 12–14, 19; early travels of, 10–12; as envoy to Asian governments, 117; and first daughter, Sarah Lee, 10, 13, 121–22; foreign travel of, 114, 118; and frustration with customs house, 17–18, 19, 33, 109; and Gadsden negotiations, 55–56, 109; and Gadsden Purchase, 113; and Gadsden Treaty, 55–56, 69, 89; and Gila Trail, 80–82, 84–85; and government boarding house discussions, 4, 21, 27, 32–34, 68, 109; and Guaymas, 56–57, 96, 110; and Hardin County Court job, 9, 14; and Hart Fellows, 16, 19; and ignoring Indian claims to land, 60; and Iturbide Grant, 109, 114; known as Father of Arizona, 3, 155n1; legal training of, 10, 156n6; and letters of introduction, 13–14, 53; and locating mines, 6, 110; and Louis J. F. Jaeger, 86; and Major Samuel Heintzelman, 87, 88; and marriage to Margaret Haycraft, 10, 13, 120–21; and marriage to Mattie Tucker, 120–21; and Mrs. John Bigelow, 118; narrative roles of, 7, 105, 106; and Arizona Mining Company, 117; pensions of, 121; and prospective port at San Juan Bautista Bay, 6, 58, 60–62, 89, 90, 98; and quest for wealth, 4, 12, 113, 115, 122; and San Francisco customs house, 4, 16–20, 45, 46, 49; and San Francisco syndicate, 4, 6, 44–45, 47–48, 57, 58, 67, 90, 97, 101, 109, 113; and San Juan Bautista land, 65, 70, 113; and Santa Rita Mining Company, 118; and Charles T. Hayden, 120; and Sierra Madre Mining Company, 120; and settlement of Arizona, 3, 114; and silver mining, 3, 71, 114; and Sonora Exploring and Mining Company, 29, 103, 108, 109, 115–17, 118, 119, 123; and Sonoran expedition, 3, 6–8, 10,

27, 29, 37, 45–46, 70, 71–72, 105, 122; and speculation in real estate, 18–19, 45–46, 101; and stay with Haycraft family, 9–10; and transcontinental railroad, 68, 89–90, 99, 101–3, 108; and treaty to acquire land from Mexico, 25, 55–56; as trustee of Colorado City, 91, 94, 98; and uncertainty about border between Mexico and United States, 72; and U. S. government jobs, 118, 119; and Washington, D.C. trip, 99, 100; and wealthy Sonoran landowners, 6, 45, 57, 61, 62, 66; and wife and daughter in Kentucky, 4, 12, 101; and William Blackmore, 118, 173n18
Poston family: Elizabeth Ann, 9, 18; John Lee, 9; Judith Debrille (mother), 9, 10; Lee Ann Debrelle, 9; Sanford James, 9, 12; Sarah Lee (daughter), 10, 12; Temple (father), 9, 10. *See also* Pope family
Poston, Margaret (first wife), 12, 13, 101; and birth and death of second daughter, 18; and birth of Sarah Lee Poston, 10; death of, 120; and marriage to Charles Poston, 10, 13, 121
Pumpelly, Raphael, 104, 111, 112, 116

San Francisco, California, 69, 95, 96, 97; and Charles Poston, 109, 110, 112, 117; and customs house, 16, 17, 21, 18, 19, 44, 47–49, 70, 102, 123, 125, 157n9; description of, 15–16; as destination for Charles Poston, Herman Ehrenberg, and Samuel Heintzelman, 94; and government boarding house, 21; and real estate market, 18–19, 45–46, 101; and unemployed Frenchmen, 39
San Francisco syndicate, 4, 61, 101, 109, 110; and annexation of Mexico, 67, 74; and Colorado City, 99; and exploration of the Colorado River region, 99, 102; and financial support of Poston, 72; and lack of interest in Poston's plans, 6, 97, 99; possible members of, 44–45, 48; and property acquisition, 45, 57; and San Juan Bautista Bay port site, 75, 90; and Texas Western Railroad, 62, 65, 90
San Juan Bautista Bay, 103, 113; and Poston's agreement, 70, 72; and dismissal of as a port site, 96, 97; map of, 59; and failure of project, 7, 109, 114; and Gadsden Treaty, 75; and Joaquin de Astiazarán, 64; and Lieutenant Stanley, 58–59; and proposed port city on, 62, 75; as prospective port, 6, 58, 60–61, 67–69, 74, 89, 90, 95, 98
Santa Anna, Antonio Lopez de, 31; and colonization to populate northern Mexico, 38; and decree against armed foreigners, 39, 50; and Mexican revolution, 65, 66, 67; and negotiations for land with Gadsden, 4; as president of Mexico, 25, 26, 51
Seri Indians, 59–62
Sonora, Mexico, 35, 70; agricultural potential of, 52, 57; and Alamos, 52, 53, 54; annexation of, 67, 69, 74–75; and Apaches, 66; and *bolas y planchas de plata* (balls and slabs of silver), 27–28; and General José María Yáñez, 39–40, 66; and Emigrant trail, 68; filibusters in 38–40; and General Miguel Blanco, 37, 38; and Governor Manuel Gándara, 61, 63–64; and grants and *denuncias*, 61–62, 64; and invasion of by Walker, 40–41; and Iturbide Grant, 31; map of, 59; mineral wealth of, 32, 68, 73; and mining, 88–89, 120; and negotiations for boundary, 26; and notable families, 63–64; and possibility of separation from Mexico, 65, 90, 95; and Poston's expedition, 3, 6–8, 25, 89, 98, 106; silver mines of, 26–28, 30–31, 45, 53, 71, 114; and Sopori grant, 64, 172n2; and Vega and Almada families, 51, 52–53
Sonora Exploring and Mining Company, 123; and abandonment of mines, 116, 120; establishment of, 103, 108, 109, 115; financial problems of, 116; founders of, 29, 103; and General

Heintzelman as president, 109, 115; and Herman Ehrenberg, 47; major investors in, 115, 116; Poston as director of, 116; promotion of, 103; and purchase of Arivaca Ranch, 115–16; and purchase of, by Arizona Mining Company, 117; Samuel Colt as president of, 116, 117; and Santa Rita Mining Company, 116; and Thomas King, 123, 125; and William Wrightson, 29, 109, 115, 117, 123

Texas Western Railroad, 6, 65, 165n50; and Charles Poston, 90; charter of, 100; and name change to Southern Pacific Railroad, 100; and plan for railroad, 24, 75, 89–90; and possible annexation of Mexico, 69–70; and proposal of the San Diego and Gila Southern Pacific and Atlantic Railroad Company, 95; and purchase of by Atlantic & Pacific Railroad Company, 97; and southern route of transcontinental railroad, 100; and syndicate's plans for a port city, 62, 90

transcontinental railroad, 52, 72, 111, 159n29, 165n41; and access to trade, 74; and acquiring land rights for, 6–7; and Atlantic & Pacific Railroad Company, 97; and Charles Poston, 99, 101–2, 103, 112, 113, 114; and Colorado City, 98; and Colorado River, 90, 95, 99; control of, 89; debate over route for, 3–4, 24, 69, 70, 72–75; and Emigrant trail, 68; and Gila River, 22, 95; and port city as terminus, 7; and proposal of the San Diego and Gila Southern Pacific and Atlantic Railroad Company, 95; and risk in development of, 99; and San Diego Gila Railroad, 100; and Senator Thomas J. Rusk, 95; and southern route, 4, 22–26, 68, 72, 95, 100, 102, 115; and terminus on the Gulf of California, 45

Treaty of Guadalupe Hidalgo: and acquiring of territories by the United States, 31; and boundary between United States and Mexico, 22, 24, 73–74; and ceding of states to United States, 25; and failure to annex Baja California, 26; and Mexican war, 22, 176n23; problems with, 24–25

United States, 104; and annexation of Mexico, 37, 65, 67–69, 159n27; and Civil War, 116; and boundary with Mexico, 21–22, 26–27, 55–56, 72, 89; and Consul Juan Robinson, 42, 47, 56; and New Mexico, 22; and purchase of land from Mexico, 26–27, 96; and Utah, 98

Zoraida, 47, 50, 53, 171n6; stranded and delayed at Navachiste, 49–51, 108; voyage of, 110

About the Author

C. Gilbert Storms has a B.A. degree in English from Trinity College (Connecticut) and M.A. and Ph.D. degrees in English from Rutgers University. He taught American literature and writing for twenty-nine years at Miami University in Oxford, Ohio, after which he worked in industry for several years as a technical writer and documentation designer. He currently lives in Tucson, where he researches and writes on Arizona history, focusing especially on the history of southern Arizona. He has published articles in the *Journal of Arizona History* and the *Wild West History Association Journal*.